Cooperative Learning &

Hands-On Science

Laura Candler
In consultation with Laurie Kagan

Kagan

Kagan Publishing
981 Calle Amanecer
San Clemente, CA 92673
1(800) 933-2667
www.KaganOnline.com

ISBN: 978-1-879097-26-1

Table of Contents

Table of Structures

Lesson	1	2	3	4	5	6	7	8	9	10	11	12	13	14	15
Blackboard Share (pg. 18)													✔		✔
Brainstorming (pg. 20)				✔										✔	✔
Corners (pg. 24)									✔					✔	
Formations (pg. 26)						✔								✔	
Jigsaw (pg. 28)									✔		✔	✔			
Numbered Heads Together (pg. 32)			✔	✔		✔				✔			✔		
Pairs (pg. 34)	✔							✔							
RoundRobin (pg. 36)	✔	✔				✔					✔			✔	✔
RoundTable (pg. 38)	✔	✔		✔		✔			✔			✔		✔	✔
Send-A-Problem (pg. 40)							✔			✔					
Spend-A-Buck (pg. 42)													✔	✔	✔
Team Discussion (pg. 46)												✔		✔	✔
Teammates Consult (pg. 48)											✔	✔	✔		
Team Projects (pg. 50)	✔		✔		✔	✔				✔	✔			✔	✔
Think-Pair-Share (pg. 54)		✔	✔		✔	✔	✔	✔		✔		✔		✔	✔
Three-Step Interview (pg. 56)		✔			✔			✔							

Laura Candler: *Hands-On Science*   1 (800) 933-2667 • *Kagan Publishing*

Table of Process Skills

Lesson	1	2	3	4	5	6	7	8	9	10	11	12	13	14	15
Classifying	✔			✔		✔	✔		✔			✔			
Communicating	✔	✔	✔	✔	✔	✔	✔	✔	✔	✔	✔	✔	✔	✔	✔
Experimenting										✔		✔			✔
Identifying	✔	✔	✔	✔	✔	✔	✔	✔	✔	✔	✔				
Inferring	✔		✔		✔	✔	✔	✔	✔	✔	✔	✔	✔		✔
Measuring		✔								✔		✔			
Model Making			✔		✔	✔		✔		✔					
Observing	✔	✔	✔	✔	✔	✔	✔	✔	✔	✔	✔	✔			✔
Organizing Data	✔		✔			✔	✔		✔	✔	✔	✔	✔	✔	✔
Predicting						✔				✔				✔	✔

Table of Blackline Masters

Table of Icons

 Adaptations for Age

This symbol denotes lesson modifications for younger students.

 Advanced Preparation

This symbol is located throughout all lessons to indicate advanced preparation is needed for specific activities.

 Content Ideas

The lightbulb icon denotes quick and easy ideas for using cooperative learning structures with science content.

 Curriculum Links

Look for the links icon when you need ideas for extending science concepts into other curriculum areas.

 Literature Link

Look for the open book icon next to activities which use children's literature.

 Safety Spotlight

Be sure to read the safety reminders next to the spotlight icon in many lessons.

 Science Journal Ideas

You'll find the journal icon at the end of each lesson adjacent to specific journal writing ideas.

Structure Variations

You'll find useful information about cooperative learning structure variations next to this symbol.

Foreword

We at **Kagan Publishing** are quite proud to publish *Hands-On Science.* Consistent with the Cooperative Learning philosophy, the book represents the creativity and hard work of a team: Laura Candler, author; Laurie Robertson, project consultant; Celso Rodriguez, designer and artist; and Michael Cifranic, formatter.

Laura and Laurie worked together integrating the best of cooperative learning with the best of process science. Without the brilliant and hard work of Celso and Mike, the wonderful ideas of Laura and Laurie could not appear in such an attractive, teacher-friendly format.

Successful science instruction involves learning both **scientific knowledge** and **scientific process** — attitudes, ways of thinking, methods. At the heart of *Hands-On Science* is a belief in the foundational importance of scientific process. The success of science education rests on our ability and willingness to "do science" with our students.

Our success as science educators from kindergarten on is a function of how well we teach the process of science — the attitudes, skills, ways of thinking, and methods of science. If we teach process well, scientific knowledge will follow.

It is because of this belief in process that Laura begins by identifying ten key process skills of primary science: *Classifying, Communicating, Experimenting, Identifying, Inferring, Measuring, Model Making, Observing, Organizing Data,* and *Predicting.* In each of her model lessons she explicitly includes at least four of the ten process skills. The content of science is taught, but only in the context of meaningful, hands-on experimentation.

With her "curriculum links" Laura provides broader context as well, relating each science lesson to diverse areas such as art, health, language arts, creative movement, literature, music, social studies, math, as well as journal writing. In this way science is taught in a context which gives it meaning. Laura's extensively field-tested lessons leave primary students demanding to "do more science."

If we go the other route, if we emphasize scientific knowledge over scientific process, students learn neither. We will continue to produce generations of students "turned off" toward science. Our traditional approach to science has reduced science to dull, non-relevant history. It is not a surprise that we have a nation which is not scientifically literate. "One only has to look at the international studies of educational performance to see that U.S. students rank near the bottom in science and mathematics — hardly what one would expect if the schools were doing their job well." (American Association for the Advancement of Science, 1989, p. 13).

Hands-On Science is an antidote to traditional science textbooks which emphasize content over process:
 "The present science textbooks and methods of instruction, far from helping, often actually impede progress toward scientific literacy. They emphasize the learning of answers more than the exploration of questions, memory at the expense of of critical thought, bits and pieces of information instead of understandings in context, recitation over argument, reading in lieu of doing. They fail to encourage students to work together, to share ideas and information freely with each other, or to use modern instruments to extend their intellectual capabilities." (American Association for the Advancement of Science, 1989, p. 14).

Hands-On Science turns the table on the traditional approach to science education: At the top of the agenda are exploration of questions, critical thought, collaborative effort, contextual understanding, discussion, and hands-on manipulation. *Hands-On Science* nourishes students' inherent love of science, nourishment which, if made more common, will prepare our society with the scientific literacy necessary for healthy functioning in our increasingly technological world.

Dr. Spencer Kagan

Reference

American Association for the Advancement of Science. *Science for All Americans. A Project 2061 Report on Literacy Goals in Science, Mathematics, and Technology.* American Association for the Advancement of Science. Washington, D.C., 1989.

Acknowledgements

I am indebted to so many people for their help and support with this writing project. First of all, I want to thank **Spencer Kagan** for opening the doors of cooperative learning to me. His dedication to this field has given educators all over the country the tools to better reach and teach children. His ideas rejuvenated my teaching, and I am grateful for the opportunity to work with him.

I am also indebted to **Laurie Kagan** for her guidance while writing this book. She invested many hours of her valuable time into making sure these lessons uphold the standards of *Kagan Publishing.* She also provided encouragement and ideas when I desperately needed both.

I want to thank **Celso Rodriguez** for the cover design, as well as the illustrations through this book. I feel honored to have had such a talented illustrator bring my pages to life through his artwork.

I am grateful to **Michael Cifranic** for the many hours he invested in formatting *Hands-On Science.* His expertise has resulted in a book that is well organized, allowing teachers easy access to an otherwise overwhelming amount of information.

In addition, I am truly grateful to **Joan Zeberlein,** especially for her help during the early stages of this book. She showed me how to apply the multi-structural approach to the independent science activities I had previously taught. She also field-tested many of my lessons and gave me invaluable advice on how to improve those lessons. Above all, her friendship and support sustained me through many hours of writing.

I also want to express thanks to my principal, **Donald Dawson,** and the entire faculty of E.E. Miller Elementary School for their support throughout this project. I appreciate the help of **Judy Compton** and **Pam Armfield** in tracking down children's science literature. I especially want to thank the following teachers for field-testing one or more lessons: **Cheryl Collazo, Brenda Bethea, Monika Morse, Theresa Short, Dorine Beauchamp, Deborah O'Neil, Michelle Laferte, Sue Moyer, Karen Zimmerman, Norm Melvin, Elena McKoy, Pat King, Kathy Howell, Jackie Albritton, Deborah Dees,** and **Rachel Pinkham.**

In addition to the teachers at my school, others also field-tested my lessons. I am grateful to **Barbara Burgess, Patty Wonderly, Kathie Matthews,** and **Bonnie Noyes** for their help in this area.

Most of all, I want to thank my husband **Marco Candler.** I could not have completed this project without his love and understanding. He assumed so many responsibilities and gave me the gift of time - time to write.

Science is a verb, not a noun. Children must *do* science in order to learn the skills needed in today's technologically advanced world. But even more importantly, children must do science *together*. Throughout this book I intertwine those two threads of science education: *hands-on* instruction and cooperative learning.

Hands-On Science

Along with other science educators, I proclaimed the importance of science process skills for years. However, I faced a dilemma: most curriculums and testing programs focus on science content. Should I sacrifice skills in the name of content? Or should I trim content in order to make time for skills?

Fortunately, my dilemma is being resolved by recent curriculum reforms. From the national to the district level, science process skills and science content are being seen as equally important. Curriculum writers are no longer treating science as a body of knowledge to be memorized. They now recognize that science content must be acquired by using science skills to manipulate objects and ideas. The term "hands-on science" refers to the integration of process skill instruction with appropriate science content.

The American Association for the Advancement of Science is currently spearheading a curriculum reform movement entitled "Project 2061." This long-term project outlines what students need to know to become scientifically literate and suggests ways to reach those goals. Their recently released report, *Benchmarks for Science Literacy,* states "Knowledge and skills are both essential and can be learned together. In fact, they should be learned together most of the time." (AAAS, 1993)

Perhaps more influential than curriculum changes, however, are the changes being made in science testing. Proponents of change are realizing something that teachers have recognized for years. Testing methods often have a bigger impact than curriculum on classroom instruction. The curriculum might advocate more emphasis on science skills, but if the testing program focuses on knowledge, teachers will continue teaching at the knowledge level.

Therefore, educators are experimenting with a new type of testing called "authentic assessment." Authentic assessment involves hands-on testing of basic science skills. A typical test involves students rotating through stations, using materials like thermometers, batteries, and pulleys to carry out science tasks. Students make charts or write sentences to explain their results. They apply both science knowledge and science skills to accomplish the tasks at each station.

I was recently invited to field-test an authentic assessment test. The tasks seemed relatively simple to me, but it was clear that my students were overwhelmed by the experience. I was amazed that my 5th graders were unable to sort buttons and explain why they had placed a particular button in a particular group. They seemed to be unable to read a Celsius thermometer and make inferences about how water temperature changes over time. And comparing two pulley systems was

completely beyond them!

I realized that a year of hands-on instruction hadn't been enough to ensure success with this new type of assessment. True gains in science literacy will only be achieved when students are involved in hands-on science from their very first year in school. Hopefully, changing assessment methods as well as reforming the curriculum will encourage the necessary changes in science teaching.

We must provide daily opportunities for students to practice process skills in a meaningful context. Children don't learn science skills by reading about them in a book; they must actively observe, classify, measure, predict, and make models. Just as importantly, they must learn to communicate their findings to others.

Cooperation vs. Competition

Cooperative learning provides the ideal environment for students to learn to communicate science findings. I think I have always instinctively known that science must be experienced in small cooperative groups. What I didn't know was that there is a world of difference between cooperative learning and groupwork. And I didn't learn that lesson until I began to implement Spencer Kagan's cooperative learning model.

I had assumed that by teaching hands-on science to small groups of students everyone was actively engaged in the learning. How wrong I was! I eventually realized that even though most of my students participated in class, some of them were just going through the motions without becoming intellectually involved. I was doing nothing to ensure that my students were participating equally and still less to hold them accountable for their learning.

I will never forget the look of panic on one student's face the day I tried my first cooperative learning structure, Numbered Heads Together. When he realized that I might spin his number and call on him, he looked shocked. His expression said, "You mean I have to pay attention and *learn* this?" In turn, I was shocked because I didn't realize that I was allowing some students to choose not to learn. From that moment on, I was a cooperative learning convert.

One obvious benefit of seating students in small groups is convenience. If you only have seven magnets, you'll need to divide your students into seven groups for a magnet lesson. Also, students seated close together can help each other with difficult tasks.

However, the reasons for using cooperative learning are much more powerful than mere convenience. Textbook science may be taught using traditional methods, but science skills cannot be mastered by individuals working in isolation. Only through interacting with others will students master essential science concepts and skills. Children don't learn by memorizing facts and ideas; they must discuss, debate, and defend new concepts before truly understanding them. Using a team approach to science instruction

fosters this active processing of ideas.

Cooperative learning is becoming an increasingly important component of science education. The Project 2061 committee specifically calls for frequent opportunities for students to work in groups:

Scientists and engineers work mostly in groups and less often as isolated investigators. Similarly, students should gain experience sharing responsibility for learning with each other. In the process of coming to common understandings, students in groups must frequently inform each other about procedures and meanings, argue over findings, and assess how the task is progressing. In the context of team responsibility, feedback and communication become more realistic and of a character very different from the usual individualistic textbook-homework-recitation approach. (Rutherford & Ahlgren, 1990)

The fact that scientists no longer work in isolation reinforces the need for cooperative learning in science education. The ability to work as a part of a team is now as highly valued as pure academic brilliance. In fact, many companies hire consultants to teach their employees how to work more productively in teams. Such is the case with Zeneca, an agricultural chemical company based in Richmond, California. Over the last few years they have invested huge sums of money in a program to promote teamwork. The purpose of the program is not to teach science skills, but rather to teach social skills. Teaching people to communicate effectively in teams is a major focus of the program. Many of the same cooperation skills taught by educators are taught to Zeneca's employees: how to listen actively, how to brainstorm effectively, how to reach group consensus, and how to resolve conflicts.

The program at Zeneca is not unique. Many companies are recognizing that their employees must learn to cooperate in order for the company as a whole to compete effectively.

Competition versus cooperation in the classroom has long been debated by educators. The Project 2061 report *Science for All Americans* offers new insight on this theme with regards to science:

Overemphasis on competition among students for high grades distorts what ought to be the prime motive for studying science: to find things out. Competition among students in the science classroom may also result in many of them developing a dislike of science and losing their confidence in their ability to learn science. (Rutherford & Ahlgren, 1990)

Not only is cooperative learning important in its own right, it provides a necessary alternative to the detrimental effects of competition in the science classroom.

Doing Science Together!

Hands-on instruction and cooperative learning are both strong themes in science education reform. Reading about science is out; doing science is in. Fortunately, doing science is infinitely more fun! And doing science with teammates is even more fun than doing science alone.

The fifteen lessons in this book use cooperative learning to teach a blend of science skills and content. Choose a lesson and experience the excitement of doing science together!

References

American Association for the Advancement of Science. *Benchmarks for Science Literacy.* Oxford University Press, New York, NY: 1993.

Rutherford, J. & Ahlgren, A. *Science for All Americans.* Oxford University Press, New York, NY: 1990.

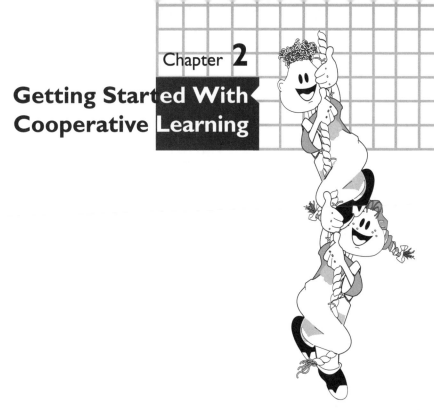

Chapter 2

Getting Started With Cooperative Learning

Cooperative Learning vs. Group Work ◆

Four Basic Principles of Cooperative Learning ◆

Cooperative Learning Structures ◆

Team Formation ◆

Seating Arrangements ◆

The Teacher's Role in Cooperative Learning ◆

Classroom Management ◆

Solving Problems within Teams ◆

Teambuilding ◆

Assessing Progress and Assigning Grades ◆

Cooperative learning methods are radically different from "traditional" teaching methods. If you aren't already using cooperative learning in your classroom, you'll need to become familiar with these new teaching techniques before attempting a full science lesson.

Since the focus of this book is on the science classroom, I'll only include an overview of the essential components of cooperative learning. If you haven't had any instruction in Kagan's structural approach, I suggest reading his book *Cooperative Learning*. I also recommend taking one of his teacher training workshops so that you can experience the power of cooperative learning firsthand.

I have found that many teachers ask the same questions when setting up a cooperative classroom. In this chapter I will answer those questions, focusing specifically on the cooperative science classroom. Basically, teachers want to know:

- *How is cooperative learning different from "group work"?*
- *What is a cooperative learning structure?*
- *How do I form teams in my classroom?*
- *How should I seat my students?*
- *What is my role in the cooperative learning classroom?*
- *How do I manage cooperative learning activities?*
- *What do I do if my students don't function well in teams?*
- *Why are teambuilders important?*
- *How do I assign grades?*

Cooperative Learning vs. Group Work

Believe it or not, cooperative learning is not a new concept. For decades teachers have experimented with allowing students to work in teams to accomplish academic tasks. However, many teachers discovered that cooperative learning was wonderful in

theory but disastrous in practice. The bright students were doing all the work, students were unable to cooperate with each other, and grades were unfairly affected. Many of us remember at least one incident in school where we worked in groups. In most cases our experiences only reinforce our ideas that cooperative learning is just an old idea that sounds great but doesn't work.

If you have ever felt this way, don't despair. The situations described above are very definitely group work, but most assuredly not cooperative learning! True cooperative learning involves students *actively* working together in a caring, concerned environment. Students' grades are positively affected by cooperative learning because each student is better able to master skills and understand concepts, not because a few people do all the work.

Cooperative learning theory and practice have undergone radical changes in the last 15 years. Educators and theorists have identified the essential components of cooperative learning which distinguish it from simple "group work." Understanding these basic concepts will help you implement true cooperative learning in your own classroom.

Four Basic Principles of Cooperative Learning

Kagan has identified four basic principles which are fundamental to the success of any cooperative learning activity: Simultaneous Interaction, Positive Interdependence, Individual

Accountability, and Equal Participation. These basic principles provide the foundation for successful cooperative learning activities. A brief overview of each basic principle is given, but true understanding and appreciation for these principles will come only through using them and observing their impact in your classroom.

1. Simultaneous Interaction
Simultaneous Interaction is the principle that separates cooperative learning from traditional teaching methods. In the traditional setting, participation is usually sequential, with one person at a time interacting overtly with the class or teacher. The rest of the time, that student is only passively involved with the instruction. For instance, in a class discussion one student at a time shares an idea with the class. The rest of the class may or may not be involved; as long as one person at a time is talking the activity is considered successful.

Contrast this with a team discussion in which one person on each team is talking simultaneously. With students in teams of four, 25% of the class is overtly involved in discussing an idea. The rest of the team is actively listening as each person considers how they will contribute to the discussion themselves. Many students are more comfortable discussing ideas with a small group and are more likely to become overtly involved in the lesson.

A pair discussion allows for even greater simultaneous interaction. When two students are discussing an idea together, one person in each pair is overtly involved. The amount of student involvement in the class jumps to 50% at this point!

Keep in mind, however, that greater simultaneity may not always meet the lesson objectives. You'll still use class discussions when you want everyone to be exposed to the greatest number of ideas or perspectives. Sometimes during team discussions you'll hear inaccurate science concepts being reinforced by other students and may want to open up a class discussion to dispel any misunderstandings.

Simultaneous Interaction is a powerful principle to apply in planning your instruction. In general, simultaneous interaction is preferable to sequential interaction because it increases the number of students actively involved.

2. Positive Interdependence
A spirit of positive interdependence is evident when students feel that they need each other in order to accomplish the assigned task. They feel that a gain for one is a gain for all and that the task can only be completed if everyone participates.

Positive interdependence can be fostered in many ways. You can limit and assign the resources available so that everyone must contribute to the final product. One person may have the scissors, another the glue, another the marker, etc. With team projects such as murals and posters, you can assign each team member one color and tell students that ALL colors must be used in the final product.

Positive interdependence can also be

encouraged by assigning roles. Divide the team responsibilities and assign roles such as Recorders, Reporters, Quiet Captains, Checkers, and Taskmasters. In science, you may need Lead Scientists, Materials Monitors, and Cleanup Captains.

3. Individual Accountability

Early attempts at cooperative learning often failed because students were not held accountable for participating and/or learning. Group grades were frequently assigned to a product without taking individual performance into account. As a result, lazy students learned to let others do the work, confident that the grade they earned would be at least as good as the one they would have obtained on their own. Hardworking students resented the fact that others received high grades for work to which they never contributed.

Understanding and applying the principle of Individual Accountability will prevent these pitfalls in your own classroom. First of all, activities should be structured in such a way that everyone must contribute to the discussion or task. Secondly, grades should never be assigned to a team product without taking into consideration the efforts of each team member. Finally, when material is studied or reviewed, each person should be tested individually on the content. Team test-taking should be reserved for practice sessions only.

4. Equal Participation

In the best cooperative learning activities, students will participate equally in each discussion or task. Not only will each person have some part in the final product, each person will make an equal contribution to that product. In a discussion, each team member will speak for an *equal* amount of time.

Without constant monitoring, equal participation may be lacking in the cooperative classroom. Some students naturally want to take over and do most of the work. In a team discussion, often one person monopolizes the conversation without allowing others to express their ideas. You'll need to observe your teams closely while members are interacting. Sometimes you'll have to modify an activity on the spot to ensure equal participation. Assigning roles can help team members contribute equally to a project, while having students take turns in a discussion will equalize verbal participation.

Cooperative Learning Structures

At this point you may be wondering how you'll ever implement cooperative learning in your own classroom successfully. How will you ensure that the four basic principles are integrated throughout your science lessons?

The Structural Approach developed by Spencer Kagan offers an easy answer to that question. This approach to cooperative learning involves building lessons with cooperative learning "structures." Structures are not tied to subject matter but rather provide ways to implement cooperative learning techniques. Examples of basic structures include **Think-Pair-Share, RoundRobin, and Numbered Heads Together.**

Cooperative learning structures are designed to incorporate the four basic principles, allowing you the freedom to plan your lessons without worrying about including these principles. As long as you build your lessons with structures, you'll automatically incorporate those four essential components of cooperative learning.

Each science lesson in this book is "multi-structural," comprising a variety of cooperative learning structures. As you teach the lessons, you'll see the same structures used over and over in many different ways. Eventually you'll want to develop your own lessons to teach science concepts which are not included in this book. To assist you in using the structures correctly, an entire chapter has been devoted to understanding and using cooperative learning structures. For each structure used in this book, you'll find an explanation of the specific steps you should follow when using that structure. You'll also find tips for adapting the structure to different age levels and suggestions for incorporating other science content.

Team Formation

Before you begin teaching science cooperatively, you'll need to form heterogeneous teams. Teams of four students are preferable since they can easily be divided for pair work. Unless otherwise stated, the science lessons in this book assume you've divided your class into teams of four.

Careful consideration should be given to forming cooperative learning teams. Teams should be balanced with regards to academic ability, ethnic background,

and gender. In general, students should not be allowed to choose their own teams.

Every teacher has his or her favorite method of forming teams. I'll share one method with you, but if you feel the need for more information on this subject you may want to read the chapter in *Cooperative Learning* on team formation.

Since you'll be forming teams of boys and girls with varying abilities and ethnic backgrounds, you'll need an organized system for planning those teams. Using manipulatives such as index cards is helpful. You'll find one easy way of forming teams below.

Steps in Forming Teams of Four

1. Gather the following supplies:
• A copy of your class roster
• Four crayons or markers (blue, green, yellow and red)
• A pencil or pen
• A stack of index cards (one per student)

2. Write one student's name on the top line of each index card. If necessary, use the rest of the card to make notes about ethnic background or gender.

3. Divide the index cards into four equal piles based on academic ability. Place all the high achieving students in one pile, the high-average students in another, the low-average students in a third, and the low achieving students in the fourth pile. Make sure the piles are approximately equal in size. If you have 28 students, you'll have 7 cards in each pile. If you have 30 students you'll have 7 cards in some piles and 8 cards in the other stacks.

4. Color-code the four piles by drawing a large dot of the appropriate color in the upper right-hand corner of each index card. Use the colors given below:
Blue: High-achieving students
Green: High-average students
Yellow: Low-average students
Red: Low-achieving students

5. Clear a large work area on the table or floor. Start by placing all the blue cards in a column. Think of these students as the academic leaders of your teams.

Team #	Blue	Green	Yellow	Red
1	□	□	□	□
2	□	□	□	
3	□	□	□	□
4	□	□	□	
5	□	□	□	□
6	□	□	□	□

6. Place the green, yellow, and red cards in columns next to the blue cards.

7. If your cards do not evenly divide into four columns, decide whether you want some teams to have three or five students. Classroom size and the nature of the lesson will play a part in this decision.

8. Each *row* of cards represents one team. Examine each row carefully to see if your teams are balanced according to race and gender. If some are not, switch cards so that your final teams are as balanced as possible.

9. Number your teams and write the team numbers on each card.

10. Draw a seating chart or make a list of team assignments to share with your students. *Do not* let students see the index cards you used in planning

teams, as they will easily be able to figure out the color-coded system.

If you don't want to bother with index cards, a Team Formation Kit is available from *Kagan Cooperative Learning.* The kit contains color-coded cards, plain cards, slotted sheets of tagboard for displaying the teams, and full directions.

Many teachers also want to know how long their teams should stay together. Generally, six weeks seems to be the optimal time. Forming new teams too frequently may prevent students from ever developing that team feeling of "we instead of me." Yet after six weeks, students are usually ready to see new faces and interact with other students in the class.

Occasionally you may want to form new teams for a particular lesson or study unit. If students don't need highly complex academic skills for the lesson, you may want to form random teams for a short period of time. Shuffle your index cards together without regard for the color-coding and deal the cards into stacks of four students. Post or announce a list of the students on each random team. When the activity is over, allow students to reunite with their "old" teammates. Using random teams in this way adds a spark of excitement and can build class unity.

Seating Arrangements

The next consideration after forming teams is how to best seat students. If your classroom is equipped with tables, seat each team of four at one table so that no one has his or her back to the front of the room. If you have flat-topped desks, four desks may be pushed together to form a table. This arrangement is ideal for the science classroom since it provides a flat surface for convenience during science activities. The desks may be separated during testing or other individual activities.

Probably the most difficult furniture to work with is the L-shaped slant-top desk found in many upper elementary or middle schools. The desks don't fit together easily to form a table, and even when pushed together the resulting surface is not flat. Activities with batteries, marbles, and containers of water become difficult to perform. Yet inadequate furniture should never be an excuse for not doing cooperative learning! The creative teacher can always find a solution. One easy way to solve the problem is to have students sit on the floor when a flat surface is required. Another is to move the activity outside or to a different room, such as the cafeteria.

The Teacher's Role in Cooperative Learning

As you begin to develop a feel for cooperative learning, you'll realize that the teacher's role in the cooperative classroom is dramatically different from his or her role in the traditional classroom. In the past, the teacher was seen as the sole classroom authority and dispenser of information. The teacher imparted knowledge and "good" students absorbed this knowledge without question, calling the facts forth at will for tests.

In contrast, the teacher in a cooperative classroom is a facilitator of learning. Just enough information is presented to stimulate individual thinking and discovery. Students are encouraged to question, defend, and discuss ideas. They learn by experimenting with materials and exploring concepts. Learning is seen as an ongoing process, not just a set of facts or skills to master. The teacher simply provides an environment in which students can learn.

Your role in the cooperative classroom is every bit as important as it was in the traditional classroom. As a facilitator, you must plan lessons which allow students the opportunity to discuss, defend, and explore ideas. You'll need to make sure that adequate materials and time are provided for students to experiment with scientific concepts. When students are working on cooperative activities, you'll need to monitor their progress carefully so that students are participating equally and are held accountable for their learning. One of your biggest roles will be to manage the excitement and activity generated by cooperative learning lessons.

Classroom Management

One reason many teachers hesitate to implement cooperative learning is a concern that the resulting noise and activity will be difficult to manage. It's a lot easier to manage a classroom when only one student at a time is allowed to speak. As teachers we like to feel "in control" of our class, and we feel that allowing many students to interact at once will become a management nightmare.

These concerns, in fact, are very valid. If a teacher tries to implement cooperative learning without adequate management strategies, the classroom environment *can* dissolve into a free-for-all of unstructured noise and activity.

Fortunately, there are a host of simple classroom management ideas which allow teachers to control the activity level without stifling the excitement of learning. Some techniques can be used in any situation, while others are more appropriate for particular activities.

Implementing a Quiet Signal is the first step towards managing the activity level in your classroom. Nothing ruins the spirit of a cooperative activity more than having to constantly yell above your students' voices to get their attention. One effective signal is to simply raise your hand when you want students to be quiet. As students see you with your hand raised, they become quiet and raise their hands also. Before long, everyone will silently have a hand in the air. Wait until *everyone* is ready before speaking. I use this signal frequently, but I have modified it a bit. Sometimes students are so intent on their tasks that I may stand with my hand raised for 30 seconds before anyone realizes that I want their attention. I now count softly, "One . . . two . . three. . . . " My students know they are to be quiet and

looking at me by the time I say "three."

Another management strategy is to plan your activities so thoroughly that students don't have the opportunity to develop off-task behaviors. Give clear, bite-sized directions. When possible, use one team to model or demonstrate the activity. Have all materials prepared and counted out for each team in advance.

Give positive attention to behaviors you want to develop. Rather than constantly reprimanding teams that are too loud or *not* working well together, compliment the teams that are behaving in a desired manner. Simply stand beside a team that is working well, use your quiet signal, and tell the class what you like about the behavior of that team. For example, "I like the way this team has their heads close together during the discussion. They can hear each other but they aren't disturbing other teams." Try to find something positive to say about each team.

As you become comfortable with cooperative learning, you'll discover many more techniques to help you manage instruction effectively.

Solving Problems within Teams

Some teachers have told me that they would like to try cooperative learning, but they are afraid their students won't get along in teams. They feel that too much time will be wasted while team members argue with each other instead of working productively together.

Once again, these are very valid concerns. You can't just seat four students together who have nothing in common and expect them to automatically treat each other with loving kindness. Many students lack the social skills necessary to work well in teams, especially if they have never been exposed to cooperative learning. The skills to be successful in a group are very different from those needed to accomplish a task individually. These skills must be actively taught and reinforced.

For instance, students need to learn to respect each other's ideas. Cooperative learning requires a warm, caring, and supportive environment. I teach my students from the first day of school that "put downs" are not tolerated and that all ideas are valued. Students should never be allowed to express put downs in front of the class or within teams. In addition, students should be taught how to express praise for each others' accomplishments and ideas.

Students also need to learn active listening skills. These skills can easily be taught through role-playing. Ask a student volunteer to come forward to tell you some exciting news (arrange this in advance so they will know how you are going to react). Pretend to be completely uninterested by avoiding eye-contact, interrupting them, and fiddling with something like a pencil or watch. Then repeat the entire scenario using *active* listening skills (leaning toward the speaker, making eye-contact, asking relevant questions, etc.). Ask your teams to discuss the difference between poor listening and active listening. Have a Recorder on each team list the things a listener to should do (or not do) to practice active listening.

In the same way, most social skills can be taught to students. Focus on one skill at a time, teaching students specific ways to improve that cooperative skill. For more information, read the social skill chapter in Kagan's *Cooperative Learning*.

Teambuilding

Teambuilding activities provide another way to foster a spirit of cooperation. Teambuilding activities provide a chance for team members to enjoy each other as individuals. Often teambuilding activities have a game-like atmosphere since they do not focus on academic skills.

When I was first introduced to cooperative learning, I felt that teambuilding was a waste of time. In fact, I decided that I wouldn't bother to use teambuilding. Before long, I found out that teambuilding was a necessary component of cooperative learning. I discovered that students need to learn to appreciate each other as individuals before they are able to perform as an academic team.

One of the first ways to build team spirit is to allow students to create a team name together. They can list hobbies and interests that they all have in common and make up a name that represents their uniqueness. After they have developed a name, they can invent a team handshake that symbolizes their team unity. Encourage them to use their handshake when they accomplish something together.

Almost any non-academic team activity can be used for teambuilding.

You can stage tower-building contests or allow teammates to interview each other about their favorite hobbies. Seasonal puzzles and activities also provide teambuilding fun, such as having teams make words from the letters in "Thanksgiving."

Assessing Progress and Assigning Grades

You now have all the elements of a successful cooperative classroom in place. You've formed your teams, fine-tuned your management skills, and solved your team-cooperation problems. However, you have one last area of concern: grading. Our current educational system dictates that a student's progress must be assessed and grades must be assigned. How do you assign grades to students who are working in cooperative teams?

First of all, remember that cooperative learning is not meant to be used every moment of the day. Students can work together on projects, they can discuss and defend their ideas, and they can study together for tests. But at some point, all students must show that they understand important concepts and can perform basic skills on their own. Cooperative learning classrooms will not be successful if students aren't held individually accountable for their learning. So make sure students understand that their teammates can help them during the learning process, but each person will have to take an individual quiz at the end just as they always have.

Another way to assess progress is to incorporate individual writing activities frequently throughout your lessons. Students can write about activities or respond to questions in Science Journals. You can collect their Journals periodically to evaluate their progress.

What about grading team products such as posters and research papers? These tangible items just beg to be graded! I struggled with the problem of grading team products and came up with two solutions.

If team members are proud of their work and don't seem to be concerned about a grade, I simply display the projects prominently in the classroom. Elementary students aren't usually as grade-conscious as older students. They are excited to see their work on display, and being graded can spoil the excitement.

Yet, sometimes I need a grade. Perhaps the class has spent a whole week on a project and the grading period is almost over. For reasons that have little to do with the learning process itself, I find myself needing to grade a project.

When I feel this way, I have each team member write a paragraph explaining his or her contribution to the project. All team members sign *all* paragraphs to show that they agree with each person's contributions. I assign a group grade to the project, but I do not record this grade for each student. If one student has contributed significantly more than the others, his or her grade is higher than the team grade. If I know that someone has not contributed as much as the others, his or her grade is lower than the team grade. For example, a team poster might be given a "B." A student who put forth a great deal of effort might still receive an "A," but a student who did very little would receive a "C" or "D."

Another way to assign grades to team projects is to divide the project into parts and hold each student responsible for one part. For example, imagine that each team is assigned to create a poster or report on a particular biome, such as the tundra. One person would be responsible for including information about the animals, another about the plants, the third about the climate, and the fourth about the location of that biome. When grading the product, grade each student's portion individually.

One of my favorite ways to evaluate students in science is to let them evaluate themselves. I ask each student to complete a Science Activity Self-Assessment (see next page). After rating themselves and writing an explanation of each assessment area, the fill in the letter grade they feel they deserve. I add my comments and assign the final grade. I didn't discover the power of this assessment tool until the second time I used it: since my students knew they would have to evaluate their own learning, they made conscious efforts to improve their science performance. They were amazingly honest in their assessments and didn't want to have to give themselves a poor grade!

With enough planning and thought, most grading problems can be solved. Just remember that a student's grades should never be influenced purely by the efforts of team members. Students who don't participate shouldn't receive a passing grade just because they are a member of a hardworking team. Students who would receive superior grades on their own should never be penalized by being on a team with unmotivated students.

If cooperative learning is implemented properly, grades in a classroom *will* improve. However, those grades will improve because students have individually mastered basic skills and understand complex concepts as a result of working with other students. This is the only acceptable "grade inflation" due to cooperative learning.

References

Kagan, Spencer. *Cooperative Learning.* Kagan Cooperative Learning, San Juan Capistrano, CA: 1994.

Science Activity Self-Assessment

Name _____ Date _____

Activity _____

1. What science ideas did you learn or understand better from this activity?

_____

_____

_____

2. How well did you use science process skills? Explain.

Poor   Great
1 2 3 4 5

_____

_____

3. How well did you participate as a team member? Explain.

Poor   Great
1 2 3 4 5

_____

_____

4. How well did you follow instructions? Explain.

Poor   Great
1 2 3 4 5

_____

_____

5. How well did you exercise self-control in behavior? Explain.

Poor   Great
1 2 3 4 5

_____

_____

_____

6 What grade do you feel you deserve on this activity? ⟶ _____

Teacher Comments:

_____

_____

_____

```
FINAL GRADE


```

Laura Candler: *Hands-On Science*   1 (800) 933-2667 • *Kagan Publishing*

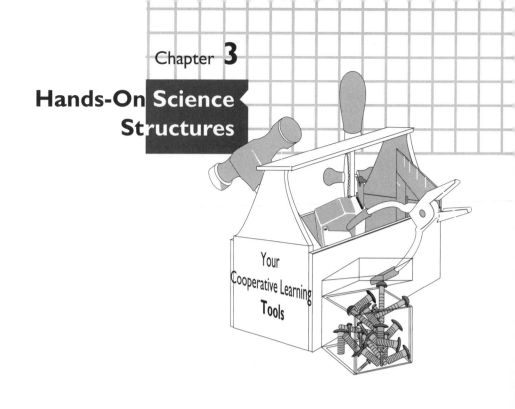

Hands-On Science Structures

Your Cooperative Learning **Tools**

Structures are the tools which ensure your success with cooperative learning. The 16 structures which follow provide an array of cooperative learning techniques designed to meet the needs of every teacher. As when learning any new tool, practice is essential. Learn to use the structures correctly by experiencing them throughout the *Hands-On Science* lessons.

When you become familiar with the structures, you will want to use them to create your own science lessons. To assist you with lesson planning, content ideas are offered for each structure. Variations of each structure are provided to help you adapt them to your specific needs. After you discover the power of these tools, you'll find yourself reaching into your structure "toolbox" each time you prepare a new lesson!

① **Teacher Selects Sharing Method**

② **Team Members Share Ideas With Class**

(See Lessons 13 and 15)

During a science investigation, teams often gather data. Sometimes it's necessary to compile that data as a class so that the results can be discussed. **Blackboard Share** provides an excellent way for teams to share written information with the class.

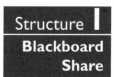

Your
Cooperative Learning
Tools

① Teacher selects sharing method—

First, determine the appropriate method for sharing information. Try to incorporate simultaneity; choose a method which allows many students to record data at the same time. For instance, you can divide your chalkboard into sections and let each team write their results simultaneously.

To compile class data from an experiment, draw a blank chart on the board and have teams add their data directly to the class chart. Sometimes small sticky notes can be used to speed up the process of recording data. Create class bar graphs by sketching a blank graph on the board and having a representative from each team shade in their teams' results.

② Team members share ideas with class—

After determining the sharing method you plan to use, explain the procedure to the class. When the time comes for students to share information, designate one person on each team to record their team's results on the blackboard. Follow with a class discussion to analyze the results of the activity.

Sharing on Paper

Butcher paper, chart paper, or poster paper can substitute for board space. A long sheet of butcher paper can be used for class graphing activities. Poster paper works well when teams prepare their part of the class presentation separately. Students can complete the posters in teams, then tape their team posters to the wall for sharing.

Overhead Projector Share

If you teach with an overhead projector, you may want to draw the class chart on the overhead instead of on the board. You can also draw the chart in black ink on paper and burn a transparency. Students can write on the transparency with a non-permanent pen. After the activity, wipe the transparency clean and save it for another lesson.

- Reporting results from an experiment
- Sharing results of a team vote
- Creating a class bar graph
- Presenting team posters to the class
- Organizing data from a class survey

① **Assign Roles**

② **Identify Topic**

③ **Generate And Record Ideas**

(See Lessons 4, 14 and 15)

Brainstorming is not a new procedure. Many of us have had students brainstorm ideas for projects or writing assignments. However, **4-S Brainstorming** tightens up the brainstorming process while enhancing its creative potential.

Brainstorming is more productive when students generate ideas quickly and without judgment. In fact, accepting offbeat ideas often stimulates creative solutions. In addition, brainstorming sessions become more fruitful when students are taught to build on each other's ideas. The structure **4-S Brainstorming** incorporates these ideas by assigning student roles. The role titles Speed, Synergy, Support, and Silly give this structure its name.

Structure **2**
Brainstorming

Your
Cooperative Learning
Tools

Assign Roles– ①

Before beginning your brainstorming session, assign roles to each team member and discuss the job of each role. The easiest way to assign roles is to have students number off within their teams and announce roles by number. Discuss the following job descriptions with the class.

Role	Job Description
Speed	Encourage your teammates to work quickly and list as many ideas as possible. Your job is to pressure your team to think of more and more ideas.
Silly	Encourage your teammates to think of silly and unusual ideas. Remember that a silly idea might make someone think of a workable idea.
Synergy	Remind your teammates to build on each other's ideas. (Synergy means that by combining two ideas you can think of an idea that's better than either original idea.)
Support	Remind your teammates that all ideas are good. An idea may seem silly or not related to the topic, but it may help someone else think of another idea. Compliment your teammates for any idea.

To help students remember their role titles and job descriptions, duplicate a set of **4-S Brainstorming** role cards for each team. Have students cut them out and fold them to make a "tent." Tell them to place the role cards on their desks with the role title facing the other students and the job description facing themselves

Silly

Identify topic– ②

After assigning roles, state the topic for the brainstorming session. I have used brainstorming for generating solutions to problems, identifying topics for surveys, listing project ideas, and naming items for classification activities.

Generate and record ideas– ③

Tell students to call out their ideas as they think of them; unlike **RoundRobin** students don't take turns when brainstorming. Remind students to use their roles as they work.

Designate one person on each team to record ideas. The Recorder can list the ideas on a single sheet or record each idea on an individual slip of paper. I like to have students record ideas on separate slips if we are going to use those ideas during the next activity. For example, ideas can be sorted or rank-ordered by priority. Sometimes I have students vote for the idea they like best; listing ideas separately simplifies the voting process.

Think Pad Brainstorming

Sometimes its best to have each person record his or her own ideas. To use **Think Pad Brainstorming** each student tears off several sheets of paper from a scrap pad (Think Pad). As each person thinks of an idea, he or she calls it out and writes it down. The individual slips of paper are stacked in the center of the team for later use. When using this variation, make sure students are verbalizing their ideas and brainstorming together. I have seen teams try to brainstorm silently when using **Think**

Pad Brainstorming! If this happens, designate one Recorder to ensure that ideas are spoken aloud.

Brainstorming Without Roles

We all face time restraints in our schedules. Sometimes you'll just want to slip in a 5 minute brainstorming session without assigning roles. As long as students are familiar with brainstorming techniques, you can omit the roles occasionally. Younger students may also benefit from this type of brainstorming since the role titles can overwhelm them.

- Listing ideas for a science experiment
- Thinking of solutions for environmental problems
- Naming possible topics for a survey
- Generating ideas for team projects
- Listing examples of mammals, birds or fish
- Listing items for sorting activities
- Naming topics of interest in science
- Brainstorming items that use energy

4-S Brainstorming Role Cards (Set A)

Directions: Cut out cards on solid lines. Fold cards on dotted lines.

Remind your teammates that
ALL ideas are good.

Support

Remind your teammates to
build on each other's ideas.

Synergy

Laura Candler: *Hands-On Science* 1 (800) 933-2667 • *Kagan Publishing*

4-S Brainstorming Role Cards (Set B)

Directions: Cut out cards on solid lines. Fold cards on dotted lines.

Encourage your teammates to think of silly and unusual ideas.

- -

Silly

Encourage your teammates to work quickly and list as many ideas as possible.

- -

Speed

1 Teacher Asks Question

2 Teacher Announces Corners

3 Students Write Choice

4 Students Move To Corners

5 Students Pair And Discuss Choices

(See Lessons 9 and 14)

In **Corners,** the teacher asks a question with four possible answers and designates a corner of the room for each answer. Each student writes down his or her choice and moves to the corresponding corner. The students in each corner then pair and discuss their choices.

I like **Corners** because it provides two benefits at once. In addition to conveying science content, **Corners** gets kids actively mixing with other class members. Students immediately identify with others who select the same choice, and strong bonds develop between class members as they recognize similarities among themselves. The classbuilding component of **Corners** makes it an excellent choice for introducing a lesson or sharing opinions.

Structure 3

Corners

Your
Cooperative Learning
Tools

① Teacher asks question—

First, choose your question or topic and identify four different responses. Students can respond to questions about their preferences, they can make predictions about experiments, or they can take a stand on scientific dilemmas. Corners can also be used to allow students to choose research topics. Below are some sample questions and responses:

What do you think will happen when the wire is attached to the battery?
Nothing
The bulb will light.
The buzzer will sound.
The bulb will light and the buzzer will sound.

Which invention would you like to research?
The airplane
The lightbulb
The microwave oven
The telephone

Which environmental problem do you feel is the worst today?
Destruction of tropical rainforests
Acid Rain
Water Pollution
Over Population

② Teacher announces corners—

After stating the question or topic, designate one corner of your room to represent each response. If possible, make a small sign from construction paper to post in each corner so that students can see all choices. If you don't make signs, write the four choices on the board or overhead projector.

③ Students write choice—

Have each student write his or her choice on a piece of scrap paper. Do not let them discuss their responses or you'll have friends influencing each other rather than individuals responding honestly to the question. Make sure to have students write their responses down so they can't change their minds later.

④ Students move to corners—

Ask students to take their written responses and move quietly to the designated corners.

⑤ Students pair and discuss choices—

After all students have moved to corners, have them pair up with a partner to discuss the reasons for their choice. Encourage them to pair up with someone they don't know well, rather than choosing their best friends or teammates.

• Making predictions
• Stating preferences
• Answering questions
• Choosing research topics
• Voting for choices
• Expressing opinions on current issues

① **Teacher Announces Object Or Concept**

② **Students Form Object Or Demonstrate Concept**

(See Lessons 6 and 14)

Formations are a fun way to make abstract concepts concrete. Students work as a class or in teams to form an object or demonstrate a concept announced by the teacher. When an entire class works together, class spirit is strengthened. Similarly, team unity is fostered when teammates cooperate to create formations.

Your
Cooperative Learning
Tools

Teacher announces object or concept—

①

Think of an object or concept which can be portrayed by the class or individual teams. Many science concepts lend themselves to formations. For instance, students can work together to form a solar system, complete with heavenly bodies revolving around the sun. Students in teams can form a tree, with each member dramatizing a different part. You can have teams portray famous science inventions or animals that live in a particular biome.

If each team is going to create a different formation, you can write the items on individual slips of paper. Have one person from each team secretly draw the name of one object or concept.

Students form object or demonstrate concept—

②

After you have announced the object or concept you want students to form, let them get to work. Try not to direct them; allow them to figure out how to best meet the challenge of portraying that object.

If teams are working independently, add some excitement to the activity by having each team present its formation to the class. The rest of the teams put their heads together and try to guess the name of the formation.

• Demonstrating how the seasons are caused
• Creating animals
• Dramatizing inventions
• Demonstrating the action of wind vanes
• Dramatizing the life cycle of an insect
• Making up a food chain or food web
• Demonstrating open and closed circuits
• Demonstrating the water cycle

① **Teacher Assigns "Expert" Topics**

② **Experts Groups Meet**

③ **Teammates Reunite And Share**

(See Lessons 9, 11 and 12)

More than any other structure, **Jigsaw** fosters interdependence. Just as a puzzle needs every piece to become whole, each team needs every team member's contributions to be effective. **Jigsaw** is an excellent structure to use when subject matter can be broken easily into four parts. You can prepare material specifically or simply use four parts of a textbook chapter. Each person on the team masters a small portion of the material by meeting with same topic experts from other teams. Then everyone returns to their original team to share what was learned.

Jigsaw provides an excellent way to meet one of the goals of Project 2061: understanding the historical perspectives of modern science. We typically teach our students about famous scientists and inventions by having each person in the class write a report on one scientist and present their findings to the class. Instead, consider making each person an "expert" on several scientists. Allow expert groups to meet and prepare brief presentations on the major contributions of their scientists. After original teams reunite and share their information, everyone takes a quiz on all the scientists.

One of my favorite ways to use **Jigsaw** in science is in setting up experiments with four variables. I assign each person one part of the experiment to prepare. All the students who are responsible for a particular part of the experiment meet together and follow written directions to prepare their materials. When everyone has finished, original teams reunite and assemble the entire experiment. The lesson "What's Wrong With the Water?" (found on pages 217-231) provides an excellent example of using **Jigsaw** this way. Bean seeds are grown in four types of water and each team member is responsible for preparing and watering one cup of seeds. However, the entire team works together to observe and graph the results of the experiment.

Your
Cooperative Learning
Tools

Teacher assigns "expert" topics— ①

No matter what the content of the lesson, plan in advance who will become a part of each expert group. Assign every member of each original four-member team to a different expert group. If you have five members on one team, pair two students together and let both of them be a part of the same expert group. Try to keep the expert groups balanced academically and socially.

I like to assign students to expert groups by using the Jigsaw Expert Group Formation chart (see pages 30-31). Using a pencil, I write the team names across the top and the names of team members in the blocks below. I write only one name per block unless I have some five-member teams. When finished, my expert groups appear horizontally on the chart. If I see that the expert groups aren't balanced, I can easily erase some names and switch them. The chart also provides me with a handy reference when I introduce the Jigsaw activity to my class.

Experts Groups meet— ②

On the day of the lesson, designate four areas of the room for your expert groups to meet. Announce all four topics to the class so that everyone will have an idea of the lesson objective. Assign the students to their groups and have them move to their designated areas. Tell them they are going to become experts on a specific topic, so later they can share what they learn with their teammates.

Monitor the expert groups carefully. One way I do this is by having a ten minute conference with each group to assess their progress. It's critical that everyone in every group becomes involved and masters the material. Some students may feel lost at first and need a little guidance.

Tell students they have two jobs: to become an expert on their topic and to decide how they are going to present that information to their teammates. Encourage creative presentations by suggesting visual aids such as posters or photographs. Challenge students to incorporate cooperative learning structures like **Numbered Heads Together** in their presentations.

Teammates reunite and share— ③

After the expert groups have met for the designated amount of time, everyone returns to their original teams. In Roundrobin fashion, each person presents a mini-lesson to their teammates. Remind students that they are completely responsible for making sure that their teammates have been given the correct information. Emphasize that the success of any **Jigsaw** activity depends upon the full participation of all team members.

- Studying a textbook chapter
- Learning about important inventions
- Setting up an experiment
- Studying famous scientists
- Learning about types of pollution
- Making weather instruments
- Studying different plant and animal habitats

Partners

A variation of Jigsaw may used if the material to be presented can be divided in half rather than in four parts. Split your teams into pairs to form two sets of partners who will become experts on half the information. Each set of partners moves to meet with a pair from a different team who is responsible for the same material. These new same-topic teams work together to prepare mini-lessons to share with their original team members.

I have found that Partners works well when I have many students of low ability who do not function well on their own. Also, even high ability students enjoy the feeling of togetherness that comes with preparing a presentation together.

Jigsaw Expert Group Formation

Team Names →	Team 1	Team 2	Team 3	Team 4	Team 5	Team 6	Team 7	Team 8
Expert Group 1								
Expert Group 2								
Expert Group 3								
Expert Group 4								

Laura Candler: *Hands-On Science*

1 (800) 933-2667 • *Kagan Publishing*

Jigsaw Expert Group Formation

Team Names ↑	Team 1	Team 2	Team 3	Team 4	Team 5	Team 6	Team 7	Team 8
Expert Group 1								
Expert Group 2								
Expert Group 3								
Expert Group 4								

① Students Number Off

② Teacher Poses Question

③ Students' Put Heads Together For Discussion

④ Teacher Chooses A Number

⑤ Numbered Students Respond

(See Lessons 3, 3, 6, 10 and 13)

Numbered Heads Together is a simple but effective mastery structure. This technique is a fun way to review science content prior to an activity or after a lesson has been taught. Using the structure can also serve as an informal assessment of your students' knowledge base. **Numbered Heads** should be used when recall of basic facts and ideas is desired; the structure is less suitable for divergent questions that have many correct answers.

Students number off— ①
Before starting the activity, ask your students to number off from 1 - 4. You may want to assign numbers according to a specific seating arrangement. Check to make sure everyone knows their number by randomly calling out numbers and having the students with that number raise their hands.

Teacher poses question— ②
Ask a question that can be answered briefly. For this structure the question should not be directed toward higher-level thinking, but rather should have one or two specific "correct" answers. For example, "Where is the dorsal fin of a fish located?" or "Does a wind vane point into the wind or away from the wind?"

Students' put heads together for discussion— ③
Team members should lean toward the center of the team so that they can quietly discuss the answer. Remind everyone that anyone could be called to give the team answer so they should all become involved in the discussion. When everyone on a team knows the answer they should sit back in their seats and stop talking.

Your
Cooperative Learning
Tools

Teacher chooses a number— (4)

When everyone has stopped talking, choose a student from each team to respond by calling out a number from 1 - 4. To be absolutely fair, you may want to use a spinner (available from ***Kagan Cooperative Learning***).

Numbered students respond— (5)

Depending on the type of answer, there are many ways to have the students with that number respond. If a numerical answer is needed, have each person hold up the correct number of fingers. If a one word answer is required, let them give a choral response when you give a signal.

My favorite response method is team chalkboards. I provide each team with a small chalkboard, a piece of chalk, and a sock for an eraser. The numbered student writes the team answer on the board and turns it upside down. On a signal from me, team chalkboards are held up for me to check.

If you don't have individual chalkboards, you can laminate a 10" x 12" piece of posterboard for each team. Distribute an overhead projector pen and a damp paper towel to each team also. Or you can also divide the class chalkboard into sections and have the designated students come forward and write the team's answer in the space provided.

No matter what response mode you choose, make sure students don't help each other during this step. Individual accountability is important. If students know that they will not be able to receive help if called upon, they will be more likely to listen when their team is discussing the answer.

After completing one round of **Numbered Heads,** continue to pose questions as needed. Try to allow all students the opportunity to answer at least one question.

Individuals Think / Numbered Heads Together

To increase student involvement and improve the quality of responses, give students think time before the team discussion. Immediately after posing the question, allow 10 or 15 seconds for each person to think of his or her own answer before allowing anyone to speak.

Individuals Write / Numbered Heads Together

To ensure even more individual participation, add in another step. Immediately after posing the question, have each person think of their own answer and write it on a slip of scrap paper. The team discussion may only begin after everyone has an idea down on paper.

Reviewing science vocabulary
• Identifying common objects (rocks, flowers, seeds, etc.)
• Finding elements on the Periodic Table
• Naming ways animals are adapted to their environment
• Reviewing science safety rules
• Stating possible effects of acid rain

(1) Teacher Designates Pairs

(2) Teacher Assigns Task

(3) Pairs Complete Task

(See Lessons 1, 2 and 8)

Pairs is the simplest of all structures; two students work together to complete an assigned task. **Pairs** allows plenty of student contact with science materials, but prevents individuals from feeling overwhelmed at having to do everything themselves. Students find comfort in knowing their partner is also listening to the directions or observing the demonstration. And sometimes all four hands are needed to hold materials together during an activity.

Pairs is an excellent structure to use when introducing cooperative learning to your students. Minimal social skills are needed for two students to work together. Both are likely to be equally involved with the task. Taking turns is easier in pairs than in teams.

The best aspect of **Pairs** is that working with a partner is fun! The magic of science doubles when students are able to share the experience with a friend.

Your
Cooperative Learning
Tools

1

Teacher designates pairs—

If your students are seated in teams of four, you can form your pairs easily by splitting the team into two sets of partners. Keep in mind the ability levels of your students. Don't place two students together who are both likely to struggle with the task. If your students are not seated in teams, you can assign partners in advance.

2

Teacher assigns task—

Assign the task to your students and explain the procedure. For example, you may have students work together to build weather instruments or to perform an experiment. Give clear, concise directions, explaining how they are to work together on the project. Tell students to ask their partner if they have a question. If neither of them knows the answer, they should both raise their hands to signal that this is a *pair* question.

3

Pairs complete task—

While your pairs are working, monitor their progress carefully. Make sure that they are participating equally. Encourage interdependence by answering questions only when both hands are raised.

- Constructing musical instruments
- Completing a survey
- Experimenting with batteries and bulbs
- Designing a paper airplane
- Graphing the results of an experiment
- Classifying rocks
- Making a kaleidoscope
- Investigating magnets
- Conducting an experiment
- Testing reflexes
- Collecting insects or leaves

① **Students Number Off**

② **Question Or Topic Is Posed**

③ **Students Take Turns
Sharing A Response**

(See Lessons 1, 2, 5, 14 and 15)

RoundRobin is one of the most simple and versatile of all cooperative learning structures. It provides an orderly framework for allowing each student within the team to share an idea, answer a question, state an observation, or make a prediction. In **RoundRobin,** students do not discuss or evaluate each other's responses, they simply listen to each other.

RoundRobin is excellent for sharing information or generating ideas. You can ask students to stop after each person has shared one idea, or you can challenge them to respond until they exhaust their all ideas.

I often use **RoundRobin** at the beginning of a class period to stimulate interest in the upcoming lesson or to review a concept I taught the previous day. I have also used it at the end of a class period to provide closure for the lesson. In this case, I ask them to **RoundRobin** something they learned from the lesson or a question they would like to investigate further.

Your
Cooperative Learning
Tools

Students number off— ①
Within each team of three to five, students number off in order.

Question or topic is posed— ②
In most cases, you will pose the topic or question. You may ask them to name as many planets as possible. Or you may ask them to share their predictions just before performing a science experiment. Sometimes you will allow them time to freely explore a set of materials then **RoundRobin** their observations.

RoundRobin may also be a part of a student-directed science experiment. In that case, the Lead Scientist will read the question to the team and each person will respond in turn. Often, a Recorder will write each person's response on the team's lab report.

Students take turns sharing a response— ③
After you pose the question, designate someone by number to begin sharing their response. After that person has answered, the next numbered person on each team responds until everyone has shared an answer. Be sure students know whether they are expected to stop after everyone has responded, or if they should continue until they run out of ideas. You may want to assign a Timekeeper in each team who will make sure that each person speaks for a designated amount of time. Encourage students to practice "active listening" skills by leaning forward, making eye contact, and focusing on what each person is saying.

RallyRobin
Students form pairs within the team and take turns sharing ideas back and forth. This calls for more active participation, since students are speaking 50% of the time.

• State observations or inferences
• Make predictions
• Ask questions
• Name zoo animals
• Name ocean life
• Name parts of a plant or types of plants
• Name parts of the body
• Name types of weather
• Name animals in a particular kingdom
• Name animals in a particular biome
• Name weather instruments
• Name planets and other heavenly bodies

① Students Number Off

② Teacher Explains Task

③ Students Take Turns Completing Task

(See Lessons 1, 4, 6, 7, 9 ,12 and 14)

RoundTable is a flexible and adaptable structure. Basically, **RoundTable** provides a method for taking turns within teams. This structure is similar to **RoundRobin** except that students are completing a task rather than just verbally sharing responses. Often, **RoundTable** involves passing a sheet of paper around and taking turns writing responses. In science, however, **RoundTable** may also be used when science materials are shared between students on a team. For example, you may want to give each person a hand lens and one object to view. As they finish viewing their object, they pass the object to the next person on the team.

RoundTable may also incorporate rotating roles. In some cases, everyone on the team may have a different role to complete. For example, each person may be asked to use a different sense to observe an object as it is passed around the team.

RoundTable is also excellent for having students complete team charts and graphs. Give each team one chart or graph. Assign each person on the team a section to complete. As the team chart is passed, everyone should watch and discuss the response being written.

My favorite way to use **RoundTable** in science is for sorting or classifying objects. Sometimes I announce the categories and sometimes I let students make up their own categories. One person "deals out" the items to be sorted so that everyone has approximately the same number. Then everyone takes turns placing their items into the correct categories. This is a great way to have students classify objects such as rocks, leaves, or seeds. Pictures of animals or plants can also be sorted this way.

Your
Cooperative Learning
Tools

Students number off— ①
Have your students number off
within their teams.

Teacher states task— ②
Begin **RoundTable** by explaining the task you
want your students to take turns completing. If
the task involves written responses, you'll want
your students to pass one or more sheets of
paper around.

If the task involves doing an activity, you'll need
to explain the procedure for carrying out the
task. For instance, if students are going to take
turns using a pan balance to weigh objects,
demonstrate the procedure as everyone watches.

**Students take turns
completing task—** ③
After you have explained the task, designate a
person on each team to begin the activity.
Everyone else offers praise and encouragement
as they carefully watch. When the first person
finishes, he or she passes the materials to the
next person on the team. Everyone continues
taking turns and passing materials until the
activity has been completed.

Simultaneous RoundTable
Normally in **RoundTable** only one
person is working at a time. In
Simultaneous RoundTable, however,
everyone has a task to complete
simultaneously. If the task involves
writing, everyone needs a piece of
paper and a pencil. For example, Person #1
may have a paper entitled "Fish," Person #2
may have a paper labeled "Amphibians,"
Person #3 may have "Birds," and Person #4
may have "Mammals." When the signal is
given, each person writes one example of
their topic. After they write a word, they pass
their papers clockwise. Each time they
receive a paper they add to the list.

RallyTable
Another way to increase participation is
to break the team into two sets of pairs. One
paper is given to each pair, and they pass the
paper back and forth. This structure is called
RallyTable.

• Listing names of animals
• Listing types of plants
• Writing observations
• Testing rocks and minerals
• Sharing microscopes
• Completing charts and graphs
• Sorting objects into categories
• Weighing and measuring items

① **Students Create Problems**

② **Teams Send Problems To Other Teams**

③ **Team Members Work Problems**

④ **Teams Continue Sending And Working Problems**

(See Lessons 7 and 10)

Send-A-Problem turns a problem-solving session into a game. By creating problems and sending them to other students, teams experience the fun of challenging others to solve their problems.

The "problems" used in this structure don't have to be stated in written form. **Send-A-Problem** has hands-on applications in science. Students can send each other objects to be identified, measured, or viewed under a microscope. They can also send each other classification schemes to be deciphered or science mysteries to be solved. Don't be afraid to apply this structure creatively!

Students create problems— ①

Students will create their own problems for this activity. For instance, the team might create a bar graph of their experiment results. Then each person writes one question about the graph on the front of an index card and the answer on the back. To make sure each problem is stated clearly and its answer is correct, team members should check each other's cards.

In cases where objects instead of written problems are sent, ask students to label each object clearly and provide answer keys on index cards. Then have them place all objects and answer keys on a paper plate or tray.

---

②

Teams send problems to other teams—

Have students number off from 1 - 4 within their teams. Since each team will be sending its problems to another team, decide the classroom rotation pattern in advance. Begin by having Person #4 deliver their team's problems to Person #1 on the next team. In the same way, at the end of each round Person #4 will deliver the problems to Person #1 on the next team.

③

Team members work problems—

When the set of problems arrives, person #1 keeps all the index cards in hand. He or she becomes the "teacher" for this round and reads the first question aloud. Everyone else is a "student" and solves the problem individually. After everyone writes their answer, they compare and discuss their solutions. The "teacher" then checks the team's answer by looking on the back of the index card. If the entire team disagrees with the answer on the back of the card, they send a messenger to the original team to get clarification.

Next, the "teacher" hands the entire stack of problem cards to Person #2. That person becomes the "teacher" for the next problem and follows the same steps outlined above. All four problems should be solved in the same manner, with a new "teacher" designated for each problem.

④

Teams continue sending and working problems—

When all four problems have been solved, Person #4 takes the stack to Person #1 on the next team. If problems pile up because one team works more slowly than the others, you may want to set a time limit for each round.

Writing descriptions of rocks or leaves to challenge other teams

• Solving brainteasers

• Writing questions about a graph of experiment results

• Writing questions about information that has been read aloud

• Measuring the volume of a selection of containers

• Solving science-related math word problems

Teacher-Created Problems →

In some cases, you may want to generate the problems rather than letting your students create them. Write the problems on individual slips  of paper or numbered index cards. If students will be sending objects, make sure all objects are labeled clearly. Provide each team with an answer key.

① **Identify And Discuss Choices**

② **Students Spend Bucks**

③ **Students Count Bucks To Find Top Choice**

(See Lessons 13, 14 and 15)

Spend-A-Buck is my favorite structure to use when teams make decisions. Before I learned this structure my students argued unproductively over choices that needed to be made. Either one student ended up telling everyone else what to do, or I had to step in and resolve the issue. After I taught my students **Spend-A-Buck,** they began to request it when making a decision.

In **Spend-A-Buck,** students are given a certain number of "bucks" (markers) to vote with during the decision-making process. The beauty of the structure is that team members can try to convince each other that a particular idea is best, but everyone has an equal voice in the final decision. Powers of persuasion aren't allowed to become powers of coercion.

Your
Cooperative Learning
Tools

Identify and discuss choices— ①

Spend-A-Buck can be used when students need to make any kind of choice or decision. The first step is to make sure everyone knows what the options are. Each choice must be written on a separate slip of paper. Sometimes students will come up with the choices on their own by **Brainstorming** their options. If the entire class is going to vote on the same choices, you can write them on a sheet of paper, duplicate one copy for each team, and have students cut apart the choices.

Next, give your students a chance to discuss the options. Depending on the decision, you can allow them a brief team discussion or even hold a class discussion. Encourage students to examine all the options carefully and to bring out the pros and cons of each choice. Don't let the discussion dissolve into an argument; teach them to respect each other's opinions.

Students spend bucks— ②

Now give each student the same number of "bucks" to spend. You can duplicate the page of bucks and have students cut them apart, or you can use any other kind of marker. Plastic bingo chips, slips of paper, dried beans, pennies, and cardboard "pogs" all work well. The number of bucks you give may depend on the activity, but five bucks work well for most decisions.

Have team members spread out all the choices so that everyone can see them easily. Then tell your students to spend their bucks on the choice or choices that they like best. Students can place all their bucks on their first choice or split their bucks between several choices. If they like five choices equally, they can place one buck on each.

Students count bucks to find top choice— ③

Designate one person on each team to count the bucks for each choice. Have them write the number of votes directly on the slips of paper that list each choice. If one choice is not a clear winner, let students retrieve their bucks and vote again for the top choices only.

Colored Bucks

I have found that students often change their minds in the middle of the voting process and want to take back some of the bucks they have already spent. Unfortunately, they can't remember how many bucks they have already put down on each idea. To solve this problem, I duplicate the bucks on white paper and let each team member decorate his or her bucks in a different color. This helps them keep track of how they are spending their bucks. After the decision has been made, one person collects all the bucks and places them in an envelope. The bucks are kept in the team supply basket, ready for any impromptu decisions.

Choosing a topic for a team project
• Voting on a class field trip
• Selecting an idea after Brainstorming
• Deciding upon a science experiment

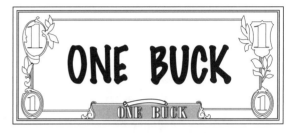

1. **Teacher Assigns Topic**

2. **Teammates Discuss Topic**

3. **To Equalize Participation, Use Talking Chips**

(See Lessons 12 and 15)

Team Discussion is a structure which can be slipped into almost any lesson. The teacher assigns a discussion topic and the members of each team share their thoughts on the subject. **Team Discussions** are useful when introducing a topic; you can have students discuss their prior knowledge to stimulate their interest in learning something new. During the lesson itself, you may want teams to discuss solutions to a problem or the pros and cons of a controversial topic. **Team Discussions** can also be used for reflection and review at the end of a lesson.

Team Discussion is a very versatile structure, but its use must be monitored carefully. It is one of the most unstructured of the cooperative learning structures, so it has the potential for unequal participation. However, there are ways to remedy that problem if it develops.

Structure **12**

Team Discussion

Your
Cooperative Learning
Tools

① Teacher assigns topic—

The best topics for team discussions are low-consensus questions. Instead of questions like "What is solar energy?" which have just one answer, try questions like "What are some common uses of solar energy?" or "What are the problems our country faces in trying to switch to solar energy?"

② Teammates discuss topic—

After the topic is announced, teammates put their heads together to discuss the topic. You may want to assign a time limit so that everyone knows just how much time they have to discuss the topic.

While your students are involved in their discussions, be sure to monitor your teams carefully. Especially at first, some teams may drift away from the assigned topic and need redirection. As you walk, listen to what your students are saying. Does everyone clearly understand the topic? You may discover that the original question was unclear, or that students don't have enough background knowledge to discuss the topic intelligently.

③ To equalize participation, use Talking Chips—

In monitoring the team's discussions, I occasionally notice that some team members are not involved while other members monopolize the conversation. When this happens, I implement **Talking Chips.**

To use this structure, give each team member an equal number of "chips," usually just 2 or 3. You can use bingo chips, small pieces of paper, or cardboard "pogs." As each member of the team contributes an idea to the discussion, he or she places a chip in the center of the team. A person may add ideas until he or she runs out of chips. When all chips are in the center of the table, everyone picks up their chips and the discussion continues.

One simple way to use **Talking Chips** is to allow students to use their pencil as a "chip." As each person voices an idea, his or her pencil is placed in the center of the table. When all pencils are down, everyone picks up their pencils and continues the discussion in the same manner.

How many items can you think of that are made of rocks and minerals?
• Can water look clean and be polluted? How?
• What are some reasons that rainforests should be saved?
• What simple machine makes up a bicycle?
• What are some examples of seeds that people eat?
• In what ways are plants different from animals?
• Do you think life can exist on Mars? Why or why not?
• How did people long ago predict the weather? Do these methods still work today?
• Why are fish shaped the way they are?
• What are some reasons that animals are endangered?
• What are some effects of acid rain?
• How is a polar bear adapted to arctic conditions?
• What is a mammal?

Pair Discussion

To encourage greater involvement, you may want to divide each team in half and involve the members in **Pair Discussions.** Younger children may find **Pair Discussions** easier than Team Discussions.

Class Discussion

Sometimes a **Class Discussion** is needed to allow all members to contribute ideas or to clear up misunderstandings. However, **Class Discussions** should be limited since they are a very weak form of cooperative learning.

(1) **Pencils Down**

(2) **Teammates Discuss Question**

(3) **Team Members Write Answers; No Talking**

(4) **Repeat Above Steps**

(See Lesson 11, 12 and 13)

Even in the midst of hands-on science, it is sometimes necessary to have students complete worksheets or lab reports individually. **Teammates Consult** is an excellent structure to use when you want each person to write their own responses to questions but you want the benefits of team interaction. When students are allowed to put their heads together before each response, the quality of the answers is multiplied. Yet students are individually accountable for writing the correct answer since they may not talk while they are writing.

Your
Cooperative Learning
Tools

Pencils down— ①

Unlike most cooperative learning structures, each person must have his or her own copy of the worksheet or lab report to complete.

To begin the activity, each person places his or her pencil in a cup (or supply basket) in the center of the team. If a cup is not readily available, students may simply place their pencils down on their desks.

Teammates discuss question— ②

When all pencils are down, Person #1 leads a discussion about the answer to the first question. Everyone should contribute ideas, but everyone does not have to agree on the answer to the question.

Team members write answers; no talking.— ③

When everyone is ready, all team members pick up their pencils and silently write their answers. They do not have to write the same answer or use the exact words of other team members. Most importantly, they may not talk or ask for help while they are writing. Similarly, team members may not copy from each other's papers.

You will have to monitor this step of **Teammates Consult** very closely at first. Many students forget that they are not allowed to talk while they are writing. Remind individual teams that they may talk and write, but not both at the same time. If a team consistently breaks this rule, remove the talking privilege and have them complete the worksheet individually. With a little practice, students get very good at monitoring themselves and their teammates during this structure.

Repeat above steps.— ④

When everyone is finished writing a response, team members place their pencils back into the cup. Person #2 leads a discussion on the answer to the next question. When all team members are ready, everyone again picks up their pencils to write the answer to the second question.

Team members should continue in the same manner until the worksheet or assignment is complete. With each round of the activity, the role of discussion leader rotates.

• Lesson review questions
• Experiment logs
• Lab reports
• Worksheets
• Interpreting graphs
• Identifying objects

① **Teacher Explains Project**

② **Teacher Assigns Roles**

③ **Teams Complete Project**

④ **Teams Present Project**

(See Lessons 1, 5, 6, 7, 10, 11, 14 and 15)

Team Projects involve the creation of a unique product by each team, and can be very simple or very involved. They may be relatively unstructured or highly structured, depending on the individual requirements of the project. **Team Projects** may take as little as five minutes or as long as several weeks to complete. I like **Team Projects** because in addition to their usefulness academically, they build team spirit. Team members take pride in the results of their work together.

Team Projects have a variety of uses in science. For example, teams may create posters showing food webs or illustrating the bones of the body. Teams can create their own rock, leaf, or seed collections. This structure is ideal for having students create team booklets. I have also discovered that **Team Projects** are useful when students work together to complete science experiments and investigations.

Teacher explains project— ①

When you assign a **Team Project**, be sure to explain the project clearly to your students. Decide in advance the basic guidelines, but be flexible to your students' input. Make sure you tell the class the amount of time you are allowing for them to complete their project.

Teacher assigns roles—

Assigning roles is one of the best ways to equalize participation. When you decide on the roles your students will need, keep in mind the purposes of the project, the number of students on each team, and the ages of your students. If you have four people on each team, you need four roles. If one team has five people, be sure to create another role for the fifth person on that team (if only Praiser or Encourager). The following roles are appropriate for many science activities:

Role	Description
Lead Scientist	Keeps the group on task. Makes sure everyone follows directions.
Materials Monitor	Gets all the materials for the team.
Cleanup Captain	Makes sure that everyone helps clean up and makes sure the area is left neat.
Time Keeper	Keeps time for the group.
Quiet Captain	Monitors noise level.
Praiser	Praises the accomplishments of team members.
Recorder	Records the ideas of the team.
Reporter	Reports the team's ideas to the class.
Question Commander	Is the only one who may ask the teacher questions, and only after checking to see that no one on the team knows the answer.

You may also want to make up roles which are appropriate only for a particular activity. For instance, the "Seed Sorting" lesson calls for Seed Keepers and Chart Checkers.

The easiest way to assign roles is by number. Have your students number off 1 - 4 and announce the role assignments by number. Make role cards to help everyone remember their roles. For each student, fold stiff paper into a "tent" and write the name of their role on both sides. You can also make one-sided role cards which can be hung from a string around each child's neck or pinned on each shirt. If you decide to rotate roles during the activity, have students switch their role cards.

I have developed an easy way to ensure that roles are rotated fairly. Construct a Rotating Role Finder with the pattern provided. Write your four roles in the spaces on the outside circle. After the device is made, simply turn the inside circle to assign new roles.

Rotating roles gives everyone a chance to perform all tasks, but the practice of switching roles can be confusing and distracting. For simple projects, you will probably want each student to keep the same role throughout the activity.

Teams complete project—

After explaining the project, distribute materials and let students get to work. If close supervision is needed with an activity, have students complete the project at a learning center. Monitor the center yourself or solicit the help of a parent volunteer.

Teams present project—

Allow some time for students to share their work with others. Providing this time shows students that you value their efforts. Teams may present to other teams or to the entire class. Teams can share the results of an experiment by taking part in the creation of a class graph.

- Creating collections of rocks, leaves, seeds, etc.
- Designing posters of seasons, biomes, types of weather
- Creating collages of mammals, birds, reptiles, etc.
- Illustrating food webs of various habitats
- Developing the best paper helicopter to enter in a contest
- Creating a musical instrument from ordinary materials
- Experimenting with plants or seeds
- Making team booklets
- Creating simple weather instruments

Planning Team Projects

Team Projects are unlike other structures because each project is unique. The steps for completing each project are different and depend entirely on a particular project's desired outcome or "product". To achieve this outcome, **Team Projects** may incorporate other structures. Yet, some products are highly creative, and a lack of structure may be needed during this creation process.

All of these factors open up the possibility of unequal participation. For this reason, keep in mind the Four Basic Principles of cooperative learning when you plan your projects. Decide in advance how you will incorporate positive interdependence, equal participation, individual accountability, and simultaneity. Since each project is unique, the manner in which you do so will vary from project to project.

Planning a **Team Project** to incorporate the Four Basic Principles is challenging, especially at first. However, without this type of planning, cooperative learning disintegrates into "groupwork." Some students take over and do everything, while others are free to do nothing. Positive interdependence, individual accountability, equal participation, and simultaneity are essential in **Team Projects.**

Positive interdependence is present when all students must participate in order for a project to be completed successfully. One way to make students interdependent is to limit the materials and assign one material to each person. For example, put one person in charge of the scissors, assign the glue to another, and give the remaining students the markers. Another way to make students dependent upon each other is to give each person only part of the information needed to complete the project. Finally, I like to assign roles so that each person has a specific job.

Individual accountability is needed to make sure that each person actually participates in the final project. Having students color-code projects such as posters can help you see how much each person has contributed. If each person is assigned a different color marker or paper, you can assess participation with a quick glance. If no obvious method of determining accountability exists, monitor your students carefully while they work. Spend a little time talking with individual students on each team to find out how they participated and what they learned from the activity.

Assigning roles also helps ensure **equal participation.** Plan carefully to make sure the tasks are divided and assigned so that no one ends up doing all the work. If some roles involve more participation than others, rotate roles throughout the project. Using other structures within the **Team Project** is another way to encourage equal participation. I often have my students use **RoundTable** and **RoundRobin** when they are doing **Team Projects.**

Finally, when planning a **Team Project** be sure to consider the principle of **simultaneity.** Cooperative learning is in its weakest form when three people are watching one person complete a task. Try to structure the activity so that everyone is doing something at the same time. One way to increase simultaneity is to use pair work within the confines of the **Team Projects.** Another way is to plan the project so that everyone works on one part simultaneously and then assembles the completed project at the end.

Rotating Role Finder Directions—

1. Cut out base and numbered dial on dark lines.

2. Write one role title on each of the four outer sections of the base.

3. Center the numbered dial on top of the base.

4. Push a paper fastener through the center of both circles.

5. Turn numbered dials to rotate roles.

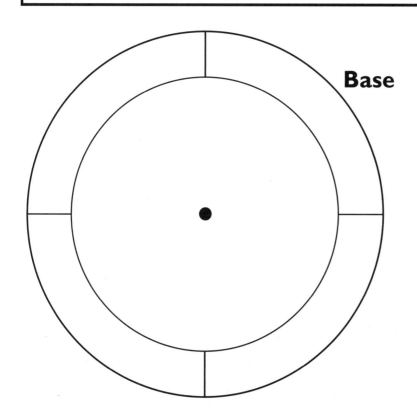

Base

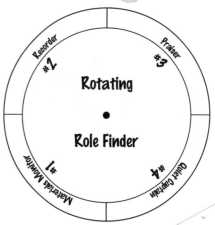

**Sample Rotating Role Finder
Spinner**

Numbered Dial

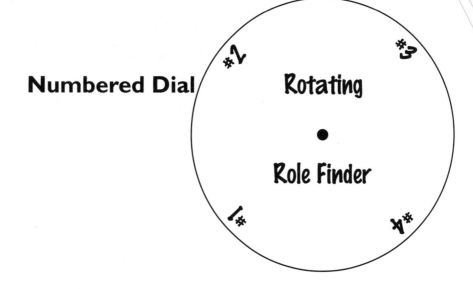

(1) **Teacher Poses Question**

(2) **Individuals Think**

(3) **Pairs Discuss Responses**

(4) **Students Share Responses With Class**
(See Lessons 3, 5, 6, 7, 10, 11, 12, 14 and 15)

Think-Pair-Share is a simple yet powerful structure. Instead of a few students answering the teacher's question, everyone in the class must respond. By its very nature, the structure demands involvement. When students know they will be expected to discuss a question or a concept, they are motivated to pay attention.

Think-Pair-Share can be used during any part of the lesson. Discussing prior knowledge is a great way to involve students from the very start. During the lesson, discussing a topic with a partner will stimulate higher-level thinking. Stopping periodically to **Think-Pair-Share** also allows students time to mentally process the lesson content. Finally, the structure can be used for review, directing students to focus on what they have learned.

① Teacher poses question—

Begin by asking a question related to the lesson. Questions which stimulate discussion are best, as opposed to those with a single, simple answer.

② Individuals *think*—

Provide necessary think time for individuals to formulate their own answers. This is a critical step, since a student who does not have time to develop a personal response will have nothing to contribute to the pair discussion. You might even ask everyone to give you a thumbs up signal when they are ready.

③ Students *pair* to discuss responses—

Now ask students to pair with a partner to discuss their ideas. You should designate partners in advance so time is not wasted deciding who will speak with whom. Monitor this step carefully. Walk around the room and listen to what the children are saying to each other. Sometimes you'll hear comments that indicate a concept was misunderstood. Occasionally you'll find a pair who are completely off the topic and need some redirection.

④ Students *share* their responses with the class—

Randomly call on students to share their responses. This part of the structure is very important for clearing up misunderstandings or focusing attention on a particular issue. To hold students accountable for listening to each other, ask them to only share what their partner said during the discussion. Students need to know that a discussion involves both speaking and listening.

- Making predictions
- Making inferences
- Discussing observations
- Explaining how to separate plastics for recycling
- Describing the pros and cons of various sources of energy
- Naming some effects of air pollution on health
- Explaining how a particular animal is adapted to its environment
- Discussing the scientific basis for weather proverbs
- Comparing and contrasting characteristics of minerals
- Describing how to construct an electromagnet

Think-Pair-Square

Sometimes you'll use the structure simply to stimulate thought or provoke a discussion. In this case, you may not need students to share their answers with the class. In **Think-Pair-Square**, students think about their responses, pair to discuss them, and then talk over their ideas with their team. In the last step, they square their responses rather than sharing them with the class.

Think-Write-Pair-Share

If some students seem to have nothing to say during the pair discussion, have everyone jot down their ideas before speaking. Students are more likely to become involved in a discussion after they have committed their ideas to paper.

① One Partner Interviews The Other

② Partners Reverse Roles

③ Team Members RoundRobin Information

(See Lessons 2, 5 and 8)

Three-Step Interview is an excellent structure for sharing information between team members. Each team is divided into two sets of partners who interview each other and then share what they learned with their teammates. The final step, **RoundRobin,** ensures that students listen to each other actively during the interview process.

Three-Step Interview is powerful, because as students share information, they also build team unity. The teambuilding benefits are present even when the information is based on science content rather than personal interests.

This structure has a variety of uses. Students can interview each other to find out their opinions about a particular subject. For instance, during a unit on the environment you can have students interview each other about which environmental issues they feel are most important. **Three-Step Interview** can also be used to share drawings or posters created for a science lesson. Students who complete science projects at home can interview each other about the results of their investigations. Students can also interview each other about current event articles.

Your
Cooperative Learning
Tools

One partner interviews the other— ①

Before you begin, divide each team of four into two sets of pairs. Within each pair, designate one person as the "A" partner and the other as the "B" partner. Tell the students that they will be interviewing each other about a particular project or topic. Explain what an interview is and have the class brainstorm a list of possible questions to ask. Teach students how to turn "yes/no" questions into open-ended questions. For example, instead of asking, "Was your prediction for your experiment correct?" they could ask "What did you learn from your experiment?"

Partner A first interviews Partner B by asking questions about B's topic or project. Give a specific time limit for this. One minute is enough for simple interviews; sometimes three or five minutes are needed for more in-depth interviews.

Tell the interviewers to listen carefully since they will have to report the information they learn to the team. I don't allow students to take notes; students pay attention better when they know they have to rely on their listening skills alone.

Partners reverse roles— ②

Now have Partner B interview Partner A for the same amount of time. Again, caution the interviewers to listen carefully and try to remember the details of the interview.

Team members RoundRobin information— ③

In the final step, team members share what they have learned with the team. Number your students from 1 to 4. Give each person 30 seconds or a minute to share. Have Person #1 begin by telling the team what they learned about their partner. Then have Persons #2, #3, and #4 in turn share what they learned.

Four-Step Interview

If your students have trouble with this structure, you might try an easier variation of **Three-Step Interview**. After the first round of interviews, let the two interviewers (the "A" partners) immediately report what they learned. This way they don't have to remember the information for a long period of time. Then conduct the second round of interviews and let the B partners immediately report what they learned.

Teams of Three

Sometimes you'll have three people left over after the remaining students are paired. You can join in as the fourth member of the team for this activity, or you can let the team of three conduct their interviews without you. In a three-person interview, each time someone is interviewed, two people on the team will interview the remaining team member. First, Partners A and B will interview C. Then B and C will interview A. Finally, C and A will interview B. Omit the **RoundRobin** stage since everyone has been involved in each interview.

Sharing science current event articles
• Interviewing about experiments
• Asking about favorite plants or animals
• Interviewing about personal opinions on science topics
• Sharing the results of research on famous scientists or inventors
• Reviewing what was learned after a lesson
• Sharing what was learned on a field trip
• Telling about science-related artwork

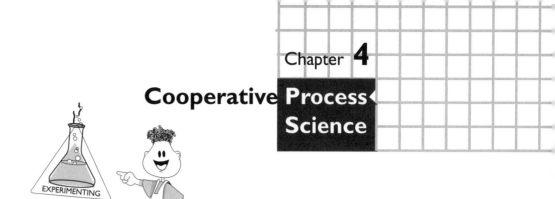

Science Process Skills ◆

Writing About Science ◆

Integrating The Curriculum ◆

Science Materials ◆

Science Safety ◆

Ready...Set...Science! ◆

To be successful, students need a broad base of science knowledge as well as the ability to think critically and perform basic science skills. The best science lessons introduce just enough science content to stimulate thinking, then develop those concepts through hands-on activities. We cannot rush students through science activities; we must give them time to play with new concepts, time to make new ideas fit with others previously learned.

Cooperative learning offers the best way to link science content with science skills. As students work together, they share the excitement of learning new ideas. By interacting with other students, they become aware of new perspectives. Working together, they develop process skills as they experiment and manipulate objects in their environment.

With this in mind, I have developed 15 multi-structural science lessons which teach science concepts through hands-on activities. Students learn to think and behave like scientists as they increase their science knowledge. Each lesson presents a tidbit of science information, followed by extensive opportunities to play with ideas and manipulate objects in order to master that information. Because of this, most lessons span several days and include a variety of activities.

If you have ever attempted to incorporate hands-on instruction into your curriculum, you know that science activities have a way of failing unexpectedly. You read about a great activity, but when you attempt it in class it doesn't work. To eliminate these frustrations, I have had many teachers field test these lessons. Since environmental factors often affect the outcome of an experiment, I can't guarantee the success of every activity. It's always best to try the activity in advance, just to make sure. However, I do give detailed step-by-step instructions and offer hints to make your experiences successful.

One concern I frequently hear is "How do I find time to teach process skills in science?" The answer to this lies in rethinking our objectives. Is it more important for students to memorize the parts of a plant or observe the wonder of a plant sprouting from a seed? Should students have to correctly identify rock samples, or might they learn more from testing rocks and classifying them according to their properties? Would it be better to read about weather instruments or to make a wind vane and use it? When moving from content-oriented to process-oriented science, you must be willing to sacrifice some content in order to spend time developing skills.

Make time for hands-on science by eliminating the clutter of extraneous facts and information. Don't try to *add* these science lessons to your

curriculum; teach these lessons *instead* of the lessons you taught previously. If you have been using your textbook to teach animal classification systems, forego the textbook in favor of the cooperative learning lesson "Animal Classification." Your students will gain a deeper understanding of the five classes of vertebrates, and they'll have fun doing it! The topic of each lesson is given on the lesson introduction page; examine the topics and decide how you will make time for the lessons which fit your curriculum.

Science Process Skills

Exactly what science process skills should we teach? Consult a dozen different resources, and you'll find a dozen different process skill lists. I have chosen to focus on ten skills that range from the simple to the complex. An overview of these skills will help you understand their importance.

1. Observing

Observation skills are essential to science. Before students can identify, classify, or infer, they must be able to use all their senses to observe their world. In addition to seeing objects and events, students must taste, touch, smell, and listen to their environment.

2. Identifying

Identification involves labelling objects and events. Naming objects often enables us to discuss those objects more easily. However, be careful not to require students to memorize names purely for the sake of memorization. Students often enjoy being able to identify local trees, rocks, and insects, but that enjoyment can easily be destroyed if students must memorize names without the opportunity to handle concrete objects.

3. Classifying

As students develop their observation skills, they begin to notice similarities and differences between objects. They begin to sort and group those objects based on their observations. You can foster these skills by teaching them various methods of classification, such Venn diagrams or dichotomous sorting "trees."

4. Predicting

Prediction involves making an educated guess about what will happen before an event takes place. When students perform experiments, making a prediction is often called "making a hypothesis." Prediction is a valuable skill for students to develop because it involves applying previously learned science concepts to new situations. Students become more involved in the outcome of a science activity when they are first given time to predict what will happen.

5. Making Models

Many science concepts involve objects so large or complex that students have a difficult time understanding them. Often these concepts can be simplified by constructing models. For instance, a camera may seem to be a magical instrument to many students. By constructing a pinhole camera, students can begin to understand how a camera captures images on paper.

6. Measuring

One of the most basic science skills students need is competence in measurement. Since the international standard for measurement in science is the Metric System, the lessons in this book involve metric measurement. Students who take "authentic" science tests are expected to have a working knowledge of the Metric System; hands-on practice with these skills is essential.

7. Organizing Data

When students conduct science investigations, they often collect data. Without some type of organization, that data is meaningless. We can easily teach students to organize the information they collect by providing charts and graphs for them to use. Eventually, we can teach them to generate the necessary charts and graphs on their own.

8. Inferring

Students have truly mastered a science concept when they can make inferences based on what they have learned. Providing plenty of opportunity for kids to "figure things out" on their own will develop the skill of inferring. Even when students don't make correct inferences, praise them for their attempts to figure things out independently.

9. Experimenting

Experimentation integrates many other process skills. Unfortunately, the term "experimenting" is often used loosely. Many people believe that any science activity is an "experiment." However, a true experiment has several identifiable characterisitics.

Generally an experiment is conducted in order to answer a question, such as "Do ants prefer sugar or artificial sweetners?" Many times the person conducting the experiment makes a *hypothesis,* or an educated guess, about the outcome of the experiment. The scientist follows a specific series of steps, called the *procedure,* in order to answer the question. Throughout the experiment, the scientist attempts to control *variables.* This simply means that he or she tries to keep most parts of the experiment the same, only changing the one part being tested. Scientists also conduct repeated *trials;* in other words, they repeat their experiments to eliminate the chance that their results were due to error. As scientists experiment, they record *data* such as observations or measurements. They organize their data with charts or graphs and state *conclusions* based on their results.

We can help students understand the process of experimentation in many ways. First, we can have them make predictions before they experiment. We can also discuss the importance of changing only one part of the experiment at a time. By having students conduct repeated trials, they learn the importance of not drawing conclusions based on one set of data. Finally, we can teach students to organize their data so that they are able to analyze it and draw conclusions about their experiments.

10. Communicating

Communication skills encompass speaking, writing, reading, and listening. With cooperative learning, many of these skills are integrated automatically. In every lesson, students must communicate their ideas effectively to their teammates or the team will be unable to function.

Writing About Science

One communication skill often overlooked in science is writing. When students are working in teams, it's especially important to have them reflect in writing upon what they have learned. Writing is a very personal task, one which forces an individual to struggle with a concept in order to get it on paper. If we don't integrate writing into our lessons, we may find that students are enjoying science immensely without retaining any concepts. For this reason, every lesson concludes with a "Writing About Science" section which offers ideas for developing this important communication skill.

An easy way to encourage writing in science is to have students keep a Science Journal. You can have students create Journals by stapling loose-leaf paper between two sheets of construction paper. Or you can ask them to purchase a composition book for this purpose. After each lesson, have them respond to the "Writing About Science" questions. Students can also illustrate their journal entries.

Integrating the Curriculum

Science knowledge is meaningless if it is not applied to life. The aim of science education is not to turn every student into a scientist, but to help students apply science knowledge and skills to everyday situations. The critical thinking and problem solving skills developed in science will enable students to become happier, more productive citizens.

Elementary teachers have a unique opportunity to strengthen the connections between science and other areas of the curriculum. Since many elementary educators teach more than one subject, they can easily link science with other subject areas. For example, students studying about the weather can graph temperatures in math, make tornado safety posters in art, and write weather poems in language arts.

To help you integrate science with other subjects, I have concluded each lesson with suggestions for "Curriculum Links." In addition, a number of the lessons introduce key concepts through children's literature.

Science Materials

Teaching hands-on science is more difficult than teaching textbook science in one respect: locating the materials for students to put their "hands on." I won't belittle this problem by saying that most of the materials used are common household items. Even though most *are* everyday items, I recognize that you will invest time, effort, and money in gathering enough materials for each lesson. Plastic cups, bean seeds, and potting soil may not be expensive, but supplying your class with such materials on a regular basis can be quite costly.

Yet, science materials are absolutely essential to hands-on instruction. Problems in obtaining materials must be addressed and resolved if meaningful science instruction is to occur. Fortunately, using cooperative learning instead of individual instruction significantly reduces the amount of materials needed. However, appropriate materials are still needed for each team.

If your school's science budget is somewhat skimpy, creative planning can solve some of your problems in locating materials. One solution is to request that parents donate some of the more common household items. Write down the materials you need for the remainder of the year, and send home this "wish list" with each student. In addition, ask your parent-teacher organization to help you purchase some non-consumable items like magnets, hand lenses, batteries, and wire. Local businesses, especially companies that rely heavily on science and technology, may support your efforts with a financial contribution.

If you are able to obtain some money but aren't sure where to order materials, consult the Science Resources at the back of this book. The companies listed specialize in supplying science books and materials to teachers. All of them have a toll-free number you can call for more information or to obtain a catalog.

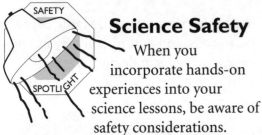

Science Safety

When you incorporate hands-on experiences into your science lessons, be aware of safety considerations. Make sure you follow any safety guidelines issued by your district or state. Remember that students who have been given more freedom to explore don't instinctively know when exploration borders on being unsafe. They trust you to set the limits. Be especially cautious when working with flames, chemicals, glass, or electricity.

Many of the lessons in this book pose no possible danger to students at all. However, some of the lessons contain potential hazards if students are not properly supervised during the activities. In these lessons, I have identified and described the possible problems. Read the "Safety Spotlight" section at the beginning of these lessons to learn about safety precautions which will enable you to avoid potentially hazardous situations.

Ready . . . Set . . . Science!

With an awareness of the process skills and an understanding of the importance of cooperative learning, you are ready to begin. First try the lessons which fit your curriculum and grade level. When you become comfortable with the multi-structural approach, try adapting some of the other lessons to meet your needs. In any event, prepare yourself for the excitement of science!

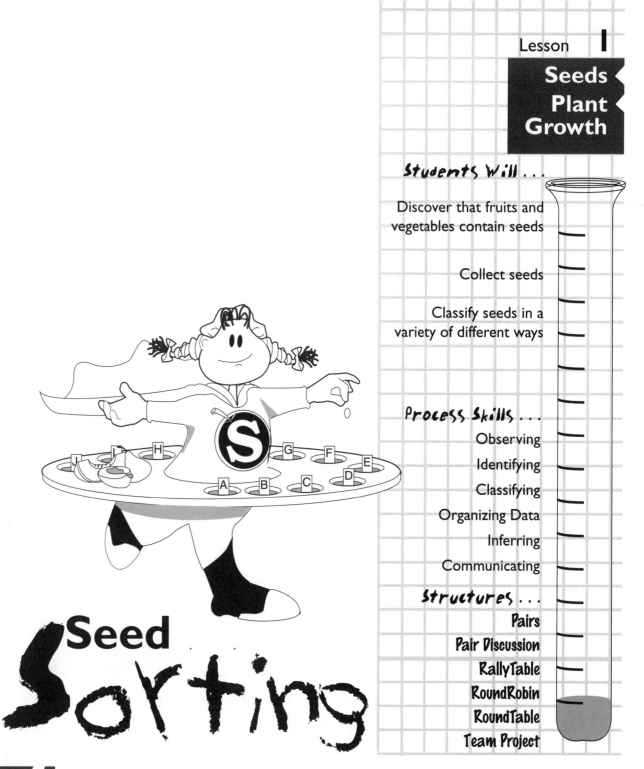

Students Will . . .

Discover that fruits and
vegetables contain seeds

Collect seeds

Classify seeds in a
variety of different ways

Process Skills . . .

Observing

Identifying

Classifying

Organizing Data

Inferring

Communicating

Structures . . .

Pairs

Pair Discussion

RallyTable

RoundRobin

RoundTable

Team Project

Seed Sorting

Seeds are one of the most simple and basic science topics to explore, yet the study of seeds never fails to fascinate children. This lesson provides the opportunity for students to investigate seeds while developing their classification skills. You will begin by reading *From Seed to Plant* (or another suitable book) to your students. Then you will show them examples of foods which contain seeds and will let them break open a green bean to discover the seeds within.

Next you will teach your students how to classify seeds according to color, size, and shape. Later, your students will take part in a Seed Scavenger Hunt. You'll help them discover the different ways seeds travel, after which they will classify their seeds according to method of dispersal.

Obtain enough whole green beans (preferably raw) for each student to have one. Collect several examples of fruits and vegetables that have obvious seeds. Some examples are: apples, peaches, corn, Chinese pea pods, strawberries, lemons, and tomatoes.

You'll also need a variety of dried beans for the first sorting activity. A few bags of beans for 15-bean soup work best, but if these are not available buy 5 or 6 types of dried beans and mix them in advance. Lentils, peas, kidney beans, lima beans, black beans, pinto beans, and red beans would work well.

Before beginning the lesson, divide your students into teams of four. Then divide each team into two sets of pairs.

1

Read about seeds using TEACHER READS

Materials for the Class:
From Seed to Plant by Gail Gibbons (or any suitable book about seeds)

Read *From Seed to Plant* aloud to your students. (If you are unable to obtain this book, *The Reason for a Flower* by Ruth Heller would work well.)

2

Naming fruits and vegetables with seeds using ROUNDROBIN

Ask your students to think of the fruits and vegetables they have eaten that have seeds in them. Then have them **RoundRobin** the names of those foods.

3

Showing examples of seeds
using TEACHER DEMONSTRATES

Materials for the Class:
several vegetables and fruits which contain seeds that are easy to observe

Show your students the fruit and vegetable examples you have brought to class. Point out the seeds in each example. If the seeds are hidden, be sure to cut open the fruit or vegetable so that everyone can see the seeds within.

SAFETY SPOTLIGHT

Be sure to tell your students not to place any of the seeds in their mouths. Some seeds are poisonous and many of them present a choking hazard. Dried beans can be particularly hazardous if swallowed, since they will swell and can be difficult to dislodge.

4

Discovering bean seeds using INDIVIDUALS EXPLORE

Materials for each Student:
1 whole raw green bean
several dried beans

Give each student a whole raw green bean. Have them feel the bean and guess what is inside. Ask them to count the number of bumps they feel. Then show your students how to slip a fingernail between the halves of the pod and split it open. Let them take out the seeds and count them.

Then give each student several dried bean seeds. Caution them not to put the seeds in their mouths. Ask them to compare the two types of bean seeds. Tell them that the dried beans are seeds just like the ones that came out of the raw green bean. They have been dried out so that they could be stored easily.

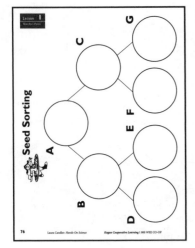

Classifying dried beans using PAIRS

Materials for each Pair:
dried beans – 15 bean soup variety (1/8 cup per pair)
1 Seed Sorting worksheet

Step One: Pair Discussion

To begin the activity, give each pair about 1/8 cup of dried beans. Tell your students that they are going to work together to sort the beans into several piles. They will need to look carefully at the beans and try to see how the beans are alike and different. First ask them to discuss with their partner the ways that some of the beans are alike. Then ask them to discuss the ways that the beans are different from each other.

Step Two: Sorting seeds

Now ask the students to sort their beans into two piles so that all the beans in one pile are alike in some way. All the beans in the other pile must be different from those in the first pile.

If they are having difficulty, lead them through an example. Have them put all the red seeds in one pile and all the rest in another one. Say "These seeds are red, and these are 'not red.'" Some children may need help with the concept "not" as in "not red." Children need to learn to describe their sets orally, using the word "not" rather than trying to describe all the different colors in the other pile.

Write the word *attribute* on the board. Tell them that color is an "attribute" that can help us sort the beans into piles. All the beans have a color, even though they are not all the same color. Tell your students that the beans have many different attributes which can be used to sort them.

Let the pairs continue to develop their own classification schemes. Walk around and talk to each pair to find out how they are sorting their beans.

(continued on page 69

5

Classifying dried beans using (continued from page 68)

Step Three: Introducing the branching classification system
Give each pair one copy of the Seed Sorting page. Tell them to put all their seeds into Circle A at the top of the page. Write the word *classify* on the board. Tell your students that to "classify" means to decide how things are alike and different so that you can put them into groups. Tell them that they will sort their pile of seeds into many different groups by thinking about the ways the seeds are alike and different.

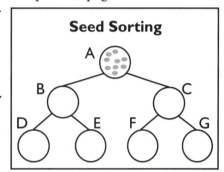

Seed Sorting

Lead the class through the entire sorting process the first time you introduce the concept of branching classification systems. Ask the pairs to put their heads together and discuss the ways the seeds could be divided into just two piles. They should be able to draw upon their earlier exploratory experiences. Let several students offer suggestions, and then pick a very easy attribute for the class to begin with. You might start with "large" and "not large" (small). You do not need to write the names of the categories on the page. If you feel words are needed, draw the illustration on the board and write the names of the attributes in the circles.

(continued on page 70)

5 cont.

Classifying dried beans using PAIRS (continued from page 69)

Step Four: Sorting seeds
Use **RallyTable** for the actual sorting process. In each pair, name one person the "A" partner and the other person the "B" partner. Ask A to take one seed from the circle at the top and think about whether it is large or small. Allow the two to discuss that characteristic,

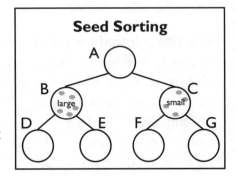

and tell them that the words large and small aren't very exact. The two of them together will have to decide together where the seed goes. There are no specific right or wrong answers as long as the general guidelines are followed. After they have agreed on the placement, A puts the seed in the correct circle.

B chooses another seed to classify. After they both discuss its placement, B moves the seed to the appropriate circle. The two continue **RallyTable** sorting until all the seeds in circle A have been moved to circles B and C.

Step Five: Discussing ways to sort seeds
Next, the students look at just circle B. Ask them to discuss ways they could divide just that set of seeds into two more categories. Let several students share their ideas with the class. Choose one to do together and write the two attributes on the board. An example would be "speckled" and "not speckled."

(continued on page 71)

5

Classifying dried beans using (continued from page 70)

Step Six: Sorting seeds
Have students use the same
RallyTable structure used earlier
to sort the seeds in circle B. All
seeds from that circle should be
moved into either Circle D or E.

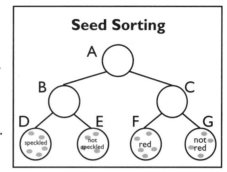

Step Seven: Discussing ways to sort seeds
Now students consider the seeds left in circle C. Ask them to
discuss ways that those seeds could be divided into two piles. The
classification scheme does not have to be the same as the one used
to divide pile B. Let several students volunteer ideas and choose
one to lead with the class. Post the names on the board.

Step Eight: Sorting seeds
Students complete the classification process by continuing with the
RallyTable method of sorting seeds.

Step Nine: Discussing the classification of a particular seed
Now hold up a particular seed from one of the bottom four
categories. Ask the students to **Think-Pair-Share** the explanation for
why that seed is in that circle. They should name both the
attributes of the seed that were used to classify it. For example,
"The seed is large and speckled." Continue holding up seed until
everyone can explain why a particular seed was placed into a
particular circle.

Step Ten: Creating classification systems
If your class has become comfortable with the classification
process, have them put all the bean seeds in Circle A again. Then
have them divide the seeds according to their own sorting schemes.
Let them challenge the pair across from them to figure out their
classification system.

Seed Scavenger Hunt using **TEAM PROJECT**

Materials for each Team:
2 Seed Scavengers worksheets
2 baggies
1 bottle of glue

Step One: Explaining the Scavenger Hunt

Distribute one copy of either Seed Scavengers worksheet to each team. Ask your students if they know what a scavenger hunt is and explain if anyone is unsure. Tell them that they will be trying to find seeds which fit the categories described on their worksheet. Tell them that the class will be doing several activities with the seeds, so they should try to collect two examples of each seed.

Step Two: Assigning roles

To make sure the project is successful, assign the roles of Leader, Materials Monitor, Seed Keeper, and Chart Checker. You may want to make rolecards for the four different roles. The students can wear their rolecards by taping them on to their shirts or hanging them by string around the neck. Explain each person's responsibilities to the class.

1) The **Leader** makes sure that everyone listens to and follows directions. He or she is the only one who may ask questions.
2) The **Materials Monitor** is the one who will get the materials that the team needs to complete the chart.
3) The **Seed Keeper** keeps the team's collections of seeds. Give that person two baggies so that they can collect two complete sets of everything. The Seed Keeper labels the baggies with the team name.
4) The **Chart Checker** makes sure that everyone agrees on the placement of any seed before it is glued down.

Step Three: Hunting for seeds

If the weather allows, take students on a walk around the school grounds to look for seeds. Autumn and spring are excellent time for collecting seeds outdoors. Let students have a little time before leaving school to plan their strategy for finding the rest of the seeds. Remind them that many fruits and vegetables contain seeds.

To equalize participation, tell everyone that they must contribute at least five different kinds of seeds to the team's collection.

(continued on page 73)

6 cont.

Seed Scavenger Hunt (continued from page 72)

Step Four: Sorting seeds

The next day have the seed keeper collect all the seeds found by team members. They split the seeds evenly between the two baggies, putting one of each type into each bag. Next, the seed keeper puts one bag away and gives everyone and equal number of seeds from the remaining bag.

Give each team a fresh copy of the worksheet. Beginning with the Leader, the students take turns placing one of his or her seeds on the chart. They shouldn't glue the seeds in place yet since some seeds may need to be moved. If a seed needs to be moved, everyone on the team should agree to the move. The person who originally placed the seed picks it up and moves it to the new location. Tell students that they are not expected to fill every square on the Seed Scavenger worksheet, just as many as possible.

After the seeds have been placed, the Chart Checker leads the team in making sure all seeds are correctly placed. When everyone has agreed, the students take turns gluing the seeds into place. They each glue down one column of seeds.

Glue the charts onto construction paper or poster board and post them where everyone can admire each others' projects. If some teams want to continue trying to find seeds to fill their chart, let them do so. Many students will bring seeds to add to the chart long after the activity is officially over.

Don't be too concerned with identifying the seeds. Discovering their unique qualities is more important than memorizing their names. While classifying the seeds, students will begin to ask questions about them. These questions will provide a bridge to the final part of the lesson.

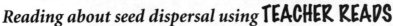

7

Reading about seed dispersal using TEACHER READS

Materials for the Class:
From Seed to Plant (or any book which describes ways that seeds travel)

Ask your students if they have ever noticed a single dandelion out in the middle of their yard or in a field of grass. Ask them to think about how the seed that made the plant may have landed there. Reread the section of *From Seed to Plant* that describes the different ways seeds travel. Explain that seeds travel in many ways. Some just drop to the ground and take root. Others are hidden by animals who forget to dig them up. Some drift with the wind, others float on water, and still others have hooks that cling to animals' fur.

8

Classifying seeds by method of travel using ROUNDTABLE

Materials for each Team:
bag of seeds saved from Activity 6
1 Traveling Seeds worksheet
1 hand lens
1 cup of water

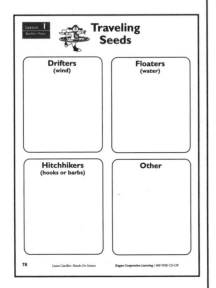

If time allows, you may want to take the class on another seed scavenger hunt. Students look for ways that seeds may move from place to place. Point out that the seeds that stick to their socks would stick to an animal's fur also.

Give each team a copy of the Traveling Seeds worksheet. Review the different ways seeds travel. The Seed Keeper give everyone an even number of seeds that were left from the previous activity. In **RoundTable** fashion, each team member places his or her seeds on the worksheet in the correct location. To do this, have one person at a time hold up a seed and tell where they think it belongs and why. The others give a thumbs up or thumbs down signal to show whether or not they agree. If all are not in agreement, the students discuss the seed further. They may want to test floaters in a cup of water or drifters by blowing them. Hitchhikers can be tested by trying to attach them to socks.

Writing About Science

Ask students to draw a picture of the way they sorted their bean seeds and explain in writing how the beans were sorted. You may also want to have them respond to some or all of the following questions in their Science Journals:

Where can you find seeds?
What does **classify** *mean? What are some things that can be classified?*
What is an **attribute?** *Name an object in the classroom and describe two of its attributes.*
How do seeds travel from one place to another?

Materials Check List

For the Class:
- ❏ *From Seed to Plant* by Gail Gibbons (or any suitable book about seeds)
- ❏ several vegetables and fruits which contain seeds that are easy to observe

For each Pair:
- ❏ dried beans – 15 bean soup variety (1/8 cup per pair)
- ❏ 1 Seed Sorting worksheet

For each Student:
- ❏ 1 whole raw green bean
- ❏ several dried beans

For each Team:
- ❏ 1 hand lens
- ❏ 1 cup of water
- ❏ bag of seeds saved from Activity 6
- ❏ 1 Traveling Seeds worksheet
- ❏ 1 bottle of glue
- ❏ 2 Seed Scavengers worksheets
- ❏ 2 baggies

Curriculum Links

1. Math - Measuring lengths of seeds
Students line seeds up in order from shortest to longest. Then show them how to measure their seeds. Children who aren't ready for standard measurement can find out how many little seeds can be lined up to make a big seed.

2. Math - Graphing a mixture of beans
Let students sort one tablespoon of mixed beans into several piles by one attribute such as color. Students count the number of each type of bean and glue the beans onto graph paper to form a bar graph.

3. Literature - Reading fiction
Read *A Tiny Seed* by Eric Carle to your class. Use Think-Pair-Share throughout the story to have students predict what will happen to the tiny seed.

4. Drama - Acting out the life cycle of a plant
Students work together in small groups to form a seed, then a sprouting seed, and finally a seed that has grown into a plant.

5. Science - Observing 15-Bean Soup
Make 15-bean soup. Follow the directions on the package, but place the ingredients in a crock pot in your classroom (out of reach of students). Make sure to soak the beans overnight before making the soup. As the soup cooks, your students will be able to smell its aroma. Before they leave at the end of the day, give each one a small cup of soup to sample.

6. Art - Making seed pictures
Let students use seeds they have collected or seeds from the 15-bean soup mix to create pictures. Students arrange the seeds in a pleasing pattern on a sheet of heavy construction paper, then let them glue the seeds in place.

Seed Sorting

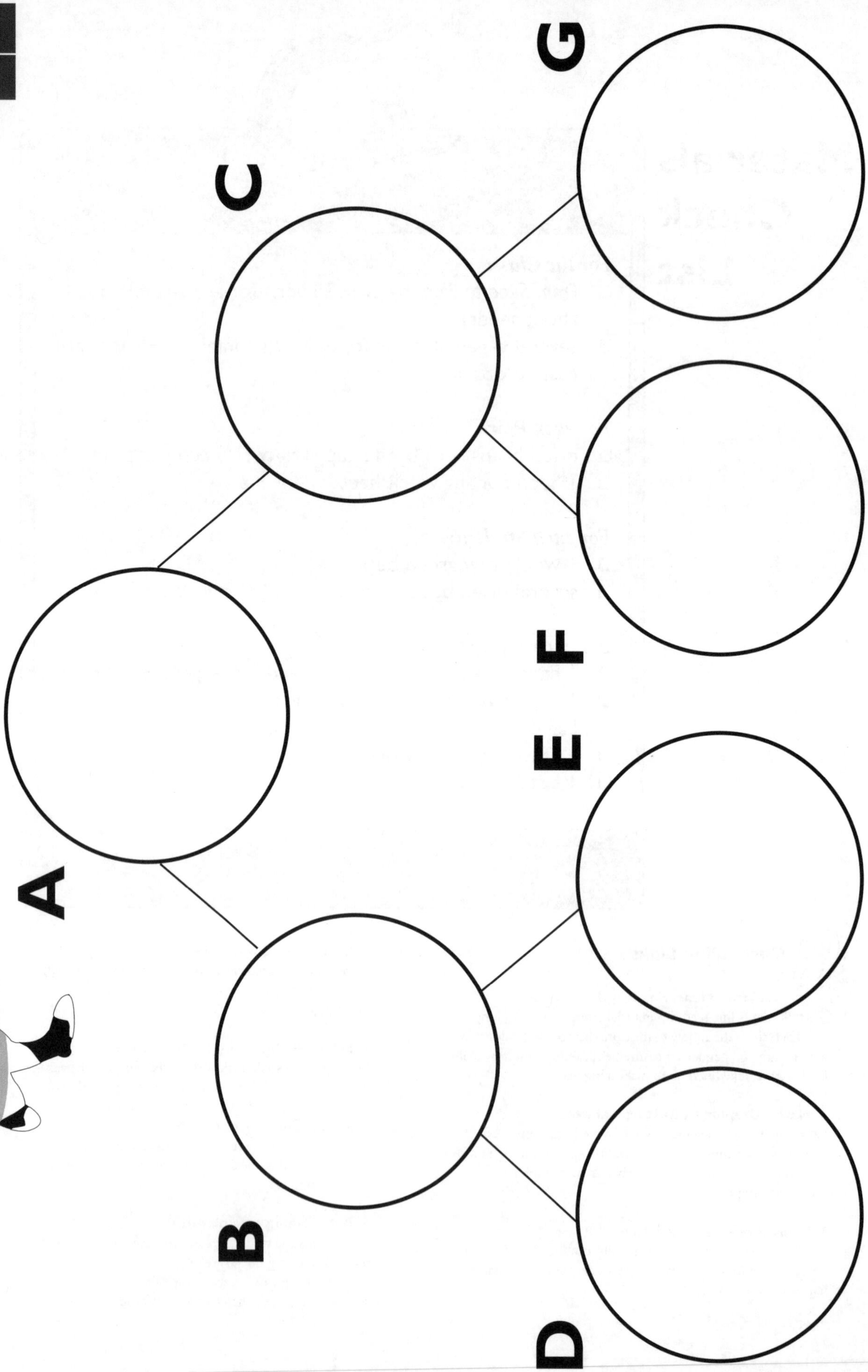

A

B

C

D

E F

G

Laura Candler: *Hands-On Science*

1 (800) 933-2667 • *Kagan Publishing*

Seed Scavengers

a brown seed	a seed that is smaller than this dot ●	a seed with barbs or hooks	a seed from a fruit
a seed that floats	a seed with one or more wings	a flat seed	a bright red seed
a yellow seed	a long thin seed	a seed with a hard seed coat	a seed with hairs or fluff
a heavy seed	a seed that is longer than this line	a seed from a vegetable	a round seed
a seed from a tree	a striped seed	a seed that people eat	a seed still in its pod

Traveling Seeds

Drifters
(wind)

Floaters
(water)

Hitchhikers
(hooks or barbs)

Other

Laura Candler: *Hands-On Science*   1 (800) 933-2667 • *Kagan Publishing*

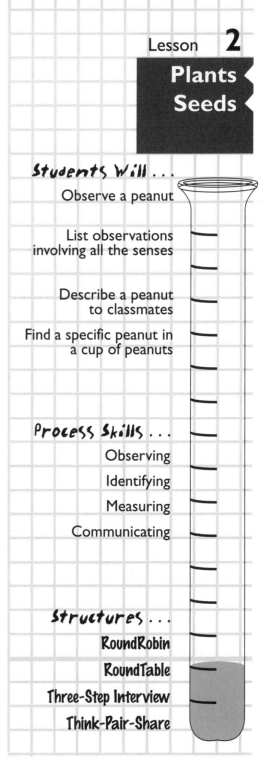

Students Will...

Observe a peanut

List observations
involving all the senses

Describe a peanut
to classmates

Find a specific peanut in
a cup of peanuts

Process Skills...

Observing

Identifying

Measuring

Communicating

Structures...

RoundRobin

RoundTable

Three-Step Interview

Think-Pair-Share

Peanut Pals

*I*n this lesson, students use all their senses to list detailed observations of peanuts. First, they break open a peanut shell and taste the roasted peanut within. Then they pass another peanut around the table and **RoundRobin** observations using all their senses. Next, each student selects a peanut which becomes his or her "Peanut Pal." Students individually sketch their peanuts and list as many observations as possible. Teammates interview each other about their Peanut Pals and then introduce their partner's Peanut Pal to the team.

Finally, Peanut Pals are placed in a cup in the center of the table along with a handful of additional peanuts. After shaking the cup, students spread the peanuts on the table and work in pairs to find their lost Peanut Pals. Students are very surprised to find they can easily locate their peanuts.

1

Explain the activity using TEACHER TALK

Tell your students that for the next activity they will need to use *all* their senses. Also tell them that if they follow your directions carefully, they will make a new friend. Do *not* reveal the surprise ending to the lesson: the fact that they will have to identify their Peanut Pals using their observations.

SAFETY

SPOTLIGHT

Remind students that we normally do not taste science materials without the direction of the teacher. However, assure them that the peanuts used in this activity are safe to eat.

2

Tasting peanuts using ROUNDROBIN

Materials for each Team:
25-30 roasted peanuts (in the shell)
1 large cup to hold peanuts

Place each team's cup of peanuts in the center of their table. Let them each choose a peanut and instruct them to remove the shell. Students slowly eat the peanut, savoring the flavor. Guide their experience by asking questions like, "How does the peanut feel in your mouth?" and "What flavor does the peanut remind you of?" When they have finished chewing, ask them to **RoundRobin** words that describe the flavor and texture of their nut.

Describing additional observations using ROUNDTABLE

Next, designate one person to select another peanut from the cup. Students pass the peanut around the table, using all their senses to observe the nut. As the peanut is passed from hand to hand, each person names something they observed about that peanut. Examples: "It rattles when I shake it." "It's about as wide as my thumb." "It has a long crack on one side of its shell." Challenge students to see how many times the peanut can go completely around the team before everyone runs out of observations. Return the peanut to the cup when finished.

4

Describing Peanut Pals using INDIVIDUALS WRITE

Materials for each Student:
Peanut Pal Observation Record
ruler

Materials for each Team:
cup of peanuts
magnifying lens or hand-held microscope

Step One: Selecting Peanut Pals
Give each student a copy of the Peanut Pal Observation Record. Tell everyone to choose a peanut from the cup. After they have done so, tell them that the peanut is their new "Pal" and that they will get to know their new friend better by making careful observations.

Step Two: Making observations
Give each student a magnifying lens or a hand-held microscope. Ask them to examine their Peanut Pal in great detail from many angles. Make sure each person also has a ruler to use for measuring their peanut.

Step Three: Sketching Peanut Pals
Instruct students to start by making a sketch of their peanut in the appropriate place on their Peanut Pal Observation Record. Encourage them to draw in as many fine details as possible.

Step Four: Listing observations
Next, students write at least 10 observations about their peanut. Don't let them shell their peanuts or put them in their mouths. Many children will list only observations made with their eyes; remind them to use all their senses (except taste).

Lesson 2	**Peanut Pal Observation Record**

My Peanut Pal Looks Like This:

Observations about my Peanut Pal:
1. _____
2. _____
3. _____
4. _____
5. _____
6. _____
7. _____
8. _____
9. _____
10. _____

86 Laura Candler: *Hands-On Science* *Kagan Cooperative Learning* | 800 WEE CO-OP

5

Introducing Peanut Pals to the team
using **THREE-STEP INTERVIEW**

Step One:
Within each team, pair students to form two sets of partners. Seat partners next to each other. Designate one student in each pair to be the "A" partner and the other to be the "B" partner.

Step Two: Partner A interviews Partner B
To begin **Three-Step Interview,** Partner A turns to Partner B and asks questions about B's Peanut Pal. Students may name their Pals if they wish, but all other information must be based on observations alone. Partner A asks about the peanut's size, shape, sounds, color, and any other physical characteristics.

Step Three: Partner B interviews Partner A
Next, Partner B interviews Partner A about A's Peanut Pal. Remind students again to discuss their peanut's physical characteristics only.

Step Four: Introducing each other's Pal to the team
Then, in **RoundRobin** fashion, each of the four team members shows their *partner's* Peanut Pal to the team and describes its characteristics. For example: "I'd like you to meet Cassandra's new friend, Nutty. Nutty is about 1 1/2 inches long, and light brown all over. Nutty has a small crack going halfway down the side and it feels rough. Nutty is fatter on top than on bottom. Nutty also rattles when shaken."

Step Five: Placing Peanut Pals back in cup
Finally, each team member says "Good-bye" to his or her Peanut Pal and places it back into the cup containing at least 10 other peanuts.

6

Finding Peanut Pals using INDIVIDUALS SEARCH

Someone on each team shakes the cup gently. Then students pour all the peanuts onto the center of the table. Challenge your students to find their Peanut Pal as quickly as possible. Allow them to use their notes and sketches if needed.

7

Discussing strategies using THINK-PAIR-SHARE

When everyone has finished, ask each person to **think** about how they knew their peanut. Then they **pair** with a different partner than their previous one to discuss the identifying characteristics. Let a few students **share** their strategies with the class.

Writing About Science

Ask to students draw a detailed picture of their peanut in their Science Journals. Then have them respond to the following:
- *Which of your five senses did you use during this activity? Explain.*
- *How did you know your peanut from all the others in the cup?*
- *Describe your peanut so that anyone in the class could read your description and find your peanut in a cup of peanuts.*

For the Younger Students

A slightly easier variation of **Three-Step Interview** involves having students introduce Peanut Pals to the team immediately following each interview. Each "A" partner interviews each "B" partner, then turns to the team and introduces B's Peanut Pal to the team. Then the two B's interview the A's and immediately turn to the team to introduce A's Peanut Pal. This modification makes the structure easier because the interviewer doesn't have to remember the information over a long period of time before reporting.

Some children may not be ready to use **Three-Step Interview** in any form. If that is the case, substitute **RoundRobin.** After students have carefully observed their own Peanut Pals, omit the interview step and let each student describe his or her Pal to the team in turn.

Materials Check List

For the Class:
❑ large bag of roasted peanuts still in their shells

For each Team:
❑ 1 plastic cup
❑ magnifying lenses or handheld microscopes

For each Student:
❑ Peanut Pal Observation Record
❑ Pencil
❑ Ruler

Curriculum Links

1. Science - Sorting peanuts
Let each team pour their cupful of peanuts on the table and develop a classification scheme for those peanuts. Let them choose 2 different attributes and draw a large Venn Diagram on a sheet of butcher paper. Challenge them to sort the peanuts without writing the attributes on the diagram. Then let teams rotate and try to figure out each other's classification schemes.

2. Language Arts - Writing about peanuts
Let students research how peanuts are harvested and made into peanut butter. Then have them write the life story of a peanut. Some students may even enjoy acting out their peanut sagas. Others may enjoying illustrating their life stories in cartoon form.

3. Math - Graphing the number of peanuts in each shell
Students open 10 peanuts each and record the number of peanuts inside each shell. Show them how to create a team bar graph of their results.

4. Social Studies - Studying George Washington Carver
Let students research the accomplishments of George Washington Carver. Challenge each team to collect items that can be made from peanuts (George Washington Carver created over 300 products.)

5. Music - Sing songs about peanuts
Teach students all the verses of the children's song "Found a Peanut." Then assign one verse to each team to act out. As the class sings the song together, let each team perform as their verse is sung.

Peanut Pal
Observation Record

 **My Peanut Pal Looks Like This:**

Observations about my Peanut Pal:

1. _____
2. _____
3. _____
4. _____
5. _____
6. _____
7. _____
8. _____
9. _____
10. _____

Students Will . . .

Color moth patterns to blend in with the classroom environment

Pretend to be moth predators and try to find hidden moths

Discuss a story about survival adaptations of Peppered Moths

Create creatures which would be well-adapted to the classroom

Process Skills . . .

Observing

Identifying

Making Models

Organizing Data

Inferring

Communicating

Structures . . .

Class Project

Numbered Heads Together

Team Project

Think-Pair-Share

Simply Survival

Scientists make models of living and nonliving things in order to study them. In this lesson, your students will create models of creatures to learn about survival adaptations. They will begin by coloring moth patterns to camouflage them in the classroom environment. After hiding their moths your students will become predators, trying to locate other moths hidden in the classroom. Later, they will connect the activity to real-life survival by discussing a story about adaptations among Peppered Moths in England. Finally, each team will invent an animal uniquely adapted to the classroom.

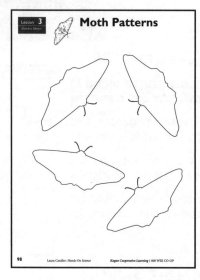

1

Simulating moth survival using CLASS PROJECT

Materials for each Team:
1 copy of the Moth Patterns worksheet
scissors
crayons or markers
tape

Step One: Coloring the moths
Give each team one sheet of moth patterns and have them work together to carefully cut around the moths. Each person should have one moth.

Tell them to color their moth so that it will blend in with something in the classroom. Explain that in a few minutes they will have to "hide" their moth by placing it somewhere in the room, but that the moth will have to remain in plain sight. Students color their moths secretly, so that no one else in the class is able to see their moth before it is hidden.

When everyone is finished, have them stick a loop of tape on the back of the moth in preparation for the next step.

Step Two: Explaining "Moth Hunt"
Tell your students that they will play "Moth Hunt," an activity in which some students will hide moths and others will hunt for them. Tell them that they will do the activity two times so that everyone will have a chance to play both parts.

Discuss the terms *predator* and *prey* with your class. Tell them that a predator is an animal that hunts another animal for food. The prey is the animal which is hunted and eaten. Divide the class in half, naming one half as the Predators and the other half as the Prey.

1 cont.

Draw two large boxes on the chalkboard or on poster paper. Label one box "Eaten" and the other "Survived." Tell your class that the Prey will hide their moths somewhere in the classroom and the Predators will hunt for the hidden moths. All the moths that are found will be taped into the "Eaten" box. The moths that are not found will be taped into the "Survived" box.

Eaten	Survived

(continued on page 89)

I cont.

Simulating moth survival (continued from page 88)

Step Three: Hiding the moths
To begin the Moth Hunt, ask the Predators to close their eyes or place their heads down on their desks so that they cannot see. Now allow the Prey to quietly "hide" their moths. Remind them not to place the moths under or behind any objects; all moths must be in plain view.

Step Four: Hunting for moths
When the Prey have returned to their seats, ask the Predators to open their eyes. Give the Predators 30 seconds to find as many moths as possible. Predators gently remove each moth as it is found. When the time is up, have the Predators tape all the moths they found into the box labelled "Eaten."

Step Five: Retrieving moths which survived
Now all the Prey students to see if the moth they hid was "eaten." Ask them to point out the location of any moth that was not found. Then the Prey retrieve the moths that survived and tape them into the box labeled "Survived."

Step Six: Repeating the moth hunt
Now have the students switch roles. The Predators become the new Prey and hide the moths they colored earlier. The Prey become the new Predators who have 30 seconds to hunt for moths. Moths which are found are taped into the box labelled "Eaten." Moths which were not found go in the "Survived" box as before.

Step Seven: Discussing camouflage
Tell your students to look at the moths that survived and think about where each one was located. Lead a **Class Discussion** about the characteristics of those moths. Explain to them that the word *camouflage* describes a situation in which an animal's color or shape blends in with its *environment,* or surroundings. Animals use camouflage as protection from predators. The moths which survived in the classroom probably blended in with some part of the classroom environment.

Make a transparency of each page of "The Story of the Peppered Moth" found on pages 94-97. If an overhead projector will not be available during the lesson, you can read the story aloud or make your own "Big Book" by transferring the story onto large sheets of paper.

2

Reading "The Story of the Peppered Moths" *using* THINK-PAIR-SHARE

Materials for the Class:
transparencies or posters of *The Story of the Peppered Moth* (see pages 94-97)

Tell students that you are going to read them a true story about moth survival. Ask them to listen and watch carefully to find out how animals can change, or adapt, to their environment. Then read "The Story of the Peppered Moths," showing each page as you read it.

At the ends of pages 3 and 6, pause after reading the question. Have students think about their own answers, then pair with a partners and discuss responses. Finally call on students to share their ideas with the class.

3

Discussing animal adaptation *using* NUMBERED HEADS TOGETHER

Number students in teams from 1 - 4. Discuss the following questions, allowing team discussion before randomly calling on students, by number, to respond. Modify the wording according to the abilities of your students:
- *Why were there more light gray moths in the beginning?*
- *How did the factories change the moth's environment?*
- *Why were there more black moths after many factories were built?*
- *Why are more light-gray speckled moths surviving now?*
- *The moths survived because their color blended in with their environment. What are some ways other animals escape their predators? (Bodies shaped like objects in the environment, imitating other harmful animals, freezing perfectly still, running away, etc.)*

4

Creature Hunt using TEAM PROJECT

Materials for each Team:
construction paper (assorted colors)
scissors
glue
crayons or markers
masking tape

Step One: Explaining the activity

Explain that *adaptations* are special body parts or behaviors that allow an animal to survive in its environment. Tell your students that as a team they are going to design a creature with adaptations that could help it survive in the classroom. They will make and hide five identical examples of that creature. Later in the activity, other teams will try to find their creatures during a class Creature Hunt.

Make sure the two boxes labelled "Eaten" and "Survived" are on the chalkboard. If you haven't done so, remove the moths so that the boxes can be used again during the Creature Hunt.

Step Two: Planning the team creature

Give at least five minutes for discussion and planning before distributing materials. Ask team members to discuss how the creature will look and what its adaptations will be. Explain that camouflage techniques should be used, but that they can invent other survival techniques also. Tell them to plan where they will hide their five creatures.

Step Three: Creating the first creature

Give each team a set of materials. Tell them to work together to make one example of their creature. Some students can be cutting while others are gluing or adding details. Encourage students to works quickly and allow no more than five minutes to actually make the animals. Tell students to keep their creatures a secret from the other teams.

Step Four: Making four more creatures

Each team uses the one creature they constructed together as a model for the other four. Each team member makes one more creature which is identical to the one designed by the team. When everyone is ready, each team should have a total of five identical creatures.

(continued on page 92)

4 cont.

Creature Hunt (continued from page 91)

Step Five: Hiding creatures
Designate one team to hide their creatures while the other students cover their eyes.

Step Six: Searching for creatures
When the animals are hidden, let everyone become Predators. After 30 seconds, have everyone tape the creatures they found into the box labelled "Eaten."

Step Seven: Identifying survivors
Have one person from the Prey team show the location of any creatures that were not found. Remove the creatures from their hiding places and type them into the box leabeled "Survived."

Step Eight: Repeating the Creature Hunt
Allow each team a turn to hide their creatures. Give Predators 30 seconds during each round of the activity to locate the Prey. Tape all creaturees into the apprrpriate "Eaten" or "Survived" boxes.

5

Discussing successful adaptations using THINK-PAIR-SHARE

Students think about the answer to the following questions, then pair with a partner to discuss them. After each question, call on students randomly to share their responses with the class.
• *Which teams' creatures survived the best?*
• *What adaptations helped those creatures survive?*
• *How could you improve the creature your team designed?*

Writing About Science
Have students respond in writing to the discussion questions listed above. Ask them to sketch a picture of a creature that could survive in their bedroom at home.

For the Younger Students
Spend some time preteaching the following terms before beginning the activity: *predator, prey, environment, camouflage,* and *adaptations.*
Throughout the lesson, modify the vocabulary as needed to meet the needs of your students.

Materials Check List

For the Class:
❏ transparencies or posters of The Story of the Peppered Moth (see pages 94-97)

For each Team:
❏ 1 copy of the Moth Patterns worksheet
❏ scissors
❏ crayons or markers
❏ tape
❏ construction paper (assorted colors)
❏ glue

Curriculum Links

1. Literature - Reading about camouflage
Your students will enjoy books from the "How to Hide" series by Ruth Heller. Examples include *How to Hide a Polar Bear*, *How to Hide an Octopus*, and *How to Hide a Crocodile*. All of the books show animals and their camouflages. Students enjoy trying to find the animals within their natural habitats.

2. Science - Worm Hunt
Locate at least five different colors of yarn and cut ten 3-inch pieces from each color. (Colored toothpicks may be substituted for the yarn pieces.) Scatter them on a grassy area. Let one team of students at a time become hungry birds who have 15 seconds to hunt for worms. After they have collected the worms, they sort the yarn by color. Tell them that there were ten pieces of each color on the grass. Students make a bar graph showing how many worms they found of each color. Discuss which colors were the easiest and most difficult to find. Repeat the experiment on pavement or on dirt.

3. Math - Calculating percentages
Each team calculates the percentage of their creatures which survived during the Creature Hunt. Display one sample of each creature along with its rate of survival.

4. Social Studies - Researching the Industrial Revolution
Tell your students that the time when England and the United States began to build factories is known as the Industrial Revolution. "The Story of the Peppered Moth" tells about Industrial Revolution's impact on the environment. Tell students that this historical period also had an enormous impact on our culture. Students research the Industrial Revolution and discover other ways it has affected our lives.

Page 1

The story of the peppered moth began long ago in Manchester, England. Two types of peppered moths lived there. One was light gray with dark gray speckles. The other was black all over. Until the 1850's, there were more light gray moths than dark gray ones.

The Story of the Peppered Moth

Laura Candler: *Hands-On Science*

1 (800) 933-2667 • *Kagan Publishing*

Page 3

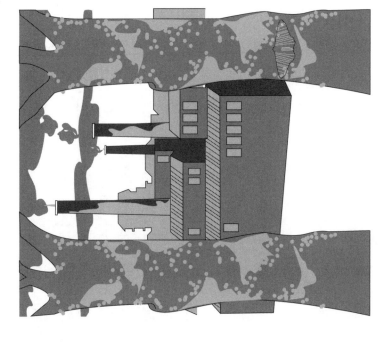

Between 1850 and 1900, England began to change. Factories were built which pumped tons of black smoke and soot into the air. The leaves and bark of trees became covered with dark soot. During this time, scientists noticed that almost all the light gray moths had disappeared. Black moths became the most common peppered moths in England. What caused this change?

Page 2

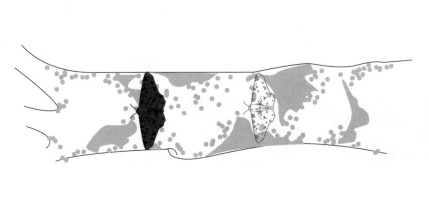

Peppered moths loved to rest on birch trees. The color of the light gray moths matched the color of the birch bark almost perfectly. Hungry birds had a hard time finding the light moths. Instead, the birds ate the dark moths which were much easier to see against the bark of the birch tree.

Page 5

Fewer and fewer gray moths lived long enough to have light colored babies. At the same time, more dark moths survived and had dark baby moths. In less than 50 years, the number of dark moths became greater than the number of light moths.

Page 4

Scientists realized that the light gray moths no longer blended in with the birch bark. The birch trees were black with soot. Hungry birds could easily spot any light moths resting on the trees. Now the dark moths blended in with the bark and were able to escape the birds.

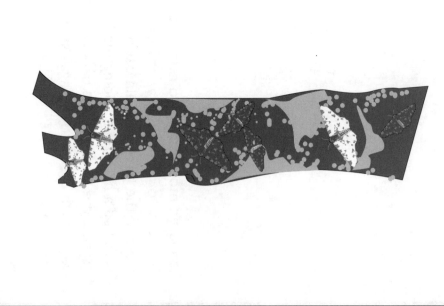

Laura Candler: *Hands-On Science*   1 (800) 933-2667 • *Kagan Publishing*

Page 7

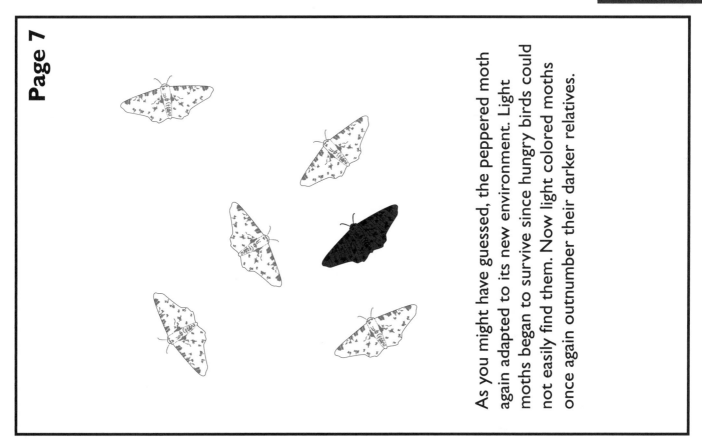

As you might have guessed, the peppered moth again adapted to its new environment. Light moths began to survive since hungry birds could not easily find them. Now light colored moths once again outnumber their darker relatives.

Page 6

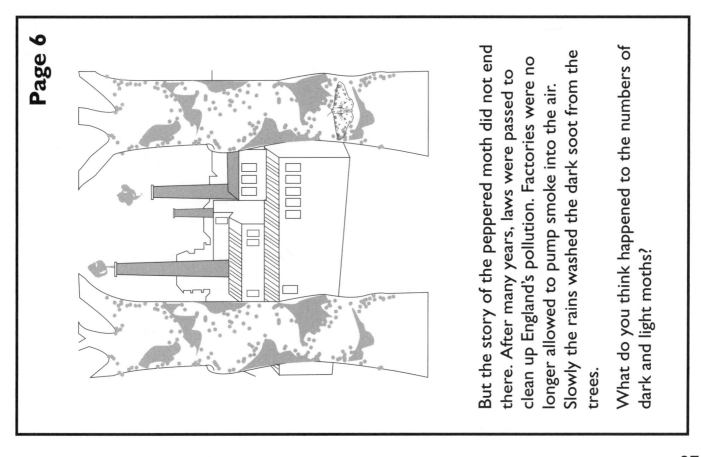

But the story of the peppered moth did not end there. After many years, laws were passed to clean up England's pollution. Factories were no longer allowed to pump smoke into the air. Slowly the rains washed the dark soot from the trees.

What do you think happened to the numbers of dark and light moths?

Moth Patterns

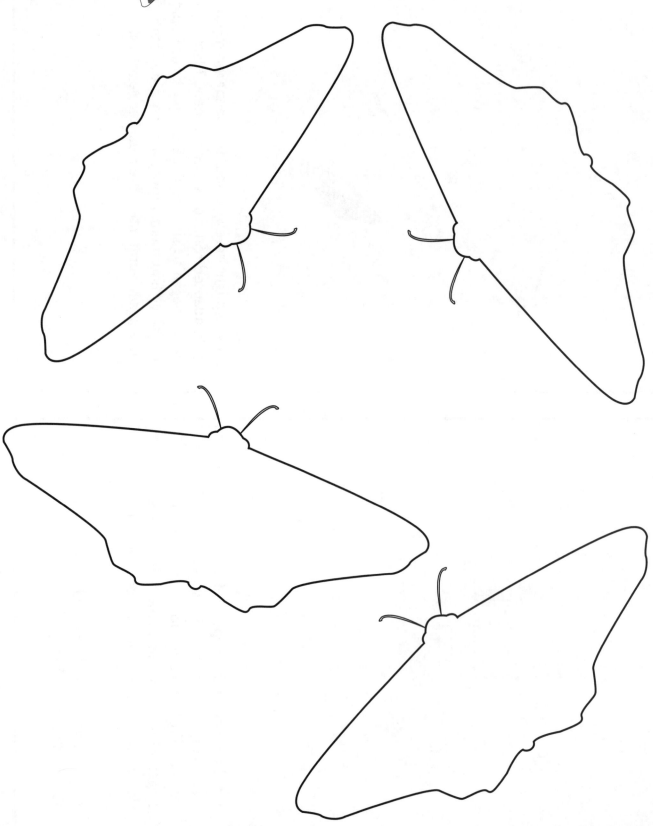

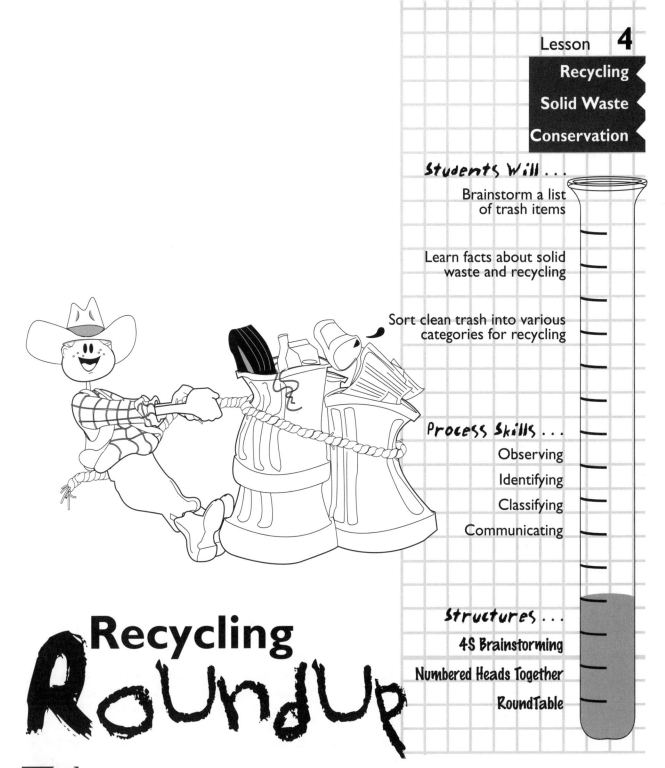

Students Will . . .

Brainstorm a list
of trash items

Learn facts about solid
waste and recycling

Sort clean trash into various
categories for recycling

Process Skills . . .

Observing

Identifying

Classifying

Communicating

Structures . . .

4S Brainstorming

Numbered Heads Together

RoundTable

Recycling
RoUNdUp

◀▌he 1990's are being hailed as the "Decade of the Environment." We are
recognizing that we must change our wasteful lifestyles. We need to reduce the
amount of waste we create, and we need to recycle as much of our trash as possible.
Before materials can be recycled, however, they must be sorted into categories. This
lesson provides the opportunity for students to learn how to sort trash properly. Your
students will first brainstorm a list of trash items that they have recently thrown away.
Then they will learn about the solid waste problem by discussing some "Trash Trivia."
Finally, they will sort clean trash into various categories for recycling.

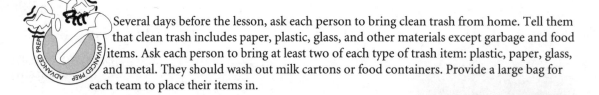

Several days before the lesson, ask each person to bring clean trash from home. Tell them that clean trash includes paper, plastic, glass, and other materials except garbage and food items. Ask each person to bring at least two of each type of trash item: plastic, paper, glass, and metal. They should wash out milk cartons or food containers. Provide a large bag for each team to place their items in.

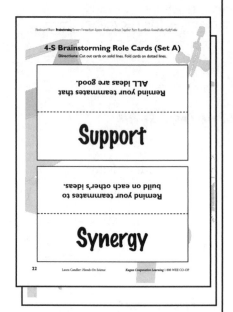

Listing types of trash using 4-S BRAINSTORMING

Materials for each Team:
1 set of 4-S Brainstorming Role Cards (both pages)
1 sheet of paper
1 pencil

Step One: Assigning roles
Ask your children to think of the many items they throw out each week. Tell them that they will be working as a team to brainstorm as many types of trash as they can think of in five minutes.

Number students on each team from 1 to 4. Assign and discuss the roles listed below. Give a set of **4-S Brainstorming** Role Cards to each team. Have each person cut out his or her role card on the solid line and fold it on the dotted line. Ask them to place their cards in front of them as a reminder of their roles during the brainstorming session.

Role Assignments
#1 - Speed (encourages everyone to work fast)
#2 - Silly (encourages silly and unusual ideas)
#3 - Synergy (encourages everyone to build on each other's ideas)
#4 - Support (reminds everyone that all ideas are good)

Step Two: Recording ideas
Make sure each team has a sheet of paper and a pencil. Remind them that brainstorming means listing ideas as quickly as possible without discussing those ideas. Designate Person #4 as the Recorder on each team who will write the ideas of all the team members. Give students five minutes to list as many types of trash as possible. When the time is up, have the Recorder count the number of different trash items on the list.

Remind students to be extremely careful when handling glass and metal. If you are uneasy about students bringing these items from home, collect them yourself before the lesson. Try to collect several colors of glass. Check metal items to make sure they don't have sharp edges. Remove metal lids from cans.

2

Discussing Trash Trivia
using NUMBERED HEADS TOGETHER

Materials for the Class:
Trash Trivia master list

Step One: Explaining the solid waste problem
Ask everyone to think about the number of different items on their team list. Then tell them that the average person throws away about four pounds of trash every day. That amounts to over a thousand pounds of trash a year! The Earth is running out of places to put all this trash.

Tell them that you are going to read them some statements about the trash problem, but they will have to decide if each statement is true or false.

Step Two: Reading a Trash Trivia statement
Now read one statement from the Trash Trivia list. Students put their heads together and discuss whether or not they think the statement is true. After about a minute of discussion, call a number from 1 to 4. The student whose number is called responds with the team's decision. If the team thinks the statement is true, that person holds his or her thumb up. If the team feels the statement is false, the person whose number was called gives a thumbs-down signal.

Step Three: Discussing responses
Tell the students whether or not the statement was true. Discuss the explanation with them. Repeat with the remaining Trash Trivia statements.

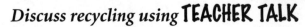

3

Discuss recycling using TEACHER TALK

Materials for the Class:
an assortment of clean trash items
1 set of 6 labeled Trash Sort pages (see Advanced Prep below)

Tell students that one solution to the trash problem is to recycle some of the items. Explain that when an item is recycled it is made into a new product. To do this, trash must be sorted into categories before it is brought to the recycling center.

Show students the six Trash Sort pages labelled: Paper, Cardboard, Glass, Plastic, Metal, or Other. Discuss the various categories and show examples of each. Items that are made of a variety of materials should be placed in the "other" category. Generally, items are not recyclable unless they are made of one substance.

Duplicate six copies of the Recycling Roundup page for each team and use them to make sets of recycling category signs. Make one set for each team. Label each sign with one of the following words: Plastic, Glass, Cardboard, Metal, Paper, or Other.

4

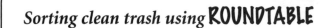

Sorting clean trash using ROUNDTABLE

Materials for each Team:
6 labeled copies of the Trash Sort page
20-30 items of clean trash
1 magnet

Materials for the Class:
8-10 garbage bags to hold sorted trash items
transparency of "Plastic Categories for Recycling" (optional)

Step One: Getting ready
Each team clear a large area for sorting the trash. If tabletops are not available, each team should find a space on the floor. Team members spread out the six Trash Sort pages in the middle of the team. Ask one person on each team to divide the clean trash items between all team members.

(continued on page 103)

4 cont.

Sorting clean trash (continued from page 102)

Step Two: Sorting into basic categories

Using **RoundTable** format, one person on each team begins by holding up one trash item and naming its category. All students who agree give a thumbs up signal. Those who disagree hold their thumbs down. If everyone doesn't agree, a team discussion takes place. When all are in agreement, the item is placed in its proper category. Then the next person holds up an item and names its category. Follow the same procedure for all trash items.

Collect all the non-recyclable items from the class in large bags. Label the bags as "other." Place all the recyclable paper into one bag. Collect all the cardboard in another bag. Make sure each bag is labelled with its category and place all bags to the side. Leave the plastic, glass, and metal items in front of each team for the next part of the sorting activity.

Step Three: Sorting metal

Now tell your students that steel or aluminum are two metals that are commonly recycled. Metal items must be sorted before recycling. Aluminum is easy to recycle, but some parts of the country do not have recycling programs for other metals.

Aluminum can be separated easily from other metals because it is not attracted by a magnet. Show students how to test a can by touching a magnet to it. If the magnet is not attracted to the can, the can is probably made of aluminum. Students should take turns testing and sorting their metal items.

After the sorting process is complete, collect all the cans from the class in labelled bags. Set them aside with the previously bagged items.

Step Four: Sorting glass

Now students sort the glass items by color. Caution them to be very careful when handling glass. Collect all glass items and bag them separately according to color. Label the bags and set them to the side.

(continued on page 104)

Sorting clean trash (continued from page 103)

Step Five: Sorting plastic

Plastic items are not recyclable in all parts of the country. If your recycling center does not accept plastic, proceed with the rest of the lesson, but place the plastic items in with the "other" trash.

Plastic recyclables need to be sorted by type of plastic. Show students how to find the triangular recycling symbol on most plastic items. The number inside the triangle is coded 1- 7 according to type of plastic. Refer to the chart "Plastic Categories for Recycling" for a description of each category. You can put a transparency of this on the overhead to share with students.

Begin the sorting activity by ask one person on each team to divide the plastic items between all team members. Again in Roundtable format, everyone takes turns finding the recycling symbol on each container and showing it to the team. Once the plastic type is identified, the item is placed in a pile according to number. At the end of the activity, collect all plastic items and place them in numbered bags.

Step Six: Taking items to a recycling center

Finally, discard the non-recyclable items and take the others to a recycling center. If possible, arrange a class trip to deliver the bags. If not, take the items yourself and snap a few pictures to share with the class.

Writing About Science

Have students respond in their Science Journals to one or more of the following questions:
- *Why is it important to recycle materials?*
- *What are some ways you and your family can help solve the solid waste problem?*
- *Which Trash Trivia statement was the most amazing to you?*
- *How can you tell if a plastic item can be recycled?*

For Younger Students

Younger students will need more time than older students to complete this activity. The Trash Trivia statements may need to be reworded using vocabulary appropriate to your students' developmental level. Also, young students may need more guidance during the various parts of the sorting activity.

When having young students brainstorm, omit the four roles. Simply encourage students to write down all ideas. Tell them to use each other's ideas to help them think of new things to add to the list. Remind them to try to list as many ideas as possible in the five minutes.

Materials Check List

For the Class:

- ❏ Trash Trivia master list
- ❏ an assortment of clean trash items
- ❏ 1 set of 6 labeled Trash Sort pages
- ❏ 8-10 garbage bags to hold sorted trash items
- ❏ transparency of Plastic Categories for Recycling (optional)

For each Team:

- ❏ 1 set of 4-S Brainstorming Role Cards (both pages)
- ❏ 6 labeled copies of the Trash Sort page
- ❏ 20-30 items of clean trash
- ❏ 1 magnet
- ❏ 1 sheet of paper
- ❏ 1 pencil

Curriculum Links

1- Math - Graphing solid waste

Students create circle or bar graphs to show the percentages of various types of trash in a landfill. Use a recent encyclopedia or almanac to find the amount of trash thrown away each year.

2. Language Arts - Writing letters

Students write letters of concern to the mayor or other elected officials. Before writing, give them the opportunity to brainstorm some of the solid waste problems in the community and some possible solutions.

3. Art - Creating posters

Students create environmental awareness posters for the school or community.

4. Science - Creating mini- landfills

Ask students which types of solid waste they think disintegrate (break down) the fastest. Then let them make mini-landfills to test their ideas. Each team will need a 2-liter plastic drink bottle. Use a sharp knife to cut each bottle almost all the way around about 1/3 of the way from the top. Pull each top back and fill the bottles halfway with soil. Then let each team test a different type of trash (plastic, paper, metal, foods, wood, etc.) by placing a few pieces on top of the soil. Fill the bottle completely with soil and place the top back on. Tape the top in place. Leave the landfills alone for 3 - 4 weeks. Then open them and compare the results. Which items have begun to break down? Are any completely disintegrated?

5. Math - Weighing classroom trash

Students chart the amount of trash created in the classroom. Collect your classroom trash each day in a plastic bag. Weigh each bag and record the weights. Figure the average per day and the total for the week. Calculate the amount that would be created in a school year. Then brainstorm ways to reduce trash in the classroom.

Trash
Sort

Laura Candler: *Hands-On Science*

1 (800) 933-2667 • *Kagan Publishing*

Trash Trivia

In a single day, Americans throw away 15,000 tons of packaging material.

True: This amount would fill up 10,000 tractor trailer trucks. If they were lined up end to end, they would stretch for 120 miles!

Recycling paper uses twice as much energy as making paper from raw material.

False: The good news is that recycling paper uses only half the energy of making paper from raw materials.

If the diapers Americans toss out each day could be lined up end to end, they would stretch halfway around the world.

True!

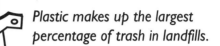
Plastic makes up the largest percentage of trash in landfills.

False: Actually, less than 10% of the trash in a landfill is plastic. The largest percentage is paper (between 30% and 50%).

About 20,000 old TVs end up in the trash everyday.

True: If all those TVs were stacked one on top of the other, they would be taller than Mt. Everest!

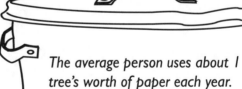
The average person uses about 1 tree's worth of paper each year.

False: Actually, each person uses the equivalent of 2 trees per year!

Recycling 1 ton of paper saves 1 tree.

False: Recycling 1 ton of paper actually saves 17 trees!

Plastic Categories for Recycling

PETE (PET)

Polyethylene terephthalate
soft drink bottles

HDPE

High Density Polyethylene
milk bottles, detergent bottles, orange juice bottles

V

Vinyl
shampoo bottles, salad dressing bottles, vinyl seats

LDPE

Low Density Polyethylene
shopping bags

PP

Polypropylene
catsup bottles, yogurt cups

PS

Polystyrene
foam cups, prescription bottles, plastic utensils

OTHER

Other

Students Will...

Observe the smoke
produced when paper burns

Illustrate a scene
in nature before acid rain

Illustrate the same scene
in nature after acid rain

Carve a "statue" from
a piece of chalk

Simulate the effects of
acid rain on a statue

Process Skills...

Observing

Identifying

Making Models

Inferring

Communicating

Structures...

Team Project

Think-Pair-Share

Three-Step Interview

Acid Rain
Encounters

In this lesson your students will learn about the destructive effects of acid rain on nature and artwork. They will begin by learning how acid rain is formed. Next, they will take an imaginary journey to a beautiful place in nature. After drawing the spot they imagined, they will picture the devastating effects of acid rain on their special place. They will again draw their nature spot, this time showing the effects of acid rain. Finally, they will learn about the harmful effects of acid rain on marble statues. After carving a statue from chalk, they'll drip vinegar over their artwork to simulate years of acid rain on marble.

Follow normal fire safety precautions when burning the paper.
Do not let students stand close to the flames.

1

Explain how acid rain is formed
using TEACHER DEMONSTRATES

Materials for the Class:
   I sheet of paper
   matches
   clear glass jar (I quart canning jar or large pickle jar)
   metal pie plate

Explain that air pollution does more than make the skies dirty and the
air smell bad. Tell your students that in this lesson they will learn
about *acid rain*, a problem caused by air pollution.

Crumple the paper into a wad and place it in the metal pie plate.
Carefully touch a lit match to the edge of the paper and allow it to
burn for several seconds. Place the glass jar upside down over the
paper and ask your students to observe closely. They should see the air
inside the jar become dark and smoky. Small black particles of soot
will cling to the glass and settle in the pie plate.

Tell your students that when things like paper, wood, plastic, or fuels
are burned they give off harmful smoke as well as invisible poisonous
chemicals. Factories, cars, trucks, airplanes, and even barbecue grills
all contribute to the pollution in the air. The harmful chemicals
released into the air mix with the water in the clouds and form acid
rain. Acid rain falls to the earth and pollutes the soil and water. Clouds
may drift far away and cause acid rain to fall on places that did not
create the smoke and pollution.

2

Reviewing the causes and effects of acid rain *using* THINK-PAIR-SHARE

Stop briefly and give your students a chance to think about what they have learned. Ask them to **Think-Pair-Share** the following questions:
- *What happens when things are burned?*
- *How is acid rain formed?*
- *How can acid rain affect places that don't have factories or cars?*
- *What are some of the effects of acid rain?*

3

Reading Part I of the Acid Rain Imagery story *using* TEACHER READS

Materials for the Class:
1 copy of the Acid Rain Imagery story (page 118)

Materials for each Student:
1 Acid Rain Effects worksheet
crayons or colored pencils

Give each student a copy of the Acid Rain Effects worksheet and each team a supply of crayons or colored pencils. Dim the lights and tell your students to find a comfortable, relaxed position. Tell them that you are going to take them on an imaginary journey to a beautiful place.

Begin reading only Part I of the Acid Rain Imagery story. Read slowly and softly. Pause between each sentence to allow your students time to image their nature scene in detail.

4

Illustrating a nature scene using INDIVIDUALS DRAW

After reading Part I only, turn up the lights. Ask students to draw their nature scene in the first box on the Acid Rain Effects worksheet. Allow as much time as needed. Students are usually very quiet and absorbed in drawing what they have imagined. Do not encourage them to share their drawings at this time.

5

Reading Part II of the Acid Rain Imagery story
using **TEACHER READS**

Dim the lights again and read Part II of the story. Read slowly and allow students to picture the destruction caused by acid rain.

6

Illustrating the effects of acid rain
using **INDIVIDUALS DRAW**

Turn on the lights and ask students to find the second box on the worksheet. Ask them to draw the changes they imagined in their nature scene. Caution students not to draw acid rain falling from the clouds, but rather to draw the *effects* of acid rain. Remind them to draw the exact same scene pictured in the first box; the only difference should be the destruction caused by acid rain. Monitor this activity carefully. Many students will draw bottles and cans floating on the water and trash on the ground. Explain that these items are examples of pollution, but are not caused by acid rain. The most accurate illustrations will only picture the damage caused by acid rain.

7

Sharing illustrations with teammates
using **THREE-STEP INTERVIEW**

Step One: Assigning partners
Within each team, divide the four students into two sets of pairs. Designate one person in each pair to be Partner A and the other person to be Partner B.

Step Two: Partner A interviews Partner B
Partner A turns to Partner B and ask questions about B's acid rain artwork. Tell the A's to make sure they understand each part of the illustration, especially the differences between the before and after pictures. Give students one minute for this interview.

Step Three: Partner B interviews Partner A
Now the students switch roles so that Partner B interviews Partner A for one minute. Partner B also should become thoroughly familiar with A's picture.

Step Four: Sharing partners' pictures with the team
Finally, in **RoundRobin** fashion each person shows his or her *partner's* picture to the team. The person explaining the illustration should describe the features of the first picture, then tell how acid rain affected that nature scene. Give each person approximately 30 seconds to tell teammates about the illustration.

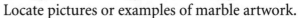

Locate pictures or examples of marble artwork.

SAFETY SPOTLIGHT

When carving the statues from chalk, caution students to be careful with the sharp nails used to carve the features. Also, caution children not to touch their eyes if they get vinegar on their hands during the last activity. Make sure everyone washes their hands when finished.

8

Observing other effects of acid rain using **TEAM PROJECT**

Materials for the Class:
pictures of marble statues and buildings

Materials for each Student:
1 unbroken piece of chalk
1 sharp large nail
1 small piece of modeling clay
2 damp paper towels

Materials for each Team:
1 plastic plate or tray
1 eyedropper
1 small cup
1/4 cup white vinegar

Step One: Explaining the project
Tell your students that acid rain is harmful to manmade items also. Explain to them that marble statues and buildings can suffer damage from the strong acids that continually rain upon them. If possible, show your students pictures or examples of marble artwork.

Give each person a piece of chalk and a sharp nail. Tell them that they are going work together to make tiny statues out of their chalk. Explain that chalk is made of the same material as marble, but that chalk is much softer.

Show them how to carve designs on their chalk with their nail. Caution them to be very careful not to cut themselves with their nails. To minimize the risk of harm, have them place their chalk flat on their desktops while they carve. *Do not allow them to hold their chalk in the palm of their hand.*

(continued on page 115)

8 cont.

Observing other effects of acid rain (continued from page 114)

Step Two: Carving statues using Simultaneous RoundTable
Students carve their statues using **Simultaneous RoundTable.** To begin, give everyone one minute to carve designs in their chalk statues. Everyone passes their incomplete statues to the person on their right. They may explain their work if they want to. Give everyone one more minute to work on the statue they just received. Ask everyone to pass the statues again. Continue until everyone has worked on every statue. Stress that the statues all belong to the team rather than to individuals.

Caution students against digging too deeply into the chalk, since the piece may break. If a statue does break, have the student treat the chalk as two small statues. Or if you have extra chalk, give that person a new piece.

When finished, have students use the damp paper towel to clean up the powder creating during the carving process.

8 cont.

Step Three: Erecting the statues
Give each person a small ball of clay. They shape the clay into a base for the chalk statue they have on their desk. Give each team a plate or a tray and everyone places their statues upright on it.

Step Four: Observing the effects of acid rain
Now give each team a cup containing 1/4 cup white vinegar. Show the class how to fill the eyedropper with the solution. Explain that vinegar is a weak acid similar to acid rain. Ask one person on each team to become the first "Rainmaker" by sprinkling the "acid rain" on one of the statues. They slowly drip the whole dropperful over the statue they selected. Ask everyone to observe carefully. The vinegar will fizz when it comes in contact with the chalk.

The first Rainmaker passes the eyedropper and cup to the next person on the team. The new Rainmaker sprinkles one full eyedropper of the solution over any statue. Allow your students to continue passing the cup and sprinkling the vinegar water over the statues for about 10 minutes. The chalk will begin to dissolve very quickly in the acid solution.

9

Making the connection using THINK-PAIR-SHARE

Make sure students understand how the model represents acid rain damage to marble. Ask them to **Think-Pair-Share** the following questions:

- *What does the chalk represent (stand for)?*
- *What does the vinegar solution represent (stand for)?*
- *How can acid rain damage marble statues and buildings?*

Writing About Science
Have students respond to the questions below in their Science Journals or on sheet of paper.
- *What causes acid rain?*
- *What are some of the effects of acid rain?*
- *How can you help prevent acid rain?*

For Younger Students
Younger students are capable of completing this lesson, but they may need more time and guidance. The lesson vocabulary will need to be adjusted according to their level of understanding. Monitor the carving activity carefully to make sure they do not cut themselves on the sharp point of the nail.

Materials Check List

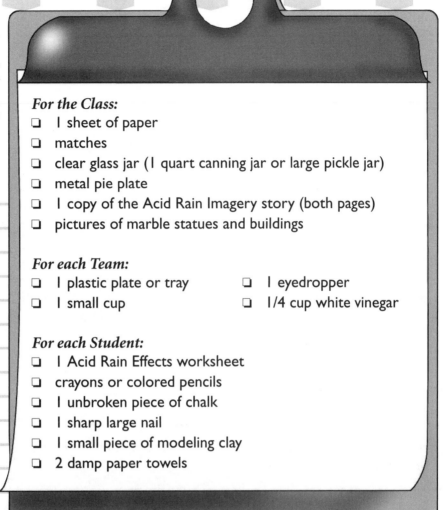

For the Class:
- ❏ 1 sheet of paper
- ❏ matches
- ❏ clear glass jar (1 quart canning jar or large pickle jar)
- ❏ metal pie plate
- ❏ 1 copy of the Acid Rain Imagery story (both pages)
- ❏ pictures of marble statues and buildings

For each Team:
- ❏ 1 plastic plate or tray
- ❏ 1 small cup
- ❏ 1 eyedropper
- ❏ 1/4 cup white vinegar

For each Student:
- ❏ 1 Acid Rain Effects worksheet
- ❏ crayons or colored pencils
- ❏ 1 unbroken piece of chalk
- ❏ 1 sharp large nail
- ❏ 1 small piece of modeling clay
- ❏ 2 damp paper towels

Curriculum Links

1. Social Studies - Discussing current events
Ask students to look for news articles about air pollution and acid rain. Read the articles aloud and conduct Team Discussions about why the acid rain problem is difficult to solve.

2. Science - Testing rain samples
The next time it rains, ask your students to set out a clean jar and collect a sample of the rain. When students bring their samples to class, use pH paper to test the acidity of the water. (You can purchase pH paper from a science supply catalog.) Normal rain has a pH above 5.0 and acid rain has any pH below 5.0.

3. Science - Experimenting with bean seeds
Conduct an experiment to test the effects of acid on bean seeds. Students soak lima bean seeds overnight and plant 4 seeds in a cup of potting soil. Two students on each team

water their seeds with pure water. The other two students should water with a mixture of 1 part vinegar to 6 parts water. When the seedlings sprout, have them measure the young plants each day and figure the average size of the bean plants in each group. Create double bar graphs comparing the growth of bean seeds in water and vinegar.

4. Health - Researching effects of air pollution
Students research the effects of air pollution on the human body. Some cities declare "smog alerts" when conditions in the air are determined to be extremely harmful.

5. Language Arts - Writing letters
Students write Letters to the Editor or letters of concern to elected officials. They should write about local air pollution problems and suggest ways of solving those problems.

Acid Rain Imagery

Part One: Before

Close your eyes . . . breathe deeply . . . and relax. Imagine a beautiful nature scene as it was before people lived on the earth. In a few moments you are going to draw this scene, so picture it clearly in your mind. You can imagine anything you want . . . rugged mountains . . . a lively stream bubbling over rocks . . . a small quiet pond . . . a thick green forest . . . or an open field of wildflowers.

Take a few moments to walk through your special place in nature. Look up at the clear, blue sky . . . Listen to the twittering and chirping of the songbirds around you . . . Watch small animals scurrying through the grass and large animals drinking the cool, pure water . . . Fish leap and sunlight sparkles on the drops that splash around them . . . Listen to the wind rustling the green leaves of the strong, healthy trees . . . Feel the breeze on your skin . . . Breathe deeply of the fresh, clean air.

Relax for a few moments, enjoying the special place you have created.

 Have students draw their nature scenes on the top portion of the Acid Rain Effects worksheet.

Part Two: After

Close your eyes again . . . breathe deeply . . . and relax. Imagine that many years have passed since you last visited your special place. People now live on the earth, polluting the air with smoke and soot. It's not raining now, but the effects of acid rain can be seen everywhere.

The air no longer smells fresh and sweet . . . Smoke from a nearby town has polluted the skies, causing acid rain to fall on the landscape . . . Pine trees are losing their green needles and the leaves of other trees are brown and withered . . . Fallen trees lie on the ground . . . The soil has become polluted with acids, causing the trees to slowly die . . . Animals no longer drink from the polluted waters . . . The fish are dying from the acids that have polluted their water . . . Everything is strangely quiet . . . even the songbirds have died or left to search for new homes.

Your special place has been destroyed by acid rain.

Acid Rain Effects

Before Acid Rain

After Acid Rain

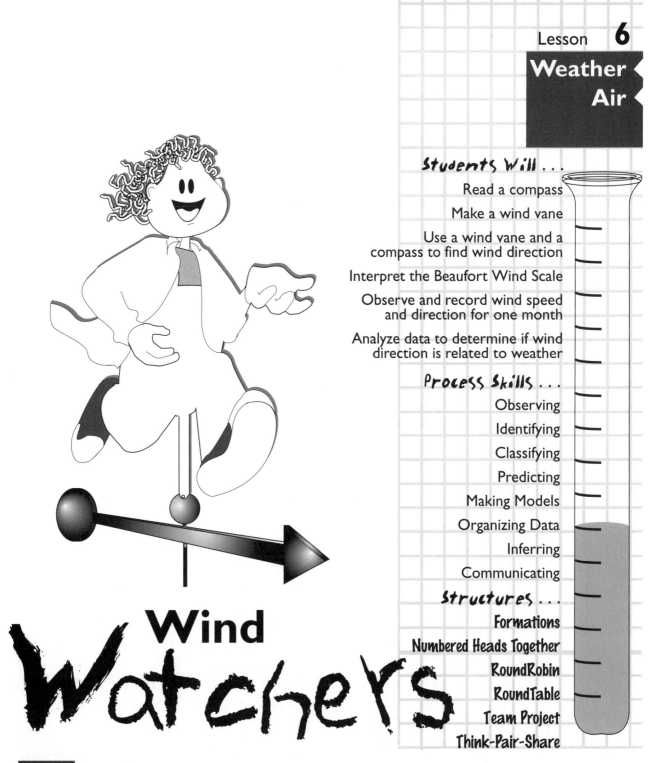

Wind Watchers

Effective science instruction cannot be limited to the classroom; science involves observing the world around us. Observing and recording weather changes provides a perfect opportunity to take science out-of-doors. In this lesson, students will make wind vanes and learn to identify wind direction. They will also estimate wind speed and identify types of wind using a chart called the Beaufort Wind Scale. Working in teams, students will record daily observations about the wind's speed and direction. They will also note the type of weather each day. Finally, they will analyze their data to determine if there is a relationship between the wind and the type of weather.

SAFETY
SPOTLIGHT

One part of the Team Project involves the use of matches. Do this activity yourself as a demonstration for the whole class. Do not allow individual students to light matches outside. Follow all fire safety guidelines established by your school.

I

Discussing prior knowledge using THINK-PAIR-SHARE

To introduce this lesson, ask questions to find out what your children already know about the wind and instruments used to measure the wind. After you ask each question, tell students to **think** about their own answer. Then have them **pair** with the person beside them to discuss their ideas. Finally, call on several students randomly to **share** their answers with the class. Use this time to clear up any misunderstandings and provide the general background needed for the lesson. The following questions are suggested:

- *What is the wind?* (Moving air)
- *How can you tell if the wind is blowing?* (You can feel it, you can see leaves blowing, you may have trouble walking, wind socks and flags are blowing, etc.)
- *How can you tell which direction the wind is blowing from?* (By watching the movement of wind vanes, wind socks, and flags)
- *How can you tell how fast the wind is blowing?* (By seeing how fast leaves are blowing, seeing how far trees bend over, measuring it with an anemometer)
- *Do you think the type of wind can affect the type of weather we're having?* (Don't give away the answer, but the type of wind does have a big impact on the weather that follows it.)

Draw an example of a compass rose on the board or make a transparency of the one on the Making a Wind Vane pattern.

2

Introducing the compass using TEACHER TALK

Materials for the Class:
  1 illustration of a compass rose

Materials for each Team:
  1 magnetic compass

Give each team one magnetic compass. The students pass it around so that each person can examine it. Ask them to notice which way the needle always seems to point. (You may not get a true reading inside the school since electrical systems can interfere with the magnetic field). Tell your students that when they use a compass out-of-doors the needle always points to the north. In this way they can find any of the directions on the compass rose.

Show the illustration of the compass rose. Review the cardinal directions (North, South, East, and West). Discuss the ways we name the directions in between. Make sure students understand all the symbols that are used in naming directions (NW, SE, W, etc.).

 Duplicate the Wind Vane pattern on construction paper and follow the directions on the worksheet to make a sample for the class.

3

Predicting wind vane action using THINK-WRITE-ROUNDROBIN

Materials for the Class:
1 wind vane (see Advanced Prep above)
1 electric fan

Materials for each Team:
scrap paper

Show your students the sample wind vane you put together before the lesson. Tell them that a wind vane can be used with a compass to find the wind direction.

Ask your students to predict whether they think a wind vane will point to the direction the wind is coming from or to the direction the wind is going. Write the following on the board:

1) Where the wind is coming from
2) Where the wind is going

Each person thinks about about his or her answer and writes it on a sheet of scrap paper. Next, team members **RoundRobin** their predictions.

Now turn on the electric fan and hold the wind vane in front of it. The wind vane will point *to the direction wind the wind is coming from.* The reason is that the tail is larger and is pushed with greater force by the wind. The wind pushes the tail away, which causes the tip of the wind vane to point into the wind (fan).

4

Becoming wind vanes using FORMATIONS

Materials for each Team:
  1 sheet of construction paper
  scissors

Tell students that they are going to take turns pretending to be wind vanes. Give each team one sheet of construction paper. Designate one person on each team to cut a large triangle out of one end as shown in the diagram. The triangle will become the pointer and the remaining piece will become the tail of the wind vane.

One person on each team will become a wind vane by holding his or her arms straight out to the sides. That person should hold the tail of the wind vane in one hand and the pointer in the other hand. The rest of the students on the team will become the wind. Tell the class that the front of the classroom is "north." Then call out a statement such as, "The wind is coming from the southeast." The students who are the wind work together and gently turn the wind vane so that it is pointing in the correct direction.

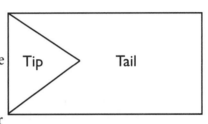

After one round of the activity, students switch roles so that a new person is the wind vane. Continue until all students have had a chance to be the wind vane.

Duplicate the parts of the Wind Vane on construction paper and the directions on regular bond paper. Each team will need one copy of each page.

5

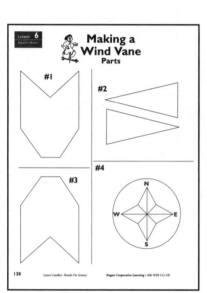

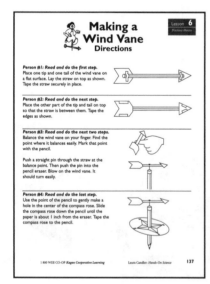

Making wind vanes using TEAM PROJECT

Materials for each Team:
1 copy of Making a Wind Vane (both pages)
tape
scissors
1 drinking straw
1 straight pin
1 new pencil, sharpened
1 magnetic compass

Step One: Introducing the project
Show the sample wind vane again and tell your students that they will be working together to make one wind vane for the team. Assign each person a number from 1 - 4. Give each team one set of materials. Ask Person #1 to cut apart the sections on the dashed lines and give one part to each person on the team.

Step Two: Constructing the wind vanes
Ask everyone to cut out the part of the wind vane that they have been given. Person #1 on each team reads the first step aloud and follows the instructions. Everyone else watches to make sure Person #1 follows the directions carefully. Then each person takes turns reading and doing the steps in the order described.

(continued on page 127)

5 cont.

Making wind vanes (continued from page 126)

Step Three: Testing wind vanes

If time allows, students take their wind vanes outside for a trial run. Stand well away from any buildings that might interfere with air flow. Keep clear of electrical power lines also, since this may affect the compass reading.

Show your students how to locate north. Students face that direction and orient the compass rose on their wind vane so that it is pointing north also. Designate someone on each team to push the pencil point into the ground. Everyone stand back to observe the movement of the wind vanes. All wind vanes should behave in the same way.

Let your students huddle together in teams to discuss the wind direction. Move from team to team, checking to be sure that everyone has interpreted their wind vanes correctly. Return to the classroom when finished.

6

Introducing the Beaufort Wind Scale *using* TEACHER TALK

Materials for each Team:
1 copy of the Beaufort Wind Scale

Tell your students that meteorologists (scientists who study weather) have instruments that measure wind speed. One type is called an anemometer; another is a wind sock. (If you can obtain examples of these, show them to the class.) However, scientists also have a method of estimating the wind speed by its effect on smoke, flags, trees, and buildings.

Give each team a copy of the Beaufort Wind Scale. Tell them that meteorologists measure wind speed in miles per hour. They have identified 12 different levels of wind speed. Scientists have assigned each type of wind a number and a name. They have listed the effects that such a wind would have on the environment. Point out some examples on the chart.

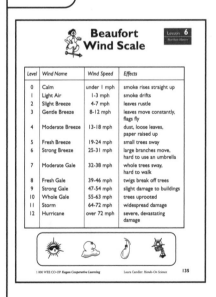

Beaufort Wind Scale

Lesson 6
Blackline Master

Level	Wind Name	Wind Speed	Effects
0	Calm	under 1 mph	smoke rises straight up
1	Light Air	1-3 mph	smoke drifts
2	Slight Breeze	4-7 mph	leaves rustle
3	Gentle Breeze	8-12 mph	leaves move constantly, flags fly
4	Moderate Breeze	13-18 mph	dust, loose leaves, paper raised up
5	Fresh Breeze	19-24 mph	small trees sway
6	Strong Breeze	25-31 mph	large branches move, hard to use an umbrella
7	Moderate Gale	32-38 mph	whole trees sway, hard to walk
8	Fresh Gale	39-46 mph	twigs break off trees
9	Strong Gale	47-54 mph	slight damage to buildings
10	Whole Gale	55-63 mph	trees uprooted
11	Storm	64-72 mph	widespread damage
12	Hurricane	over 72 mph	severe, devastating damage

1 800 WEE CO-OP *Kagan Cooperative Learning*   Laura Candler: *Hands-On Science*   135

7

Checking for understanding
using NUMBERED HEADS TOGETHER

Step One: Call out question from chart
Begin by posing a question such as "What is the name of a wind that causes smoke to drift but doesn't make leaves rustle?"

Step Two: Heads together
Tell your students to put their heads together to discuss the question and study the chart. They should make sure everyone on the team knows the answer.

Step Three: Call a number
Choose a number from 1 to 4. If you have team chalkboards, have the person whose number was called write the answer on the chalkboard. Or divide the class chalkboard into sections and have those students come forward and write their answers in their team's space.

Step Four: Checking answers
When everyone is ready, have the students hold up their chalkboards. Discuss the answers and correct misunderstandings. Continue posing new questions and calling new numbers until everyone understands the concept. Use the questions below or create your own.

- *What is the name for a wind with a speed of 25-31 mph?*
- *What type of wind causes twigs to break off trees but does not damage buildings?*
- *What are the effects of a gentle breeze?*
- *Which wind is stronger, a Moderate Breeze or a Fresh Breeze?*
- *What is the name for a wind with a speed of less than 1 mile per hour?*

Prepare one Rotating Role Finder for each team. Duplicate the pattern on page 134 on construction paper. Follow the instructions on that page to assmble the Role Finder.

8

Recording weather data using TEAM PROJECT

Materials for the Class:
1 Rotating Role Finder
box of matches

Materials for each Team:
3 copies of the Wind Watchers Weather Log
1 wind vane
1 Beaufort Wind Scale

This activity needs to be completed each day for a full month to provide enough weather data for the **RoundTable** sorting activity. Since it only takes 15 minutes a day to complete, you will probably want to move on to another science unit in the meantime. When weather data has been collected for at least 20 days, complete the sorting activity which concludes this lesson. If you are unable to continue the recording weather data for a full month, omit the **RoundTable** sorting activity. Students will be unable to draw conclusions without enough weather data to analyze.

(continued on page 130)

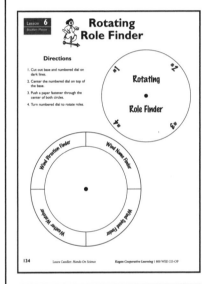

8 cont.

Recording weather data (continued from page 129)

Step One: Introducing the activity

Tell your children that they will make daily weather observations for a whole month. They will record their data on the Wind Watchers Weather Log. Give each team one copy of the Weather Log. They will need more copies later, but it would be best for you to keep the extras until needed.

Tell them that there are four roles needed for this activity. The roles will change each day to give everyone a chance to do a different job. Show the class the Rotating Role Finder. Turn the dial so that Person #1 is the Wind Direction Finder for the first day. Call out all the roles by number so that everyone knows what job they will do first.

Step Two: Making observations

It's best to make your observations at approximately the same time and in the same location each day. Leave the Weather Logs inside, but take out the wind vanes, compasses, and Beaufort Wind Scales. Students work together to determine the wind direction, wind speed, wind name, and type of weather. Each person is responsible for making sure they do their own job, but they can confirm the answers of other team members, too.

(continued on page 131)

8 cont.

Recording weather data (continued from page 130)

If the wind is very light, you will need to observe smoke to determine if the wind is "calm" or "light air." In a safe location, well away from flammable materials, strike a match and quickly blow it out. Let your students observe the way the smoke is drifting. Do not allow students to use matches out-of-doors.

Step Three: Recording observations

When the students return to the classroom, have them record their data in **RoundTable** fashion. The Wind Direction Finder writes in the day and the date, followed by the direction the wind was coming from. The Wind Name Finder writes in the name of the wind and the Wind Speed Finder fills in the estimated wind speed in miles per hour. Finally, the Weather Watcher draws the appropriate symbol for the day's weather. The symbols may be combined if needed.

Store the Weather Logs, wind vanes, and Beaufort Scales in team folders. Use the Rotating Role Finder to assign new roles each day. Continue making observations for 20 days, if possible.

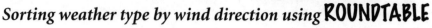

Sorting weather type by wind direction using ROUNDTABLE

Make sure students have completed at least 20 days of weather observations before completing this part of the lesson.

Step One: Thinking about the relationship between wind direction and weather
Ask your students to recall the question you asked at the beginning of the activity: "Is the type of weather related to the direction that the wind is blowing?" Have them again **think, pair,** and **share** their responses.

Step Two: Sorting weather strips
If possible, make a copy of each team's Weather Log before beginning this activity. Tell your students to cut the Weather Log apart on the horizontal lines so that each day's weather data is on a separate strip of paper. They should end up with 20 strips of paper. One person mixes up the strips and passes them out to team members so that each person has 5 strips.

Tell your students to sort the strips by wind direction only. Person #1 begins by putting one strip down in the center of the team. Person #2 puts down the next strip. If the wind direction is the same as the first one, the strip goes in that pile. If the wind direction is different, the person starts a new pile. Team members continue until all strips are sorted into categories by wind direction.

Step Three: Analyzing the data
The final part of the activity involves looking at the weather data strips and trying to find relationships between wind direction and type of weather. Students examine each pile carefully to see if one type of weather is associated with a particular wind direction. Does a north wind tend to bring rain? Does a southeast wind bring sunshine?

Step Four: Reporting results
Ask one person on each team to stand and summarize the findings of the team. Discuss the findings as a class.

Have students respond to some or all of the following in their Science Journals:
- *What is wind?*
- *How can you find out which way the wind is blowing?*
- *Explain how to use the Beaufort Wind Scale.*
- *Does the direction of the wind affect the type of weather?*

Materials Check List

For the Class:
- ❏ I illustration of a compass rose (overhead transparency)
- ❏ I Rotating Role Finder
- ❏ I wind vane
- ❏ I electric fan
- ❏ box of matches

For each Team:
- ❏ I sheet of construction paper
- ❏ I copy of Making a Wind Vane (both pages)
- ❏ I copy of the Beaufort Wind Scale
- ❏ 3 copies of the Wind Watchers Weather Log
- ❏ tape
- ❏ I drinking straw
- ❏ I straight pin
- ❏ I magnetic compass
- ❏ scrap paper
- ❏ scissors
- ❏ I new pencil, sharpened
- ❏ I wind vane

Curriculum Links

1. Art - Making wind socks

Let each team make its own wind sock. Cut a 4" x 18" piece of construction paper and staple the ends together to form a paper loop. Cut crepe paper streamers into 2-foot lengths. Staple or tape the streamers onto the loop. Punch holes in the top edge of the loop in 3 places. Tie 3 pieces of string through the holes and knot them together at the top. Hang the wind sock in the wind. If it is allowed to turn freely it will show both wind speed and direction by the way it moves.

2. Science - Making weather predictions

After children have identified relationships between wind direction and the weather, ask them to make predictions about the next day's weather based on today's wind direction.

3. Literature - Listening to weather lore

Students find examples of weather lore. (A collection of Mother Goose rhymes can provide a number of weather poems.) For example, many people are familiar with "Red sky at night, sailor's delight. Red sky in the morning, sailor take warning." Ask your students to read their examples to the class. Discuss whether or not these sayings have any scientific basis.

4. Math - Measuring and graphing temperature

Teach your students to measure temperature. Students take daily temperature readings at about the same time each day. Let each team keep temperature log. Have students make line graphs of the temperature data they collect.

Rotating Role Finder

Directions

1. Cut out base and numbered dial on dark lines.

2. Center the numbered dial on top of the base.

3. Push a paper fastener through the center of both circles.

4. Turn numbered dial to rotate roles.

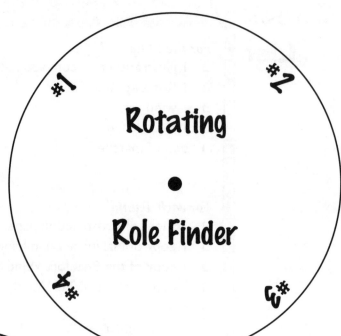

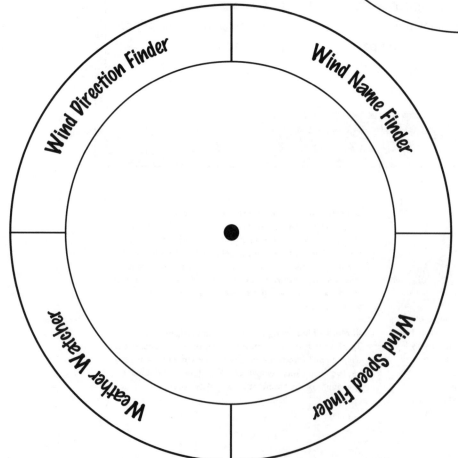

Beaufort Wind Scale

Level	Wind Name	Wind Speed	Effects
0	Calm	under 1 mph	smoke rises straight up
1	Light Air	1-3 mph	smoke drifts
2	Slight Breeze	4-7 mph	leaves rustle
3	Gentle Breeze	8-12 mph	leaves move constantly, flags fly
4	Moderate Breeze	13-18 mph	dust, loose leaves, paper raised up
5	Fresh Breeze	19-24 mph	small trees sway
6	Strong Breeze	25-31 mph	large branches move, hard to use an umbrella
7	Moderate Gale	32-38 mph	whole trees sway, hard to walk
8	Fresh Gale	39-46 mph	twigs break off trees
9	Strong Gale	47-54 mph	slight damage to buildings
10	Whole Gale	55-63 mph	trees uprooted
11	Storm	64-72 mph	widespread damage
12	Hurricane	over 72 mph	severe, devastating damage

Lesson **6**
Blackline Master

Wind Watcher Weather Log

Day and Date	Wind Direction	Wind Name	Wind Speed	Type of Weather

Key to Weather Symbols

Sunny   Cloudy   Rain   Snow

     Laura Candler: *Hands-On Science*   1 (800) 933-2667 • *Kagan Publishing*

Making a Wind Vane
Directions

Person #1: Read and do the first step.
Place one tip and one tail of the wind vane on a flat surface. Lay the straw on top as shown. Tape the straw securely in place.

Person #2: Read and do the next step.
Place the other part of the tip and tail on top so that the straw is between them. Tape the edges as shown.

Person #3: Read and do the next two steps.
Balance the wind vane on your finger. Find the point where it balances easily. Mark that point with the pencil.

Push a straight pin through the straw at the balance point. Then push the pin into the pencil eraser. Blow on the wind vane. It should turn easily.

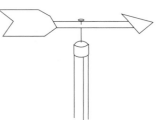

Person #4: Read and do the last step.
Use the point of the pencil to gently make a hole in the center of the compass rose. Slide the compass rose down the pencil until the paper is about 1 inch from the eraser. Tape the compass rose to the pencil.

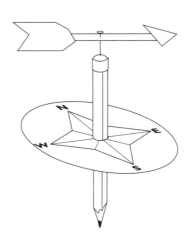

Making a Wind Vane
Parts

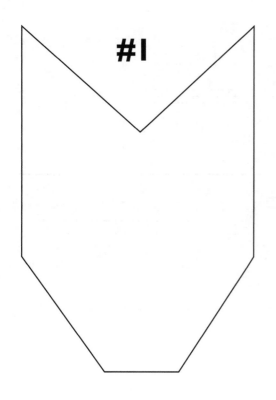

#1

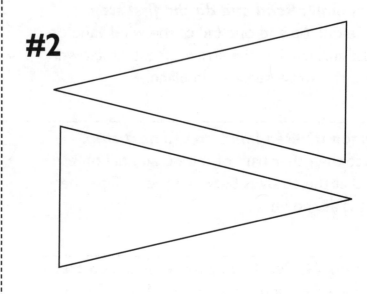

#2

#4

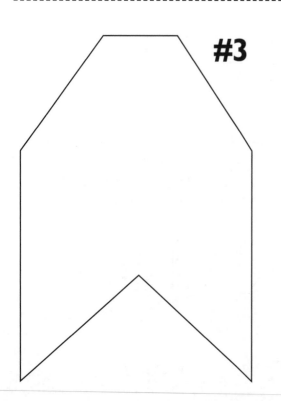

#3

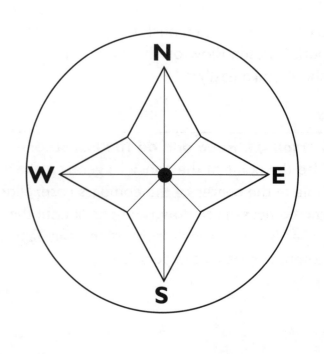

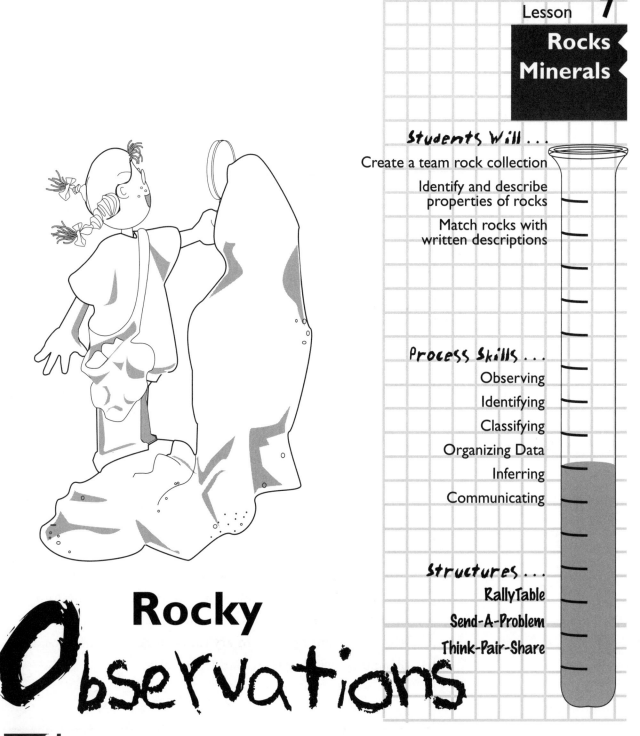

Students Will . . .

Create a team rock collection

Identify and describe
properties of rocks

Match rocks with
written descriptions

Process Skills . . .

Observing

Identifying

Classifying

Organizing Data

Inferring

Communicating

Structures . . .

RallyTable

Send-A-Problem

Think-Pair-Share

Rocky
Observations

tudying rocks and minerals provides a perfect opportunity for
practicing observation skills. In this lesson, teams work in pairs,
performing simple tests to determine the physical and chemical properties of
rocks. Next, each team member uses the test results to help them write a
detailed description of one rock in the collection. The team's descriptions is
sent, along with the collection, to another team. Receiving teams read the
descriptions and try to match the rocks with their descriptions.

Even though the emphasis is not on identifying and labelling rocks, many students enjoy learning the names of common rocks and minerals. If your school has a labelled rock collection, this would be an appropriate time to share it with the class. You may also want to gather a small collection of rock and mineral identification books. Your students will then be able to identify many of the rocks they find by comparing them to rocks in the labelled collection.

Background Information

The question often arises: "What is the difference between a rock and a mineral?" Minerals are the building blocks of rocks; rocks are made up of minerals. Minerals are generally thought to be naturally-occurring substances with a particular crystal structure. Some examples of minerals include quartz, gold, copper, feldspar, and talc. Rocks are made up of some combination of basic minerals. Common rocks include granite, obsidian, slate, and sandstone.

Rocks are formed in three ways. *Igneous rocks* are formed from cooled magma. Examples include granite, basalt, and pumice. *Sedimentary rocks* are formed when other rocks erode and become sediment on the bottoms of oceans and lakes. These sediments become pressed and cemented over millions of years into rock. Examples include shale, sandstone, and limestone. Metamorphic rocks are formed when great heat and pressure change igneous or sedimentary rocks into entirely new rocks. Examples include gneiss, marble, and slate.

SAFETY SPOTLIGHT

Some rocks found by students may be too large for their collection. If you want to break a rock into smaller pieces, be sure to protect your eyes by wearing safety goggles. Also, wrap the rock in several layers of paper or a towel before striking it with a hammer.

Each team needs a collection of rocks for this lesson. An egg carton numbered from 1 - 12 makes an excellent storage container. The rocks do not need to be from a purchased rock collection; in fact, students enjoy bringing rocks from home to contribute. Several days before the lesson, ask students to gather rocks for their team collection. Try to make sure that each team has a wide variety of specimens. You might want to have a few extra rocks available for teams with incomplete collections.

Materials for each Team:
1 egg carton
12 rocks

Gather the rest of the materials in advance also. The only material which is not commonly found in the home is a streak plate. These may be ordered from a science supply company (see Resources List). Since a streak plate is just an unglazed porcelain tile, you may also want to check your local home improvement store. If you can't find an unglazed tile, use the back of an ordinary tile. Each student only needs a 2" square piece, so you may be able to use broken tiles that you can obtain for free. A streak plate is used to find out the color of a rock's "streak," or the color left behind when you scratch a rock on the tile. If you absolutely can't locate streak plates, proceed with the lesson and omit the steps which refer to their use.

1

Reading an adventure story using TEACHER READS

Materials for the Class:
The Magic School Bus Inside the Earth by Joanna Cole (book or video)

Write the terms *rock, mineral, igneous, sedimentary,* and *metamorphic* on the board. Ask your students to listen for the meanings of the words as you read *The Magic School Bus Inside the Earth* to them. Each page includes sidebars and captions which are important to the development of the concepts, so be sure to read everything. If you have access to the Reading Rainbow collection of videotapes, you might want to show the videotape of *The Magic School Bus Inside the Earth* instead of reading it.

2

Discussing the story using THINK-PAIR-SHARE

Ask students if they remember the difference between a *rock* and a *mineral.* Have them **think** about the meaning, then **pair** with a partner to discuss it. Finally, ask several students to **share** their ideas with the class.

Use the same procedure to discuss the meanings of *sedimentary, igneous,* and *metamorphic.* Be sure to clear up misunderstandings about any of these terms before continuing the lesson.

Draw the Hardness Scale on the chalkboard or posterboard.

3

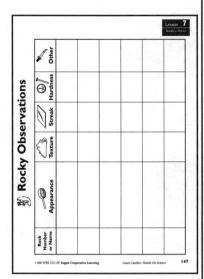

Observing and testing rocks
using TEACHER DEMONSTRATES

Materials for the Class:
transparency of the Rocky Observation
worksheet
1 rock

Materials for each Team:
2 Rocky Observation worksheets
1 team rock collection
2 trays
2 small cups vinegar
2 straws or eyedroppers
2 magnifying lenses
2 magnets
2 small cups water
2 streak plates (unglazed porcelain tiles)
2 pennies
2 iron nails

Hardness Scale	
Very Soft	Can be scratched by a fingernail.
Soft	Can be scratched by a penny.
Hard	Can be scratched by an iron nail.
Very Hard	Cannot be scratched by a fingernail, penny or nail.

If your students are not already in teams, seat them in teams of four. Then divide each team into two pairs of partners. Give each pair one copy of the Rocky Observations worksheet and a tray containing all the materials needed. If you don't have enough supplies for every team to have two of each item, give them one set of materials to leave in the center of the team. The partners can share materials, though they may have to wait for the other pair to finish occasionally.

Tell your students that they will be working with their partner to observe and test six of the rocks in their collection. They will examine the physical and chemical properties of those rocks, and will record this information on their Rocky Observations worksheets.

Use an extra rock to demonstrate each of the tests. Place a transparency of the Rocky Observations worksheet on an overhead projector and complete it as you demonstrate. If the students don't know the names of the rocks, just have them use the numbers (1-12) from each rock's position in the collection. Complete the observations in the following order:

1) **Appearance** - Describe the colors and sizes of the grains. Ask if they can see any layers of minerals or whether the,grains are mixed evenly throughout the rock. Notice if the rock is shiny or dull. Discuss the rock's "luster" or whether it has a metallic or nonmetallic look. Ask if anyone can see any fossils in the rock. Can they see any holes? Use a magnifying lens to observe the rock closely. Record all observations.

(continued on page 143)

Observing and testing rocks (continued from page 142)

2) **Texture** - Show students how to hold the rock and describe its smoothness or roughness. Tell them to close their eyes to concentrate on the textures.

3) **Streak** - Show students how to scratch the rock on an unglazed tile and observe the color left behind. Many times the color of the streak is very different from the color of the rock.

4) **Hardness**- Demonstrate how to test a rock's hardness. If it can be scratched with a fingernail, record the words "very soft." If a fingernail won't scratch the rock but a penny will, it is "soft." If the only thing that will scratch it is the nail, the rock is "hard." If nothing will scratch it the rock is "very hard."

5) **Other** - Challenge them to make any other observations and tests they can think of. They might want to try floating the rock in water or touching a magnet to it. They can drop vinegar on the rock to see if it will fizz (limestone will).

4

Observing and testing rocks using RALLYTABLE

After you have demonstrated the procedure for observing and testing the rocks, explain the **RallyTable** method of completing the chart. Each pair of students will only test six of the rocks in the team collection. In each pair, designate one person as the "A" partner and the other as the "B" partner.

Step One: Student A tests rock; Student B records results.
Student A selects the first rock and Student B keeps the Rocky Observations worksheet. *Both* students touch the rock and observe its appearance. However, Student A conducts the other four tests on that rock while Student B records the results.

Step Two: Student B tests rock; Student A records results.
The two students then switch roles. Student B conducts the tests and Student A writes the results on the worksheet.

Step Three: Continuing the tests
The students continue taking turns testing and recording data until all six rocks have been tested. Both students should be actively involved in the observation process at all times.

5

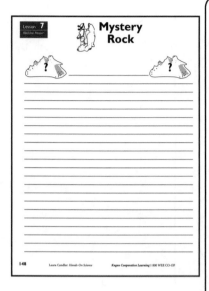

Indentifying rocks from descriptions
using **SEND-A-PROBLEM**

Materials for each Person:
I Mystery Rock worksheet
I rock
I pencil or pen

Materials for each Team:
I tray or large piece of cardboard

Step One: Explaining the activity
Tell students to place all the rocks back into their egg cartons.
Explain that each person will select a "Mystery Rock" and write a
detailed description of the rock. Then each team will send all their
rocks and their four descriptions to another team. The receiving
team will have to find the rocks which match those descriptions.

Step Two: Selecting a Mystery Rock
Let each person have a few moments to choose their Mystery
Rock from the collection. Tell them to try to keep the rock a secret
from other class members. Their own team members are allowed
to know which rock they selected, though.

Step Three: Writing descriptions
Now give each student a copy of the Mystery Rock worksheet.
Students write a paragraph description of the rock. Allow them to
use the observations recorded previously. Emphasize that they are
not trying to trick the other teams; the object is to write a clear
description so that anyone in the class can read it and find the
matching rock. Everyone reads their paragraphs to their partners
to make sure their descriptions are clear. Then, on the back of the
worksheet, students write the number of the rock that matches
the description.

(continued on page 145)

Identifying rocks from descriptions (continued from page 144)

Step Four: Sending rocks and descriptions

The team places all the rocks back in the carton and place the collection and the descriptions on a tray. Then, in a prearranged pattern, have Student #4 deliver the tray to Student #1 on the next team.

Step Five: Matching rocks with descriptions

When each tray arrives, Student #1 keeps all the descriptions and places the rock collection in the center of the team. He or she reads the first description aloud while the others look for the matching rock. Everyone jots down the number of the rock they think fits the description. When everyone is ready, Student #1 checks the team's answers. If everyone does not agree, Student #1 reads the description aloud again. When all are in agreement, Student #1 turns the description over to check for correctness.

Next, all the descriptions are passed to Student #2. This person reads the next description. The team follows the same steps as above to try to identify the rock. Repeat the procedure until all Mystery Rocks are identified.

Step Six: Continue as time allows

When all teams are finished, have Student #4 deliver each team's tray to Student #1 on the next team. Teams follow the same procedure as above to match descriptions and rocks

Writing About Science

Have students select one rock to sketch in their Science Journals. Under the sketch, have them write a detailed description of their rock. Remind them to include information about the rock's appearance, texture, streak, and any other properties they observe.

Materials Check List

For the Class:
- ❏ *The Magic School Bus Inside the Earth* by Joaana Cole (book or video)
- ❏ transparency of the Rocky Observation worksheet
- ❏ 1 rock

For each Team:
- ❏ 2 Rocky Observation worksheets
- ❏ 2 streak plates (unglazed porcelain tiles)
- ❏ 1 tray or large piece of cardboard
- ❏ 1 team rock collection
- ❏ 2 straws or eyedroppers
- ❏ 2 magnifying glasses
- ❏ 2 small cups water
- ❏ 2 iron nails
- ❏ 2 trays
- ❏ 2 small cups vinegar
- ❏ 2 magnets
- ❏ 2 pennies

For each Student:
- ❏ 1 Mystery Rock worksheet
- ❏ 1 pencil or pen
- ❏ 1 rock

Curriculum Links:

1. Science - Labelling rock collections
Provide access to rock and mineral guide books and perhaps a prepared rock collection. Teams try to identify and label the rocks in their collections. Consider inviting a local geologist to the class to help with the identification process.

2. Language Arts - Communicating about rocks
Use **Team Interview** to play "Guess My Rock." Each student visually selects a rock from the collection, without pointing to it or removing it from the collection. His or her teammates attempt to guess which rock has been selected by asking questions which can be answered with a "yes" or a "no." For example, one person might ask, "Does your rock float?" The team keeps track of the number of questions they asked and tries to improve its record (by decreasing the number of questions needed to guess the rock).

3. Science - Classifying rocks according to hardness
Use an encyclopedia or other resource to find a copy of the Mohs Scale of Hardness. Rocks can be classified and assigned a "hardness" value of 1 - 10 by following a set of simple procedures. For instance, students scratches a rock first with their fingernail, then with a penny, a knife, and a metal file. Finally students attempt to scratch glass with the rock. The results of these tests determines the hardness of the rock.

4. Art - Creating paper weights
Each student chooses a rock to decorate as a paper weight. Let them paint their rocks and glue on glitter, yarn, beads, etc.

5. Math - Creating Venn Diagrams
Use large loops of yarn to create Venn diagrams on the floor or a table. Let each team devise their own classification system. For instance, some may want to let one circle represent the set of smooth rocks, and the other to represent gray rocks. Smooth, gray rocks would be placed in the overlapping area, and rocks that are neither smooth nor gray would remain outside the circles.

6. Literature - Reading about rocks and minerals
A number of excellent rock and mineral books are available for children. *The Big Rock* by Bruce Hiscock tells the story of a rock in the Adirondack Mountains, from its creation to the present. *Rock Collecting* by Roma Gans will appeal to students who enjoyed creating the team collections. Another book, *Everybody Needs a Rock,* by Byrd Baylor, gives a child's "rules" for how to choose the perfect rock. *How to Dig a Hole to the Other Side of the World* by Faith McNulty is an adventure story similar to *The Magic School Bus Inside the Earth.*

Rocky Observations

Rock Number or Name	Appearance	Texture	Streak	Hardness	Other

Mystery Rock

? _____ ?

_____

_____

_____

_____

_____

_____

_____

_____

_____

_____

_____

_____

_____

_____

_____

_____

_____

_____

_____

_____

_____

Students Will...

Share feelings about their
favorite photograph

Construct pinhole cameras

Draw pictures of objects as
viewed through their cameras

Learn how a pinhole camera
is similar to a real camera

Process Skills...

Observing

Identifying

Making Models

Inferring

Communicating

Structures...

Pairs

Think-Pair-Share

Three-Step-Interview

Investigating Cameras

n this lesson your students will learn how a camera operates by creating
a model of a camera from simple materials. This type of model is called
a "pinhole camera," but it does not actually take photographs. However, objects
viewed through the camera will appear upside down, which provides a perfect
opportunity for students to learn that light becomes inverted as it passes
through a lens.

The pinhole cameras will be constructed from bathroom tissue tubes or empty juice cans (with both ends removed). Paper towel tubes may be used if they are cut into three pieces. The exact sizes of the tubes are not important. You will need one tube for each student, so you'll want to begin collecting these several weeks in advance.

Several days before the lesson, tell your students that they will be learning about cameras. Ask them to bring in their favorite photograph from home, but not to show it to anyone until the lesson begins.

1

Sharing photographs using THREE-STEP INTERVIEW

Materials for each Student:
1 photograph

Step One: Partner A interviews Partner B
Within each team, pair students to form two sets of partners. Partners should be seated next to each other. Designate one student in each pair to be the "A" partner and the other to be the "B" partner.

Begin the lesson by asking everyone to get out their favorite photograph to share with the team. Ask Partner A to turn to Partner B and ask questions about B's photograph. Give Partner A one minute to learn all they can about why B's photograph is his or her favorite.

Step Two: Partner B interviews Partner A
The partners reverse roles. Give Partner B one minute to ask questions about A's photograph.

Step Three: Partners tell their team about each others photograph
Finally, in **RoundRobin** fashion, each of the four team members should tell the team about their *partner's* picture. Allow each person about 30 seconds of time, or a total of two minutes.

Making pinhole cameras using PAIRS

Materials for each Student:
1 carboard tube, about 4-6 inches in length
1 square of aluminum foil (3")
1 square of waxed paper (3")
1 sheet of black construction paper (9" x 12")
1 tape
1 pin

Step One: Explaining the activity

Tell your students that they will learn how a camera operates by constructing a model of a camera, called a "pinhole camera." Let them know that the camera they create will not actually take photographs. *Tell them that each person will make his or her own camera, but that they should work with their partner to help hold materials.* Younger students will need to do the following steps right along with you. Older students enjoy the challenge of watching you make yours and then constructing their own from memory. Leave your model on display for students to refer to as they work.

Step Two: Constructing the camera

1. Place the square of foil over one end of the tube. Fold the edges down and tape them to the sides of the tube. The foil should be smooth and tight across the top of the tube.

2. Use the pin to poke a small hole in the center of the foil. (If the hole becomes too large the camera will not work properly.)

3. Place the square of waxed paper over the other end of the tube. Fold the edges over and tape them to the sides of the tube. The waxed paper should be smooth and tight across the bottom of the tube. (See illustration)

aluminum foil

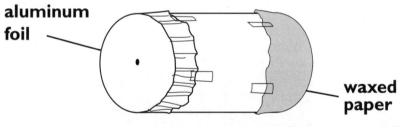

waxed paper

(continued on page 152)

Making pinhole cameras (continued from page 151)

4. The next step involves making a viewing tube from the black paper. When finished, the it will fit around the cardboard tube and will be several inches longer than the cardboard tube. If you are using a toilet tissue tube, cut the sheet of construction paper in half to form a 6" x 9" rectangle. (If you are using juice cans or other tubes you will need to cut the paper accordingly.)

5. Lay the rectangle of black paper flat and place the camera tube on top of it so that the foil end is even with one end of the paper. The paper should extend several inches farther than the waxed paper end. Roll the paper around the camera and tape the paper securely along the seam. Then tape the paper to the camera.

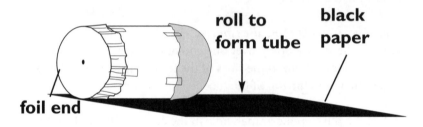

6. To use the pinhole camera, look through the waxed paper end. The black paper creates a viewing tunnel, a sort of "light shield" that keeps distracting light rays from falling on the waxed paper. Point the foil end of the camera towards a very bright object or an object in full sunlight. You'll notice that the image which appears on the waxed paper is upside down.

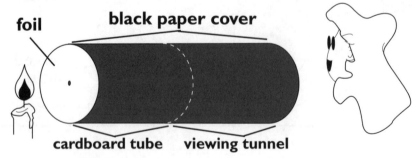

3

Using pinhole cameras using PAIRS EXPLORE

After *both* students in each pair have constructed their cameras, allow them the opportunity for free exploration. Remind them to point their cameras toward bright objects. If the weather permits, take your class outside during this exploration period. Tell them to stay with their partner for safety reasons.

4

Recording observations using INDIVIDUALS DRAW

Materials for each Student:
1 pinhole camera
1 Pinhole Camera Observations worksheet
colored pencils or crayons

Materials for the Class:
1 candle (optional)
1 box of matches (optional)

Give each student one copy of the Pinhole Camera Observations worksheet. After everyone has had time for free exploration with their pinhole cameras, ask them to choose two objects to draw on their worksheet. They should first draw the objects as they appear without the camera. Then they should draw the inverted views as they appear when seen through the camera.

Remember that objects to be viewed must be very bright. If your students are having difficulty finding an object to view, darken the room slightly and light a candle. Allow a few students at a time to approach the candle and view it through their pinhole cameras. Monitor the activity carefully so students don't move their cameras close enough to the candle to ignite them.

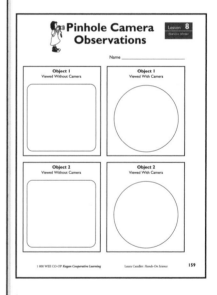

5

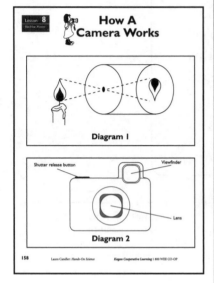

Explaining how a camera works using TEACHER TALK

Materials for the Class:
transparency of How A Camera Works
pinhole camera
commercial camera

Step One: Explaining why the camera inverts the image

By now your students will have discussed the fact that the image on the waxed paper is upside-down, or inverted. To explain why this happens, place the transparency of Diagram 1 on the overhead projector. Show the students that because light rays travel in straight lines, the light from the top of the object passes through the pinhole and appears at the bottom of the image. In the same way, light rays from the bottom of the object end up at the top of the image. The same thing happens inside a real camera. Instead of waxed paper, a real

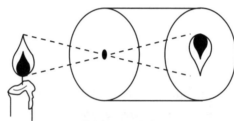

Diagram 1

camera has photographic film that is sensitive to light. The image is still formed upside-down on the film, but when the film is developed we turn the picture right-side up for viewing.

(continued on page 155)

5 cont.

Explaining how a camera works (continued from page 154)

Step Two: Demonstrating the parts of the camera
Now, if possible, show your students a commercial camera. Discuss the basic parts of the camera and the functions of those parts. Diagram 2 illustrates a very simple camera, similar to those owned by many students. You may want to use a transparency of this illustration in your discussion. Since models of cameras vary greatly, some parts may be difficult to identify on some cameras. The following basic parts can be found on all cameras:

1) **Lens** - A piece of glass that the light passes through before striking the film
2) **Shutter** - A device (usually behind the lens) that opens for a fraction of a second to allow light to strike the film. You will only be able to view the shutter if you open the back of the camera. *Don't do this if it contains film!*
3) **Shutter-release button** - Button to press when taking a picture; causes the shutter to open so that light may strike the film
4) **Viewfinder** - Place the photographer looks through to aim the camera

Depending on the model, a camera may have additional features such as a shutter speed dial, focusing ring, self-timer, flash attachment, light meter, rewind knob, etc. If the camera you are demonstrating has additional features, include them in your discussion.

6

Reflection Questions using THINK-PAIR-SHARE

Conclude the lesson by asking students to **Think-Pair-Share** the following questions. Use the class "sharing" phase to clear up any misunderstandings.

- *Why do images appear upside-down in a pinhole camera?*
- *What part of the pinhole camera is similar to the film in a real camera? (the waxed paper)*
- *What part of the pinhole camera is similar to the lens in a real camera? (the pinhole)*
- *What is the purpose of the shutter in a real camera?*
- *What is the name of the device a photographer looks through when aiming the camera? (viewfinder)*

Writing About Science

Have students illustrate the concept of light being inverted as it passes through a lens (put Diagram 1 back on the overhead if needed). Then they explain this concept in sentence form. You can also have them sketch a picture of a camera and label the parts.

Materials Check List

For the Class:
- ❏ transparency of How A Camera Works
- ❏ pinhole camera
- ❏ commercial camera
- ❏ 1 candle (optional)
- ❏ 1 box of matches (optional)

For each Student:
- ❏ 1 photograph
- ❏ 1 carboard tube, about 4-6 inches in length
- ❏ 1 square of aluminum foil (3")
- ❏ 1 square of waxed paper (3")
- ❏ 1 sheet of black construction paper (9" x 12")
- ❏ 1 Pinhole Camera Observations worksheet
- ❏ colored pencils or crayons
- ❏ 1 pin
- ❏ tape

Curriculum Links

1. Science- Examining other cameras
Allow students to bring cameras from home to examine. Help them use reference materials to identify the parts of their cameras. Allow them to draw diagrams of their cameras, labelling the parts.

2. Art - Creating photo essays
Try to find one person on each team who can bring a camera to school. Let each team plan and create a photo essay on a science topic. Possible topics include: the effects of erosion, the steps of a science project, the effects of pollution, science safety procedures, etc.

3. Language Arts - Writing about photographs
Students bring some of their favorite photographs from home. For each photograph, have them write a paragraph describing the events in the picture. Display the photographs and paragraphs in random order. Allow students to try to match each photograph with its description.

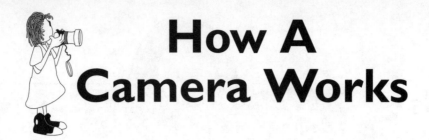

How A Camera Works

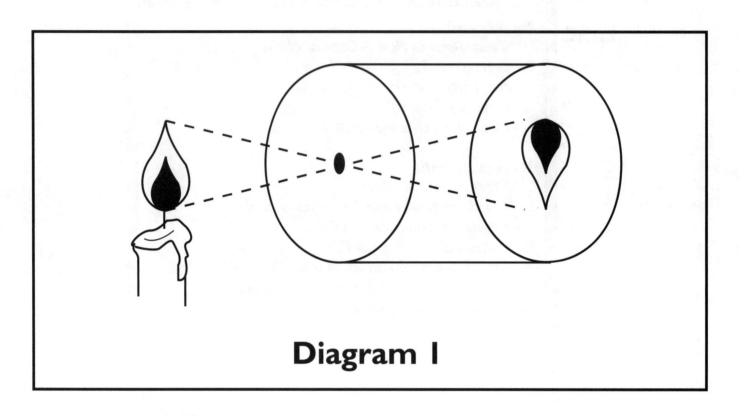

Diagram 1

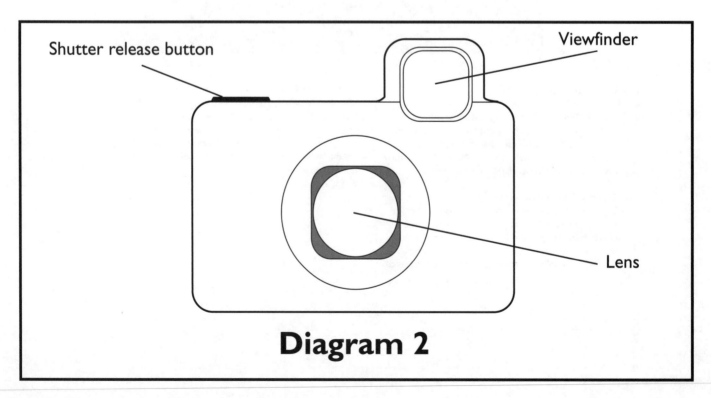

Shutter release button

Viewfinder

Lens

Diagram 2

Pinhole Camera Observations

Name _____

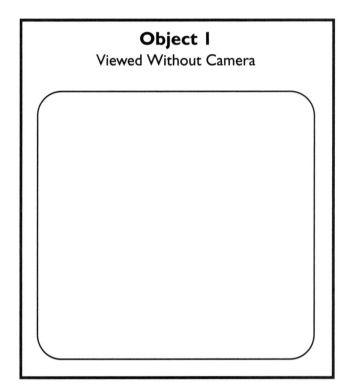

Object 1
Viewed Without Camera

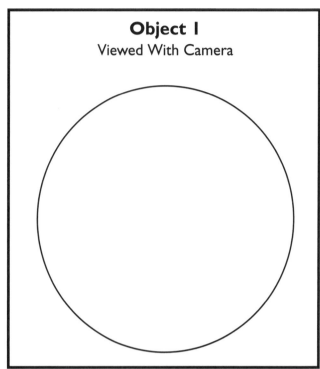

Object 1
Viewed With Camera

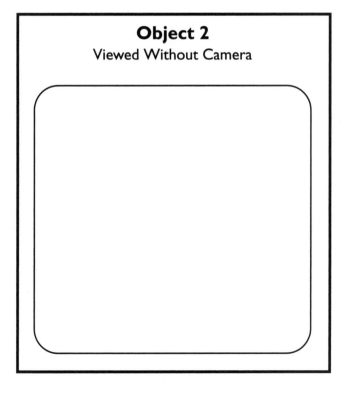

Object 2
Viewed Without Camera

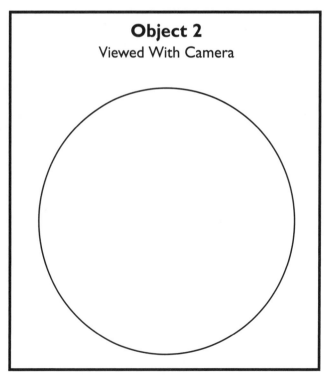

Object 2
Viewed With Camera

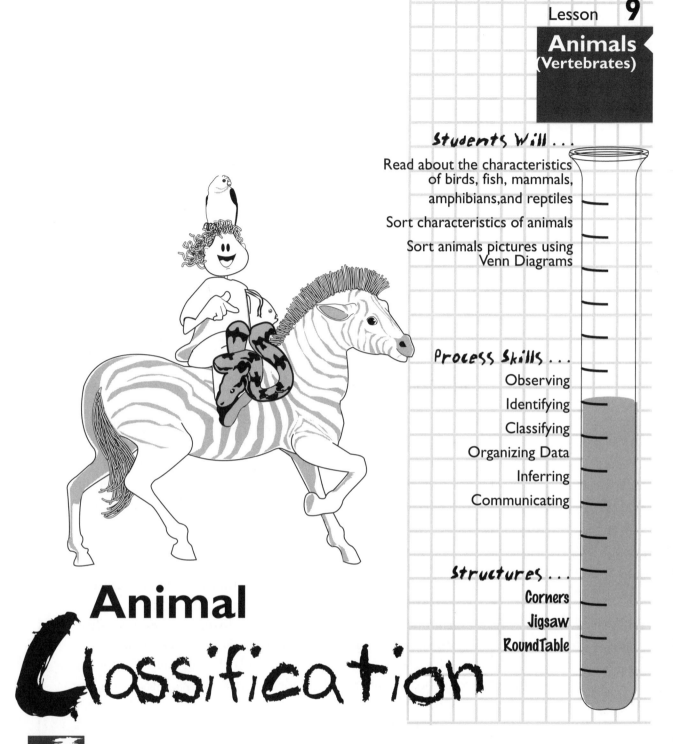

Students Will . . .

Read about the characteristics
of birds, fish, mammals,
amphibians, and reptiles

Sort characteristics of animals

Sort animals pictures using
Venn Diagrams

Process Skills . . .

Observing

Identifying

Classifying

Organizing Data

Inferring

Communicating

Structures . . .

Corners

Jigsaw

RoundTable

Animal
Classification

In this lesson, your students will learn how scientists classify animals. After using Jigsaw to become "experts" on at least one type of animal, they will help their team members sort animals by their classifications. You'll introduce your students to Venn Diagrams and will help them sort those same animals by specific characteristics like body covering, method of transportation, and habitat.

You'll need to divide your students into base teams and expert groups. Base teams of five work well since the lesson involves five types of animals (birds, fish, amphibians, reptiles, and mammals). However, if your students are already in teams of four, you can assign one person to learn about two types of animals. To form your expert groups, use the Animal Jigsaw Expert Groups worksheet provided. In pencil, write the name of each base team across the top. Then list each team's members in the column below the team's name. Your expert groups will appear across the rows. Make changes as needed to ensure that all teams are balanced academically and socially. When you are finished, list the names of the students in each Expert Group. You'll post these rosters at each table later.

♞ **Animal Jigsaw Expert Groups**

Base Teams →	Team 1	Team 2	Team 3	Team 4	Team 5	Team 6	Team 7
Mammals							
Birds							
Fish							
Reptiles							
Amphibians							

1

Explaining animal classification using TEACHER TALK

Tell your students that there are over a million different types of animals on the earth. In order to study them better, scientists classify animals, or divide them into groups. All the animals in each group are alike in some way. Animals in a particular group have similar characteristics, such as body covering, type of birth, method of transportation, etc.

One important way scientists classify animals is by whether or not they have a backbone. Animals with backbones are called "vertebrates" and animals without are called "invertebrates." Tell them that these two main groups are divided into even smaller groups, called *classes*. Over the next few days they will be studying about more about five kinds of vertebrates. On the chalkboard, illustrate these ideas by drawing a diagram similar to the one below.

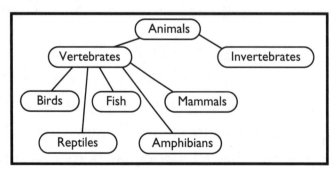

Set up five work stations around the room and label each one with the name of one type of animal (Fish, Reptile, Bird, Mammal, and Amphibian). Cut apart the Jigsaw Expert Cards and *place the appropriate card at each station.* Then place *seven sheets of construction paper, one bottle of glue, two pairs of scissors,* and *two packs of crayons* or *markers* at each station. You'll also need *books and magazines which show examples of the type of animal each Expert Group will be studying.* If you don't have room to set up the stations in advance, assemble all the materials for each station on a tray so that your students won't have to wait while you count out materials.

2

Learning about vertebrates using JIGSAW

Materials for the Class:
1 Animal Jigsaw Expert Groups worksheet
35 sheets (9" x 12") light-colored construction paper
1 copy of the 5 Jigsaw Expert Cards
10 pairs of scissors
10 packs of markers or crayons
5 bottles of glue
books and magazines which contain pictures of animals

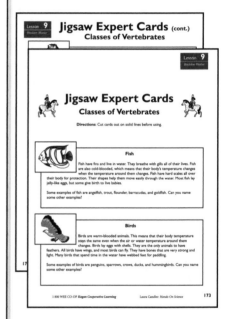

Step One: Assigning expert groups
Seat your students in their base teams. Then tell them that they will be moving to a new area of the room to learn about one of the five classes of vertebrates. They will become an expert on that type of animal and will share the information they learn with the members of their base teams. Post the roster for each Expert Group at the appropriate station and call out the members' names. Have them move to their stations.

Step Two: Learning about the five classes of vertebrates
When your students meet in their expert groups, they **RoundRobin** read the sentences on their information card. Designate one person to begin reading the first sentence, then let them pass the card around the group so that each successive person reads the next sentence. If you have provided books about each class of animal, allow your students time to look at pictures of those animals. Circulate among all the expert groups. Ask the students questions to check their understanding of the animal characteristics important for their group.

(continued on page 164)

2 cont.

Learning about vertebrates (continued from page 163)

Step Three: Making posters
When all Expert Groups seem to understand their class of animals, tell students they will each make a "miniposter" of that information. (See example.) Tell them that they will use these posters to teach their teammates about their class of animal. On their miniposters they write the name of their animal class and list the most important characteristics of that type of animal. They also draw or glue on examples of their type of animal. (Be sure they know which magazines they may cut pictures from!) When everyone has finished send them back to their base teams.

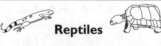

Reptiles
- *cold-blooded*
- *covered with hard, dry scales*
- *breathe with lungs*
- *lay eggs with tough leathery scales*

Step Four: Sharing information with base teams
Give each team member two minutes to stand in front of their base team and teach their team members about the type of animal they studied. Tell them to keep their miniposters handy for future reference.

3

Sorting animal characteristics using ROUNDTABLE

Materials for each Team:
1 copy Vertebrate Classification
1 copy Vertebrate Characteristics
scissors

Step One: Preparing materials
With students in base teams, number the members from 1- 4 (or 5). Give each team one copy of the Vertebrate Classification and Vertebrate Characteristics pages. Team members work together to cut apart the Animal Characteristics to form individual strips. There are several copies of some characteristics since those qualities apply to more than one class of animals.

Step Two: Dividing the characteristics among team members
Person #1 takes all the characteristics and forms a pile of slips on their desk. Then that person deals the slips out (like a deck of cards) to all team members so that everyone has approximately the same amount.

(continued on page 165)

Lesson 9 Blackline Master
Vertebrate Characteristics

are warm-blooded	are cold-blooded
are warm-blooded	are cold-blooded
are cold-blooded	breathe with gills
first have gills, then grow lungs	breathe with lungs
breathe with lungs	lay jelly-like eggs
lay eggs with leathery shell	lay jelly-like eggs
lay eggs with hard shell	give birth to live babies
make milk for their babies	have feathers
have hair or fur	have hard, dry, rough scales
have hard scales	have soft, moist skin
always live in the water	most have legs
most have legs	most have legs
have strong, light bones	have wings
breathe with lungs	most can fly

178   Laura Candler: Hands-On Science   *Kagan Cooperative Learning* | 800 WEE CO-OP

3 cont.

Sorting animal characteristics (continued from page 164)

Step Three: Sorting characteristics
Each team places the Vertebrate Classification page in the middle of the team so that everyone can read the words easily. Team members take turns reading one characteristic from their pile aloud and placing it on the correct class of animals. For instance, Person #1 might begin by reading "warm-blooded" from one slip of paper. After a brief team discussion, that person places the slip on either "Mammals" or "Birds." Then Person #2 reads the next characteristic and places it on one of the animal classes. Students take turns until all the characteristics are in place.

Step Four: Checking answers
Randomly call on students to list the characteristics of each class of animals. If team members have placed some slips incorrectly, let them make changes at this time. Students should remove the slips of paper at the end and save the sorting page for use in another activity.

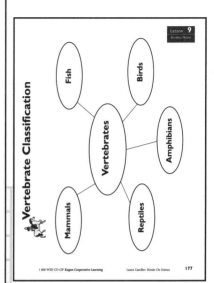

Use five sheets of construction paper to make five posters. In large letters, print the following titles on the posters (one per poster): Birds, Mammals, Reptiles, Fish, Amphibians.

4

Classifying animals using CORNERS

Materials for each Team:
1 set of Animal Cards
scissors

Materials for the Class:
5 animal posters (Birds, Mammals, Fish, Reptiles, and Amphibians)
tape

Step One: Preparing the Animal Cards
Give each team one set of Animal Cards (both pages). Ask team members to work together to cut the pictures apart. They turn the pictures face down in the center of the team and shuffle them.

(continued on page 166)

4 cont.

Classifying animals (continued from page 165)

Step Two: Explaining Corners
Display the five posters you prepared earlier in different locations. You might put one in each corner and one in the middle of the chalkboard. Tell your students that they will draw an animal card from the center of the team and will move to the area which names their class of animal.

Step Three: Moving to corners
Allow each person to draw one animal card and look at it. If necessary, allow brief Pair Discussions to make sure everyone knows which class their animal belongs to. Direct students to move to the appropriate corner.

Step Four: Justifying responses
Students pair with a partner in their corner and discuss why their animal belongs to that particular class. For instance, someone with a picture of a frog might say, "Frogs are amphibians because they are cold-blooded animals that begin life with gills and grow lungs later. They also lay jelly-like eggs."

Students return to their seats when finished. Continue with several rounds of Corners as time allows.

5

Classifying animals using ROUNDTABLE

Materials for each Team:
  1 Vertebrate Classification worksheet
  1 set of 24 animal pictures

Step One: Preparing to sort animal picture cards
To begin the activity, ask Person #2 to stack all the animal pictures into one pile. Have them deal the pictures out to team members. Place the Vertebrate Classification page in the center of each team.

Step Two: Sorting by classification
Now ask Person #2 to start by placing one of their cards in on its correct class. As they do this, they state the reason for that placement. For instance, "A turkey is a bird because it's warm-blooded, lays eggs, and has feathers." Everyone else takes turns placing their cards, one at a time, on its correct class. All team members should agree on the placement of each card.

Step Three: Checking responses
Randomly call on students to name the animals placed in each of the five classes. If team members have placed some pictures incorrectly, let them make changes at this time. Students remove the pictures at the end and save them for use in the next activity.

Make a reusable blank Venn diagram chart for each team. Use the two Animal Sorting worksheets or make your own. Use a large sheet (at least 12" x 18") of white construction paper. On one side of the paper draw two large overlapping circles. On the other side, draw three overlapping circles. (See diagram.) Laminate each sheet so that students will be able to write titles on them with an overhead transparency pen.

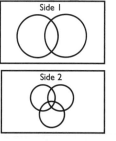

6

Classifying with Venn Diagrams using ROUNDTABLE

Materials for each Team:
- 1 Venn Diagram chart (see Advanced Preparation)
- 1 set of Animal Cards
- 1 transparency pen
- 1 damp and 1 dry paper towel
- 5 index cards (3" x 5")

Step One: Preparing to sort pictures
Ask Person #3 to divide the animal pictures evenly among team members. Point to one of the animal pictures, such as the zebra. Mention some of the characteristics that make that animal unique. For instance, "This zebra has hair on its body, four legs, black and white stripes, and breathes air with lungs." Tell your students they will be classifying their animal pictures by looking at these kinds of characteristics.

Step Two: Sorting by one characteristic
Name one characteristic such as "warm-blooded." Each team sorts their pictures into two piles: "warm-blooded" and "not warm-blooded." Person #3 starts by placing one picture in the center of the team and telling whether the animal is warm-blooded or not. The next person places an animal card on that pile or starts a new one. The rest of the team adds their pictures to one of the two piles depending on whether the animal is warm-blooded or not.

If your students need more practice with sorting by one characteristic, try some of the following ideas:
- *Has two legs*
- *Breathes with lungs*
- *Can fly*
- *Lays eggs*

(continued on page 168)

6 cont.

Classifying with Venn Diagrams (continued from page 167)

Step Three: Sorting by two characteristics

Person #4 collects all the picture cards, shuffles them, and deals them out to members of the team. Give each team a laminated Venn diagram chart, a transparency pen, and two paper towels. Tell them that a Venn diagram is two or more overlapping circles which are used for sorting objects or ideas.

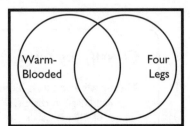

Ask Person #4 to use the transparency pen to write "Warm-blooded" inside the first circle and "Four legs" inside the second circle (see diagram). Show them how to sort their cards by leading them through several examples. Hold up the goose card and say, "The goose is warm-blooded and has only two legs, so it goes in the first circle." Then hold up the lizard and say, "The lizard is not warm-blooded but it does have four legs. Where should it go?" Place it in the second circle. Now hold up the zebra. Tell students that since it is *both* warm-blooded and has four legs it should go in the overlapping area. Finally, choose a card such as the angelfish. Ask students where they should put an animal that is neither warm-blooded nor has four legs. Show them how to place the card on the outside of the two circles, so that it is not in either circle.

Now have Person #4 take one card and tell team members where it should go on the Venn diagram. If everyone agrees, they should give a "thumbs up" signal to Person #4 who places the card in its correct location. If anyone disagrees, the entire team should discuss the item until they can agree on its placement.

In **RoundTable** fashion, students continue sorting the cards. Person #1 goes next, followed by #2 and so on until they have sorted all cards or you call time.

(continued on page 169)

6 cont.

Classifying with Venn Diagrams (continued from page 168)

While students are classifying the animal cards, circulate around the room and discuss their Venn diagrams with them. If you see any errors, ask questions that will lead students to see their mistakes on their own. It is not necessary for students to classify all the cards before you continue with the next step.

Step Four: Continuing to sort by two characteristics
Students clear their charts, wipe off the titles, and divide the cards between themselves again. Give them two more characteristics to use in sorting their animals. Remember that for a Venn diagram to work, the characteristics must be completely different. Try some of the following ideas:
- *Lays Eggs and Has Legs*
- *Can Swim and Has Fins*
- *Cold-blooded and Has Legs*
- *Lives in the Jungle and Has Fur*
- *Has Lungs and Has Two Legs*
- *Has Live Babies and Has Lungs*
- *Mammal and Has Two Legs*

Step Five: Sorting by three characteristics
If your students become proficient with sorting by two characteristics, have them turn the chart over to the other side and try three. Try some of the following combinations:
- *Has Lungs, Can Fly, and Has Two Legs*
- *Lays Eggs, Has Scales, and Warm-blooded*
- *Lives in the Desert, Lays Eggs, and Can Fly*
- *Can Swim, Lays Eggs, and Has Lungs*

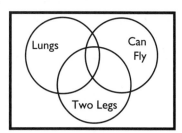

(continued on page 170)

6 cont.

Classifying with Venn Diagrams (continued from page 169)

Step Six: Adding new animals to the Venn diagrams
Give each student a 3" x 5" index card and have them cut it in half. Ask them to think of two animals that were not found on the animal cards. They write the name of each one on half of an index card. Ask them to sketch a picture of the animal under its name.

They turn to the double circle Venn diagram and write a category in each circle, such as "Warm-blooded" and "Lays eggs." In **RoundTable** format, have them take turns placing their new animals in the circles, explaining their reasons as they put down each card.

If your students have mastered the triple circle Venn diagram, give them three new categories and have them repeat the activity using the appropriate chart.

Writing About Science
Have students respond to some or all of the following questions in their Science Journals. They may use words and pictures to answer the questions.
- *What does it mean to say that scientists "classify" animals?*
- *Describe the five classes of vertebrates. Give at least one example of each class.*
- *Draw the following Venn Diagram and label it as shown. Show where a monkey, an eagle, a catfish, and a whale should be placed. Think of an animal we haven't studied and place it correctly on the Venn Diagram.*

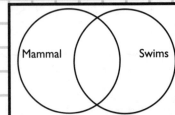

Materials Check List

For the Class:

- ❏ 5 animal posters (Birds, Mammals, Fish, Reptiles, and Amphibians)
- ❏ tape
- ❏ 1 Animal Jigsaw Expert Groups worksheet
- ❏ 1 copy of the 5 Jigsaw Expert Cards
- ❏ 35 sheets (9" x 12") light-colored construction paper
- ❏ 1 damp and 1 dry paper towel
- ❏ 10 packs of markers or crayons
- ❏ books and magazines which contain pictures of animals
- ❏ 5 bottles of glue

For each Team:

- ❏ 1 copy Vertebrate Classification
- ❏ 1 copy Vertebrate Characteristics
- ❏ 1 two-sided Venn Diagram chart
- ❏ 1 transparency pen   ❏ scissors
- ❏ 5 index cards (3" x 5")   ❏ 1 set of Animal Cards

Curriculum Links

1. Art - Creating posters

When students are in their expert groups, you may want to have them create a full-sized poster together about their class of vertebrates. Give them old magazines and books to cut pictures from. Display the five posters during the remainder of the lesson.

2. Literature - Reading about animals

Read books about animals to your students. Ruth Heller has written several children's books that are excellent for reading aloud even to older students. *Animals Born Alive and Well* is about mammals, and *Chickens Aren't the Only Ones* is about animals that lay eggs.

3. Writing - Describing imaginary animals

Students invent an animal that is a bird, reptile, mammal, fish, or amphibian. Without revealing its classification, they should write and illustrate a paragraph describing the characteristics of that animal. Post all the descriptions and pictures and let students try to guess the classification of each imaginary animal.

3. Science - Comparing bars and birds

Read *Stellaluna*, a humorous yet touching story of a baby bat raised by a bird family. Compare bats and birds using a venn diagram. In **RoundTable** fashion have students write bat and bird characteristics in the appropriate places.

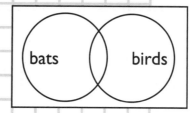

Animal Jigsaw Expert Groups

Base Teams →	Team 1	Team 2	Team 3	Team 4	Team 5	Team 6	Team 7
Mammals							
Birds							
Fish							
Reptiles							
Amphibians							

Laura Candler: *Hands-On Science*

1 (800) 933-2667 • *Kagan Publishing*

Jigsaw Expert Cards
Classes of Vertebrates

Directions: Cut cards out on solid lines before using.

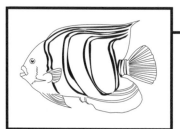

Fish

Fish have fins and live in water. They breathe with gills all of their lives. Fish are also cold-blooded, which means that their body's temperature changes when the temperature around them changes. Fish have hard scales all over their body for protection. Their shapes help them move easily through the water. Most fish lay jelly-like eggs, but some give birth to live babies.

Some examples of fish are angelfish, trout, flounder, barracudas, and goldfish. Can you name some other examples?

Birds

Birds are warm-blooded animals. This means that their body temperature stays the same even when the air or water temperature around them changes. Birds lay eggs with shells. They are the only animals to have feathers. All birds have wings, and most birds can fly. They have bones that are very strong and light. Many birds that spend time in the water have webbed feet for paddling.

Some examples of birds are penguins, sparrows, crows, ducks, and hummingbirds. Can you name some other examples?

Jigsaw Expert Cards (cont.)
Classes of Vertebrates

Mammals

Mammals are warm-blooded and can keep the same body temperature even when the outside temperature changes. Most live on land, but some live in the water. All mammals have hair or fur, though some have very little. All mammals have lungs and breathe air. Most mammals give birth to live babies that are fully formed. Mammals are the only animals that make milk to feed their young.

Some examples of mammals are deer, mice, monkeys, dolphins, whales, raccoons, and elephants. Humans are mammals, too. Can you name any other examples of mammals?

Reptiles

Reptiles are cold-blooded animals, which means that their body temperature changes when the temperature around them changes. They lay eggs with tough, leathery shells. Reptiles are covered with hard, dry, rough scales. All reptiles breathe with lungs. Most reptiles live on land, although many spend time in the water. Some reptiles have legs, while others, like snakes, do not.

Some examples of reptiles are alligators, lizards, turtles, and snakes. Can you name any other examples?

Amphibians

Amphibians are cold-blooded animals, which means that their body temperature changes when the temperature around them changes. Amphibians lay eggs which have a jelly-like substance around them. All amphibians begin their lives in the water and breathe with gills. Later, they grow lungs and can live on land. Most amphibians have soft, moist skin.

Some examples of amphibians are frogs, toads, and salamanders. Be careful not to confuse amphibians with reptiles.

Animal Cards
Set A

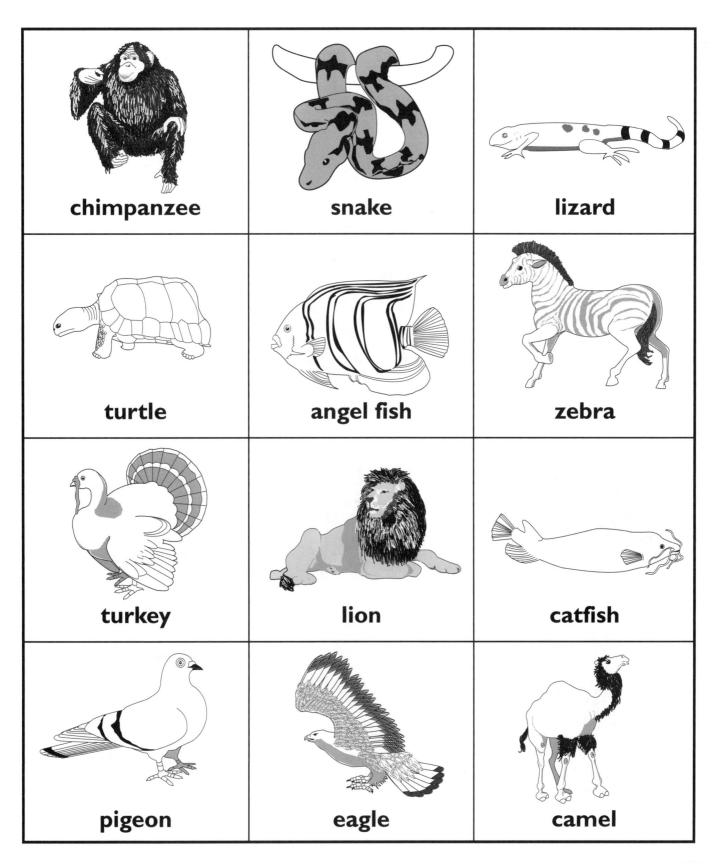

chimpanzee

snake

lizard

turtle

angel fish

zebra

turkey

lion

catfish

pigeon

eagle

camel

Animal Cards
Set B

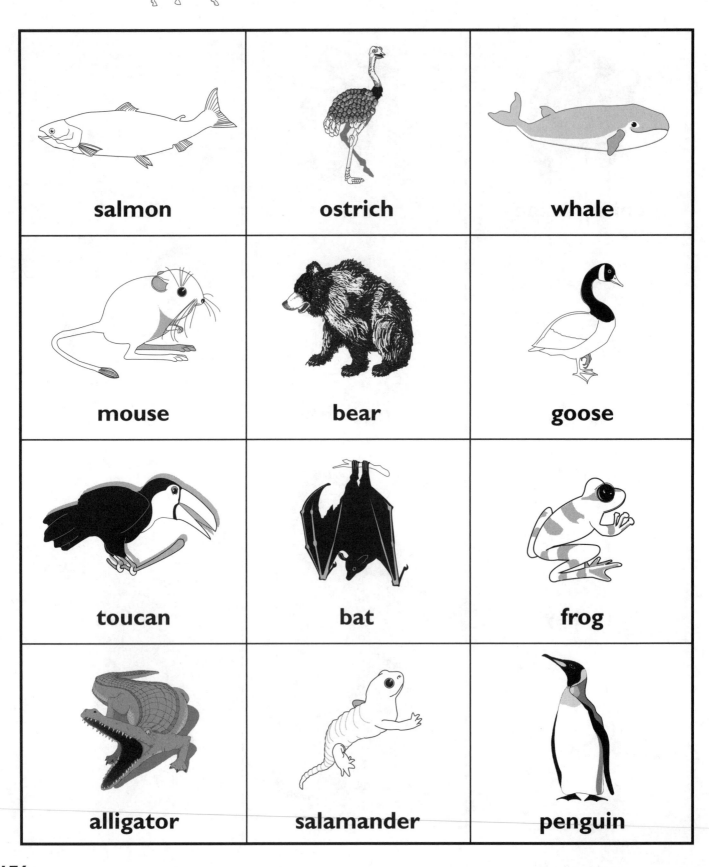

salmon	**ostrich**	**whale**
mouse	**bear**	**goose**
toucan	**bat**	**frog**
alligator	**salamander**	**penguin**

Vertebrate Classification

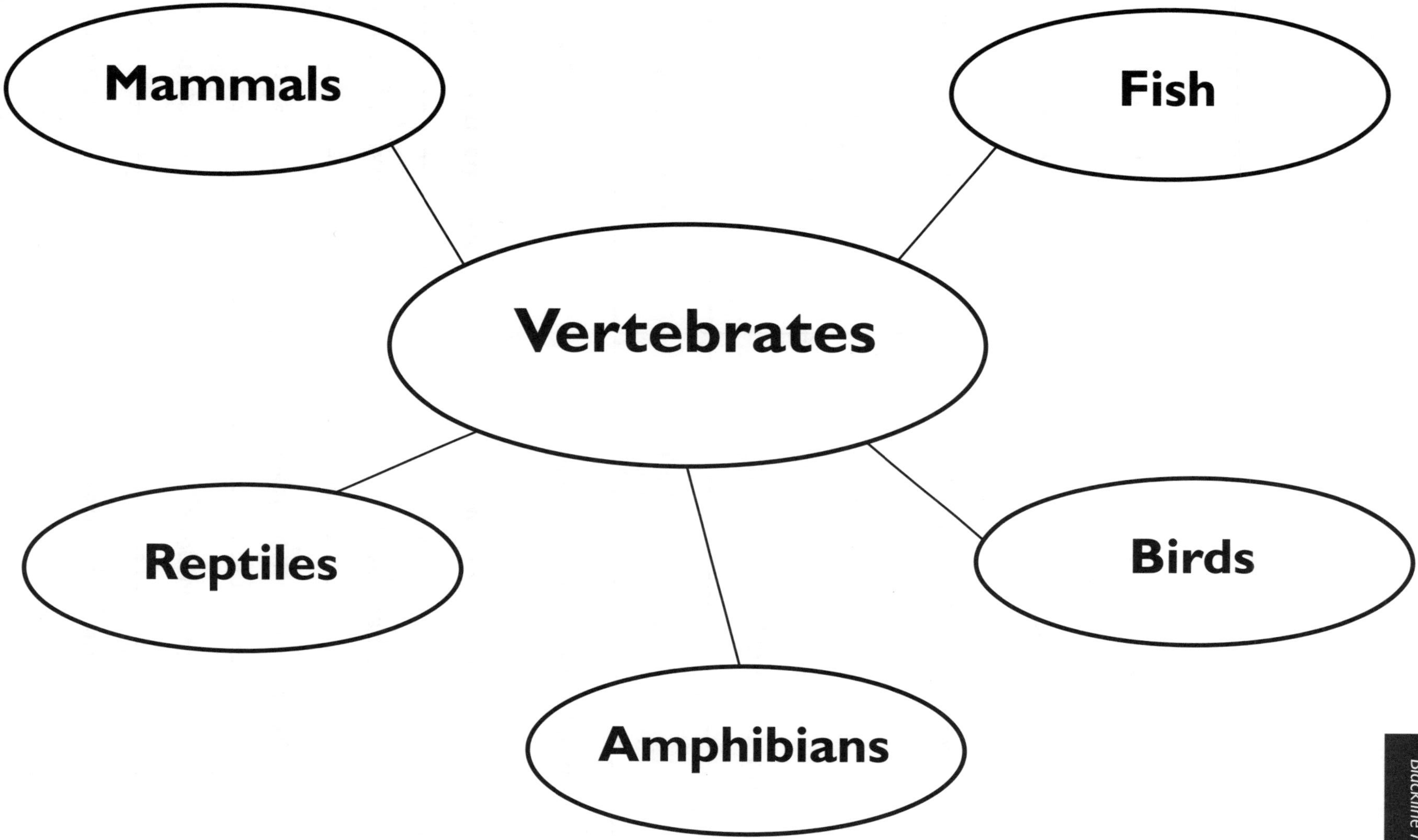

Fish

Birds

Vertebrates

Amphibians

Mammals

Reptiles

Vertebrate Characteristics

are warm-blooded	are cold-blooded
are warm-blooded	are cold-blooded
are cold-blooded	breathe with gills
first have gills, then grow lungs	breathe with lungs
breathe with lungs	lay jelly-like eggs
lay eggs with leathery shell	lay jelly-like eggs
lay eggs with hard shell	give birth to live babies
make milk for their babies	have feathers
have hair or fur	have hard, dry, rough scales
have hard scales	have soft, moist skin
always live in the water	most have legs
most have legs	most have legs
have strong, light bones	have wings
breathe with lungs	most can fly

Simple Animal Sorting

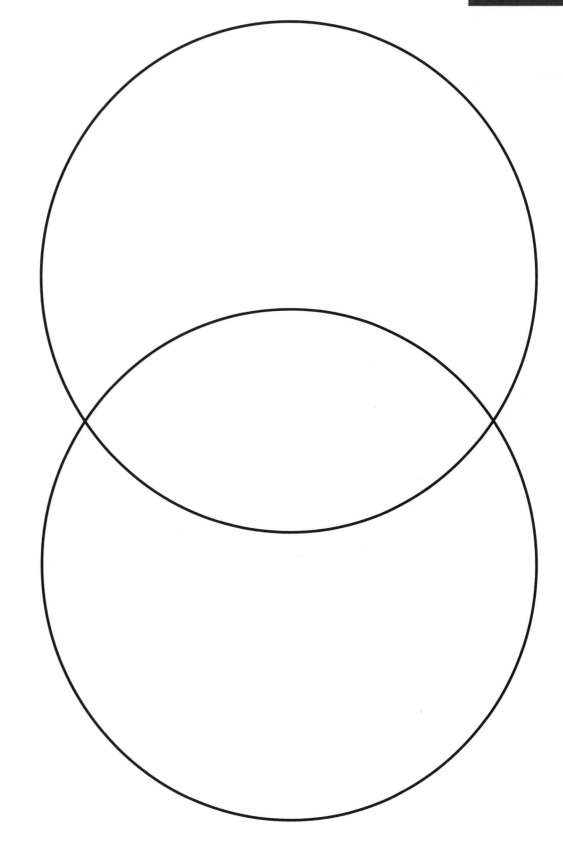

Advanced Animal Sorting

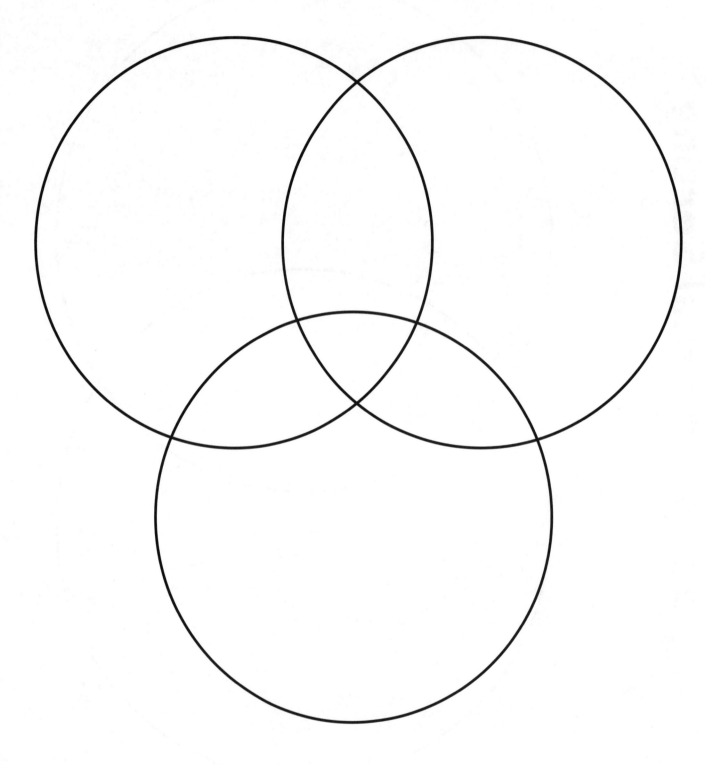

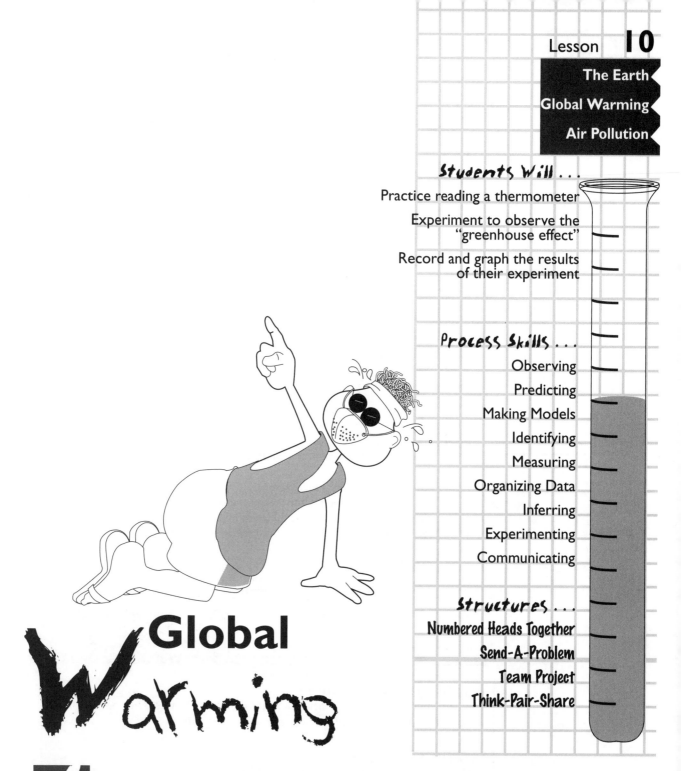

Lesson **10**

The Earth
Global Warming
Air Pollution

Students Will . . .

Practice reading a thermometer

Experiment to observe the "greenhouse effect"

Record and graph the results of their experiment

Process Skills . . .

Observing
Predicting
Making Models
Identifying
Measuring
Organizing Data
Inferring
Experimenting
Communicating

Structures . . .

Numbered Heads Together
Send-A-Problem
Team Project
Think-Pair-Share

Global Warming

tudents will learn about global warming by observing the greenhouse effect. If they aren't familiar with reading Celsius temperatures, they'll practice finding the temperature of different cups of water. Then they'll construct models of the earth out of shoe boxes and will conduct an experiment to see how the Earth's atmosphere traps heat. Working in pairs, they'll record and graph the results of their experiment. Finally, students will discuss the causes and effects of global warming.

SAFETY

SPOTLIGHT

Caution students to be careful with the cups of hot water. If any water spills during the thermometer activity, wipe it up immediately.

Ask students to be careful when handling thermometers. Thermometers for school use contain alcohol which is less dangerous than mercury; however, students can still cut themselves on broken glass.

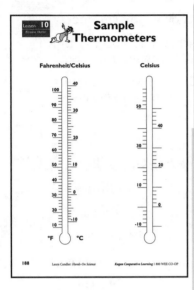

1

Reviewing the thermometer using **NUMBERED HEADS TOGETHER**

Materials for the Class:
transparency of the Sample Thermometers worksheet
overhead pen

Materials for each Team:
1 copy of the Sample Thermometers worksheet
team chalkboard (optional)
chalk (optional)
scrap paper

Step One: Introducing the thermometer
Decide which sample thermometer looks most like the ones you will be using. Place a transparency of this thermometer on the overhead projector and discuss how to interpret the scale. Give each team one copy of the Sample Thermometers page since it may be difficult to read from the front of the room.

Step Two: Shading in temperature
Use the pen to shade in the thermometer to a specific temperature. If students are having trouble viewing the thermometer, verbally describe the height of the shaded area so they can find that level on their team copy.

Step Three: Writing temperature
Make sure everyone has scrap paper. Ask each person to write down the temperature shown on the sample thermometer.

1 cont.

Step Four: Discussing temperature
Students put their heads together to Roundrobin their answers. Then have them discuss their responses until they agree on the correct answer.

Step Five: Choosing a number
When all teams are ready, choose a student from each team to respond by calling out a number from 1 to 4.

Step Six: Sharing team answers
The student on each team whose number is called writes the temperature on a team chalkboard or piece of scrap paper. Check the answers and discuss.

Step Seven: Repeating above steps
Wipe off the transparency and shade in a new temperature. Continue with until all students are comfortable reading a thermometer.

Prepare one cup of water for each team. Each cup should have a different temperature and should be labeled with a number from 1 - 8 (or the number of teams you have in your class). Do this just before you begin the lesson. For safety reasons, make sure none of the cups contain boiling water. Place a thermometer in each cup.

2

Practicing with a thermometer using SEND-A-PROBLEM

Materials for each Team:
1 clear plastic cup of water
1 Celsius thermometer

Materials for each Student:
1 copy of the Testing Temperatures worksheet (half)

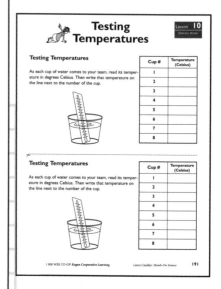

This part of the lesson is optional. If your students are comfortable using a Celsius thermometer, you can skip this practice and begin with the **Think-Pair-Share** activity that follows.

Step One: Reading the first thermometer
Ask students on each team to number off from 1 - 4. Give each team one cup of water containing a different temperature of water. The team places a thermometer in the cup. Then give each person one Testing Temperatures worksheet.

To begin, ask everyone to silently examine the thermometer and decide on the temperature of the water. On their worksheets, have them write their answer next to the number that corresponds with the number on their cup. When everyone is ready, Person #1 checks to see if all team members have the same answer. If not, team members check the thermometer again and discuss the reasons for their answers.

Step Two: Sending the cups and thermometers
When all teams are ready, have Person #1 on each team carefully deliver their team's cup and thermometer to Person #2 on another team. It's best to pass the cups in a prearranged pattern so that all teams will get to see all the cups in a particular order.

Step Three: Continuing to interpret and pass the cups
Follow the same steps to have students interpret the thermometers. Everyone silently reads and writes their answer. Person #2 leads the team in checking and discussing answers. At the end of the second round, Person #2 delivers the cup to the next team. Person #3 leads the third round, and so on.

Step Four: Checking responses
As students are working, move from team to team and confirm their answers. Water temperatures change so quickly that you must check answers before cups are passed for each round of the activity.

3

Discussing the effects of sunlight on a closed car using THINK-PAIR-SHARE

To begin the lesson on global warming, ask students to think about what happens when a car is left in the sun with the windows closed. Students pair with a partner to discuss their ideas. Then let some share students share their thoughts with the class. Many will mention that the car becomes very hot inside.

4

Explaining the "Greenhouse Effect" using TEACHER TALK

Tell them that the way a car heats up in the sun is an example of something scientists call the "greenhouse effect." A greenhouse is a place where plants are grown, and greenhouses are usually made with glass panels in the roof. The rays of sunlight come in through the glass and change into heat energy. This heat warms the inside of the greenhouse since the heat energy cannot escape back through the glass.

Tell your students that the same thing happens on the surface of the Earth. The atmosphere (air around the Earth) allows sunlight to pass through, but keeps heat from leaving the Earth easily. The Greenhouse Effect is important because it keeps the temperatures on Earth from changing greatly each day and night.

However, the Greenhouse Effect can cause problems if it allows the Earth to become too warm. People pollute the air by using things that give off harmful gases. As these gases collect in the air, they trap the sun's heat and make the Earth warmer than it should be. Scientists are worried that the Earth is slowly becoming warmer, which could be harmful to all of us.

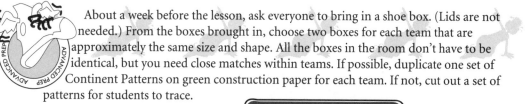

About a week before the lesson, ask everyone to bring in a shoe box. (Lids are not needed.) From the boxes brought in, choose two boxes for each team that are approximately the same size and shape. All the boxes in the room don't have to be identical, but you need close matches within teams. If possible, duplicate one set of Continent Patterns on green construction paper for each team. If not, cut out a set of patterns for students to trace.

5

Experimenting with the Greenhouse Effect using TEAM PROJECT

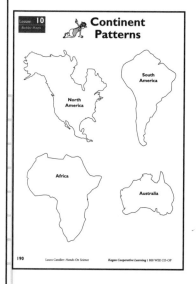

Materials for each Team:
2 shoe boxes without lids
2 pairs of scissors
1 bottle glue
1 roll tape
2 or 3 large sheets of blue construction paper (12" x 18")
2 sets of Continent Patterns duplicated on green paper or
   2 sheets of green construction paper
1 sheet plastic wrap (large enough to cover the box top)
2 Celsius thermometers
2 copies Heating Up the Earth
1 stopwatch or watch with a second hand
2 dark colored pencils (different colors)

Step One: Introducing the activity
Explain that each team will work together to make two models of the Earth out of shoe boxes. These Earth models will be used in an experiment to observe the greenhouse effect. Give each team two shoe boxes that are similar in size and shape. Place the construction paper, scissors, glue and tape in the center of each team.

Step Two: Constructing the models
Divide each team of four students into two sets of partners. Tell each pair of students that they will work together to create one model of the earth from a shoe box. They should also work together with the other pair to make sure that the models are as much alike as possible. Have them follow these steps:
   a. Line the shoe boxes completely with dark blue paper to represent the water.
   b. Cut out several of the continents from the Continent Patterns worksheet and glue them in the bottom of the boxes. (If you were unable to duplicate the Continent Patterns, let students trace a prepared set.) Both boxes should look just alike.
   c. Place a thermometer in the bottom of each box and tape it securely in place.

Step Three: Adding an atmosphere
Point out to the class that both boxes for each team now look very much alike. Now they are going to give one of the Earth models an "atmosphere" of plastic wrap. Give a sheet of plastic wrap to one pair on each team. Have them stretch the plastic wrap tightly across the top and tape it on all four sides. *The plastic wrap must be taped securely so that the air inside the box cannot escape.*

5 cont.

Experimenting with the Greenhouse Effect (continued on page 5)

Step Four: Preparing to experiment

Your students will continue to work with their team and with their partner to complete this experiment. You will need one full class period in which to make the observations. You'll also need to conduct the experiment outside on a bright, sunny day. If this is not possible, set up a lamp for each team.

Before the experiment begins, one person on each team places the boxes outside *in the shade* so that the Earth models will have time to adjust to the outside temperature.

Give each pair one copy of the worksheet "Heating Up the Earth." For simplicity in completing the experiment, in each pair designate one person as "A" and the other as "B."

Step Five: Making predictions

Allow time in the classroom for students to make predictions about what will happen to the temperature in each box. You might want to tell them that a prediction about what will happen in an experiment is called a *hypothesis*.

5 cont.

Step Six: Conducting the experiment

Take the teams outside in bright sunlight. They follow the steps on the worksheet to complete the experiment. If you are conducting this experiment in the winter, the sun's rays will be slanting across the boxes at a sharp angle. In this event, prop them up on a few books so that the sun shines directly down into each box. Make sure the boxes for each team are propped at the same angle. Tell students not to let their bodies shade the boxes at any time.

The instructions call for students to record the temperatures inside the boxes every 3 minutes. Let students know in advance what they are to do in between temperature readings. You might have them take out a book to enjoy or a homework assignment to complete.

(continued on page 6)

5 cont.

Experimenting with the Greenhouse Effect (continued from page 5)

Step Seven: Graphing results

Return to the classroom and have pairs work together to graph their results. One student will graph the temperatures in box without plastic wrap, and the other will graph the temperatures with plastic wrap. Make sure they use two different colored pencils for this.

If your class hasn't had much prior experience with graphing, make a transparency of the blank graph on the student worksheet. Demonstrate the procedure using fictitious data. Most students will need guidance in completing the scale of temperatures on the left side of the graph. Help them decide whether to write their degrees individually or by twos. Since there are 12 horizontal lines, if your students' results have a spread of more than 12 degrees they will have to write every other degree beside each line.

Step Eight: Writing a conclusion

Make sure each student writes his or her own sentence explaining the results of the experiment. Then allow students to put their ideas together and write one conclusion on the worksheet.

6

Discussing Global Warming using THINK-PAIR-SHARE

Students reflect on their results and think about the causes and effects of global warming. Ask students to discuss the answers to the following questions with their partner. They share their ideas with the class so that you can correct any misunderstandings.

- *What were the results of your experiment?*
- *Were your predictions (hypotheses) about the experiment correct?*
- *What do the results teach you about the greenhouse effect on Earth?*
- *What are some things which give off gases that increase the greenhouse effect? (factories, cars, buses, electric power plants, incinerators, and landfills)*
- *What does the term "global warming" mean?*
- *What could happen if the Earth warms up, even a few degrees? (the polar ice caps could begin to melt and raise the level of ocean water, land could become too hot and dry for growing crops, wildlife may die, people would use even more energy to keep cool)*
- *What can you do personally to help prevent global warming?*

Writing About Science

Students can respond in writing to some or all of the **Think-Pair-Share** questions above. They can also reflect in their Science Journals with pictures of the causes and effects of global warming.

Materials Check List

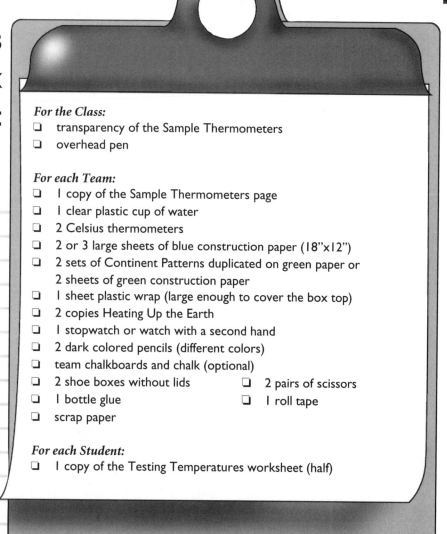

For the Class:
❏ transparency of the Sample Thermometers
❏ overhead pen

For each Team:
❏ 1 copy of the Sample Thermometers page
❏ 1 clear plastic cup of water
❏ 2 Celsius thermometers
❏ 2 or 3 large sheets of blue construction paper (18"x12")
❏ 2 sets of Continent Patterns duplicated on green paper or 2 sheets of green construction paper
❏ 1 sheet plastic wrap (large enough to cover the box top)
❏ 2 copies Heating Up the Earth
❏ 1 stopwatch or watch with a second hand
❏ 2 dark colored pencils (different colors)
❏ team chalkboards and chalk (optional)
❏ 2 shoe boxes without lids   ❏ 2 pairs of scissors
❏ 1 bottle glue   ❏ 1 roll tape
❏ scrap paper

For each Student:
❏ 1 copy of the Testing Temperatures worksheet (half)

Curriculum Links

1. Language Arts - Writing about global warming

Students write a story set in the future. Ask them to imagine that the Earth has warmed several degrees and to include descriptions of the Earth's changes in their stories.

2. Art - Drawing causes and effects of global warming

Students fold a piece of paper in half then open it again. On one side ask them to draw the *causes* of global warming (items that give off "greenhouse gases"). One the other have them draw pictures showing the possible *effects* of global warming.

Sample Thermometers

Fahrenheit/Celsius

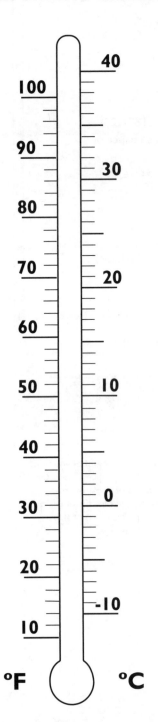

Celsius

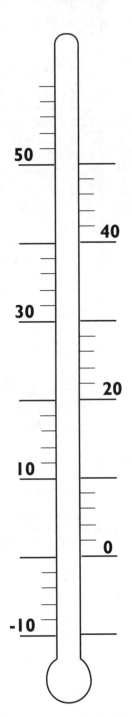

Testing Temperatures

Testing Temperatures

As each cup of water comes to your team, read its temperature in degrees Celsius. Then write that temperature on the line next to the number of the cup.

Cup #	Temperature (Celsius)
1	
2	
3	
4	
5	
6	
7	
8	

✂ -

Testing Temperatures

As each cup of water comes to your team, read its temperature in degrees Celsius. Then write that temperature on the line next to the number of the cup.

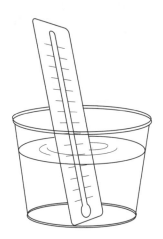

Cup #	Temperature (Celsius)
1	
2	
3	
4	
5	
6	
7	
8	

Continent Patterns

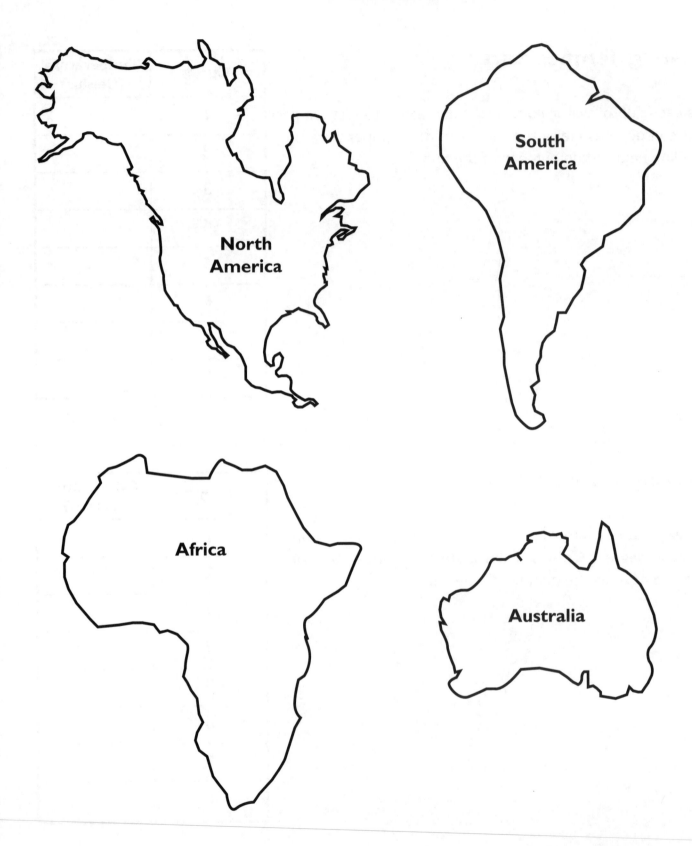

North
America

South
America

Africa

Australia

Names: (A) _____

(B) _____

Part I - Predicting Results

What do you think will happen to the temperature inside each box? Each person write your own prediction:

(A) _____

(B) _____

Part II- Experimenting

Working with your team, place both boxes in direct sunlight. The boxes should be about 10 cm apart. Student A will record the temperatures in the box with plastic wrap, and Student B will record the temperature in the box without plastic wrap. Do not remove the plastic wrap from the box at any time.

As soon as the boxes are in place, read the temperature in each box and record those temperatures in degrees Celsius beside "0" minutes. Then read the temperature every 3 minutes and complete the chart with your results.

Temperatures in Degrees Celsius

Minutes	(A) With Plastic Wrap	(B) Without Plastic Wrap
0		
3		
6		
9		
12		
15		

Heating Up The Earth

Part III - Graphing Results

Step 1 (Both) - Complete the scale of temperatures on the left side of your graph. Write your lowest temperature to the left of the bottom line and write every consecutive degree beside a line until you have written your highest temperature. If you do not have enough lines, you may have to count by two's or five's to have a complete scale.

Step 2 (Student A) - Choose a dark colored pencil and shade in the box next to "With Plastic Wrap." Plot the temperatures for the box with plastic wrap on the graph. Connect the points with straight lines.

Step 3 (Student B) - Choose a different color dark pencil and shade in the "Without Plastic Wrap" box. Plot the temperatures for the box without plastic wrap and connect them with straight lines.

Results of Greenhouse Effect Experiment

Temperature in Degrees Celsius

0   3   6   9   12   15

Minutes

☐ **With Plastic Wrap**   ☐ **Without Plastic Wrap**

 # Heating Up The Earth

Part IV - Writing A Conclusion

Step 1 - Each person think about the results of the experiment and write your own conclusion on a sheet of scrap paper. (A conclusion summarizes in words the information found on your line graph.)

Step 2 - Discuss your conclusions.

Step 3 - Work together to write one conclusion on the lines below. Then sign your names at the bottom of your work.

Conclusion:

_____

_____

_____

_____

_____

_____

_____

_____

_____

_____

_____

_____

Completed by: (A) _____

(B) _____

Students Will...

Test four kitchen powders

Record observations on
a data table

Identify the powders in
a mystery mixture

Solve a mystery by identifying
the components of the mixture

Process Skills...

Observing

Identifying

Organizing Data

Inferring

Communicating

Structures...

Jigsaw

RoundRobin

Teammates Consult

Team Project

Kitchen
Detectives

People of all ages love the challenge of solving a mystery. This lesson gives kids a chance to do a little scientific detective work in order to determine who committed an imaginary crime. In so doing they will learn about the ways in which scientists can identify unknown objects by comparing them to familiar objects.

First, you will show them a mixture of two white kitchen powders, telling them that it is the only evidence found at the scene of a crime. You will tell them that four people were seen leaving the crime scene: Salty Sam, Baking Soda Bob, Cornstarch Calvin, and Sugar Sue. Your students' job will be to find out who the culprits were by examining samples of sugar, salt, baking soda, and cornstarch. Then they will identify the two powders which make up the mystery mixture, thereby exposing the culprits.

This lesson does not introduce the concept of physical and chemical properties of matter. However, if you have previously studied these terms, you can refer to the characteristics of each powder as its physical and chemical properties.

Students should be divided into teams of four for this activity. If you must have a team of five, pair two students together as "twins" who will work together throughout the activity. You may also have a team of three students as long as you don't end up with more than seven teams all together.

For the first part of the activity, you will need to prepare the Mystery Powder by mixing 1/4 cup sugar with 1/4 cup baking soda. Place the mixture in a clear cup or jar. Label the container "Mystery Powder."

When performing tests on the four kitchen powders, the teams will rotate through seven different stations. You will need to gather the materials needed for each station in advance, placing all the materials for one station on a labelled tray or in a box. Duplicate and laminate one set of instructions for each station. Cut on dashed lines. Fold the instruction page to make a "tent." The instructions will be on one side; a list of materials and roles will be on the other. Place one instruction tent at each station.

The stations should be set up on flat surfaces such as flat desks, tabletops, or counters. If such areas are not available, you may want to use the floor.

At each station, you will need one small cup of each of the four kitchen powders (sugar, salt, baking soda, and cornstarch). Label each cup with the name of one of the four powders. Place a heaping tablespoon of powder into each cup.

Materials for each Station:

Station 1: Apperance
4 kitchen powders
4 spoons
4 sheets of black construction paper
4 magnifying lenses or hand-held microscopes
1 cup for discarding used powder

Station 2: Taste
4 kitchen powders
4 spoons

Station 3: Texture
4 kitchen powders
4 spoons
1 cup for discarding used powder

Station 4: Reaction to Water
4 kitchen powders
4 spoons
30 small squares of waxed paper (about 3" x 3")
1 small cup of water
1 eyedropper or drinking straw
30 toothpicks
1 small trash bag

Station 5: Reaction to Vinegar
4 kitchen powders
4 spoons
30 small squares of waxed paper (about 3" x 3")
1 small cup of vinegar
1 eyedropper or drinking straw
30 toothpicks
1 small trash bag

Station 6: Reaction to Iodine
4 kitchen powders
4 spoons
30 small squares of waxed paper (about 3" x 3")
1 small cup of diluted iodine (mix 1 teaspoon
  iodine into 1/2 cup of water)
1 eyedropper or drinking straw
30 toothpicks
1 small trash bag

Station 7: Reaction to Heat
4 kitchen powders
4 spoons
30 medium squares of aluminum foil
  (about 6" x 6")
4 pairs of goggles
4 candles
4 candle holders (drip wax onto metal lids and
  press the candle onto the warm wax)
1 small trash bag
1 metal or glass bowl of water
matches

This activity must be monitored carefully at all times. Several stations need particularly close attention. Station 7 involves the use of candles, so you will need to position yourself near this area. Matches should not be left out for students; you will need to light the candles for each round of the activity. If you are not comfortable with your students working around flames, you may do the Station 7 test as a demonstration in front of the class. Let them record the results on the appropriate part of their "Kitchen Detectives" worksheet. If you have 7 teams, set up a science reading center in place of the last station.

Before allowing students to move to any of the stations, review the following safety guidelines with the class:

At station 2, students will be tasting a bit of each powder. Show them how to sprinkle a little powder into the palm of their hand before they taste it. Do not let students lick their fingers and dip them into the cups of powder. Tell them that this is the only station at which they may taste the powders.

At station 6, students will be mixing the powders with an iodine solution. Pure iodine is a poison when ingested. Emphasize that students should not taste the powders or touch the iodine with their fingers. Toothpicks are provided for stirring.

At station 7, students will be heating the powders over a candle. Review basic fire safety guidelines with your students. Remind them not to wear loose, baggy sweaters or jackets at this station and to roll up long sleeves. Long hair should be tied back, and all students should wear goggles. All papers should be kept well away from the flames.

1

Introducing the activity using TEACHER TALK

Materials for the Class:
jar of Mystery Powder (1/4 cup sugar mixed with 1/4 cup baking soda)

Tell your students that you need them to help you solve a mystery. Read them the following scenario and show them the jar of Mystery Powder.

Last night an apple pie disappeared from the school cafeteria. Several clues have been discovered. The first clue is a mysterious white powder which was found on the floor. Two sets of footprints were left in the powder. In addition, witnesses reported that four people were seen in the area: Salty Sam, Sugar Sue, Baking Soda Bob, and Cornstarch Calvin. Which two people took the apple pie?

2

Planning ways to solve the mystery using **THINK-PAIR-SHARE**

Step One: How can we solve the mystery?
Ask "How can we figure out who took the apple pie?" Tell them to think for at least 15 seconds about how they might begin to solve the problem. Then have them pair with the person beside them to discuss some possible ideas. Finally, call on students randomly to share their ideas with the class. Hopefully someone in the class will mention the idea of trying to identify the ingredients in the Mystery Powder. If not, suggest the idea yourself.

Step Two: How can we identify the ingredients in the Mystery Powder?
Now ask, "How can we identify the ingredients that make up the Mystery Powder?" Again, let them think, pair, and share their ideas.

If they suggest sending the powder off to a lab to be tested, tell them that there is not enough time and that they can identify the ingredients themselves. Remind them that Salty Sam, Sugar Sue, Baking Soda Bob, and Cornstarch Calvin were seen in the area, but only two people committed the crime. Eventually someone should suggest examining samples of salt, sugar, baking soda, and cornstarch. After studying those samples, a person should be able to examine the Mystery Powder to find out which two powders it contains.

3

Testing kitchen powders using **TEAM PROJECT**

Materials for the Class:
7 stations for testing powders

Materials for each Student:
1 copy of the Kitchen Detectives worksheet

Step One: Explaining the testing procedure
Tell students that they are going to become Kitchen Detectives. They will examine and test samples of sugar, salt, baking soda, and cornstarch. Give each person one copy of the "Kitchen Detectives" worksheet.

Tell them that they will become an expert on one powder, but will work together as a detective team, rotating through 7 different stations. At each station they will be making specific tests and observations. Each expert will lead the team in observing and discussing the results for their powder, but everyone will record the results of each test. They need to make careful observations and record the data in as much detail as possible in order to solve the mystery.

(continued on page 200)

3 cont.

Testing kitchen powders (continued from page 199)

Assign roles by having students number off from 1 to 4. Person #1 is the Sugar Expert, #2 is the Salt Expert, #3 is the Baking Soda Expert, and #4 is the Cornstarch Expert. The teams write the name of each expert in the appropriate place on the worksheet.

Explain that directions can be found at each station. On the instruction card they will find a list of the roles they will use for that station. They will also find exact directions for completing the observation or test. The Reader will read the instructions, but everyone will take turns performing the tests. The Taskmaster will make sure the job gets done in the amount of time provided. The Quiet Captain will monitor the noise level, and the Cleanup Captain will lead the team in cleaning up the station at the end.

Discuss the safety guidelines for each station at this time. Emphasize that they should not taste the powders at any other station than Station 2.

Step Two: Rotating through stations

Assign one team to each station to begin the investigation. Explain the procedure for rotating. Allow approximately 10 minutes for each team to complete their observations at each station. About 2 minutes before it is time to rotate, announce the remaining time. Remind students to leave their station in an orderly manner.

While the teams are testing their powders, be sure to monitor the stations as closely as possible. After lighting the candles for each round of the activity, stay with the team at that station until they finish heating their powders.

4

Discussing results using JIGSAW

Step One: Moving to Expert Groups

After all teams have completed each station, tell your students that all the experts on each type of powder will meet briefly to compare their results. Designate four areas of the room where the Salt, Sugar, Baking Soda, and Cornstarch Experts can gather.

Step Two: Comparing results

After your children have moved to their expert groups, have them **RoundRobin** the results of their investigations. For example, in the Salt group the first person might say, "When I looked at Salt under the microscope the grains looked like small cubes." The next person would read the results for the second station and so on.

Step Three: Discussing characteristics which identify powders

Now tell everyone that they will soon be able to examine the Mystery Powder. How will they know if their powder is one of the two ingredients? Ask them to discuss the characteristics of their powder that will definitely identify it. For example, baking soda bubbles in vinegar. After several minutes of discussion, ask everyone to return to their original teams.

5

Sharing results using ROUNDROBIN

After students return to their original teams, they **RoundRobin** the most important characteristics of their powder. For example, the salt person might say "Salt tastes salty and looks like cubes under the microscope. It doesn't react with water, vinegar, or iodine."

Lesson 11
Kitchen Detectives

Remind students of the dangers of iodine.

6

Who Stole The Apple Pie?

Lesson 11
Blackline Master

Team Name _____ Student Name _____

Mystery Powder Test	What Happened	Possible Powders
1. We heated it over a flame.		
2. We tasted it.		

I think the culprits were (circle 2):
Salty Sam   Sugar Sue   Baking Soda Bob   Cornstarch Calvin

I think the 2 ingredients in the Mystery Powder are _____ and _____ because:

_____

_____

1 800 WEE CO-OP *Kagan Cooperative Learning*   Laura Candler: *Hands-On Science*   207

Solving the mystery using TEAMMATES CONSULT

Materials for each Student:
   1 copy of the Who Stole the Apple Pie? worksheet

Materials for each Team:
   small cup of Mystery Powder
   assorted test materials:
      small cups of water, dilute iodine, and vinegar
      eyedroppers or straws
      spoon
      toothpicks
      waxed paper
      black construction paper
      magnifying lenses

Step One: Explaining procedures

Give everyone a copy of the worksheet "Who Stole the Apple Pie?" Explain that each person will have to write his or her own solution to the mystery, but they will be allowed to work together to test the Mystery Powder.

Give each team a small cup with about a tablespoon of the Mystery Powder inside. Place a tray or box containing all the necessary test materials in the center of each team. Explain that for safety's sake, you will heat the powder and show them the results. You will also monitor the tasting phase to make sure that no one tastes the powders during any other part of the testing. *Remind them of the dangers of tasting iodine.* Tell them that after you heat the powder and they taste it, they will each be allowed to perform one test. All team members will watch while each person takes a turn testing the powder.

If your class is not familiar with the structure **Teammates Consult**, review the rules with them. Remind them that students may discuss each part of the worksheet before they write their answers. However, after a section has been discussed, team members may not discuss their answers while they are writing them. The basic rule is that students may talk or write, but they may not do both at the same time.

(continued on page 203)

6 cont.

Solving the mystery (continued from page 202)

Step Two: Heating the Mystery Powder

Make a spoon out of aluminum foil and place about 1/2 teaspoon of the Mystery Powder in the spoon. Light the candle and heat the powder over the flame for several minutes. Then take the spoon to each team for observation. Do not allow anyone to talk until everyone has seen the heated Mystery Powder.

Then let team members discuss what they wish to write for the first test. For the "What Happened" column, they should plan how to word a description of the results. For example, "the powder melted and turned black." For "Possible Powders," they should discuss the names of any powders that behaved in a similar way during earlier testing. Allow them to consult their "Kitchen Detectives" worksheet to see how the various powders behaved.

When everyone knows what to write, they may pick up their pencils and fill in their answers for the first test. Remind them that they may not continue to discuss their responses while they are writing.

Step Three: Tasting the Mystery Powder

When all teams have finished writing, have each person sprinkle a few grains of the Mystery Powder into the palm of their hand. Then instruct them to taste the powder. Make sure they do not put their fingers back into the cup after licking them.

Remind team members that they may talk about the results and possible powders for this test, but when they start to write they must stop talking.

(continued on page 204)

6 cont.

Solving the mystery (continued from page 203)

Step Four: Testing the Mystery Powder

Person #1 will decide what the next test will be. For example, he or she might decide to mix the powder with iodine. While this person tests the powder, everyone else should observe closely. The team discusses what to write. Then everyone picks up their pencils and silently completes the corresponding sections of the worksheet.

The same procedure is followed for each person. Person #2 performs the next test, then Person #3, and finally Person #4.

Step Five: Identifying the culprits

Finally, the entire team discusses the results and tries to identify the culprits by naming the two powders that make up the Mystery Powder. Then each person individually writes an explanation for their conclusion. In writing their explanation, they should refer to the results of their tests.

Writing About Science

In their Science Journals, have students write the names of the two ingredients which make up the Mystery Powder, and a paragraph explaining how they identified those ingredients.

Materials Check List

For the Class (see Advanced Preparation):
❏ jar of Mystery Powder (see Advanced Preparation)
❏ 7 stations for testing powders
❏ 1 copy of each Instruction Tent
❏ small cups of baking soda, cornstarch, sugar and salt

For each Team:
❏ small cup of Mystery Powder
❏ assorted test materials:
    ❏ small cups of water, dilute iodine, and vinegar
    ❏ eyedroppers or straws
    ❏ spoons
    ❏ toothpicks
    ❏ waxed paper
    ❏ black construction paper
    ❏ magnifying lenses or hand-held microscopes
    ❏ aluminum foil

For each Student:
❏ 1 copy of the Kitchen Detectives worksheet
❏ 1 copy of the Who Stole the Apple Pie? worksheet

Curriculum Links

1. Science - Identifying more Puzzling Powders
Create a selection of Puzzling Powders from the four kitchen powders in this lesson. Let some be individual powders and others be mixtures. Try mixing three of the powders together. Students perform tests on the Puzzling Powders and try to identify them.

2. Language Arts - Writing Mystery Stories
Let students work in pairs to write their own mystery stories. They may enjoy mixing two or more powders to create a Mystery Powder for their own story. Then students read their story to another pair of students who have to try to solve the mystery. Encourage them to use other science ideas in their stories.

3. Literature - Reading Mystery Stories
Students who enjoyed the challenge of figuring out the Mystery Powder may also enjoy reading mystery and detective stories.

4. Literature - Reading about Mystery Powders
Students may enjoy reading *Mystery Day*, a story about a class that experiments with mystery powders.

Kitchen Detectives

Team Name _____   Student Name _____

	Sugar	Salt	Baking Soda	Cornstarch
Experts' Names →	#1	#2	#3	#4
Appearance				
Taste				
Texture				
Reaction to Water H_2O				
Reaction to Vinegar V				
Reaction to Iodine				
Reaction to Heat				

Who Stole The Apple Pie?

Team Name _____ Student Name _____

Mystery Powder Test	What Happened	Possible Powders
1. We heated it over a flame.		
2. We tasted it.		
3.		
4.		
5.		
6.		
7.		

I think the culprits were (circle 2):

Salty Sam   Sugar Sue   Baking Soda Bob   Cornstarch Calvin

I think the 2 ingredients in the Mystery Powder are _____ and _____

because: _____

_____

_____

_____

Instruction Tent

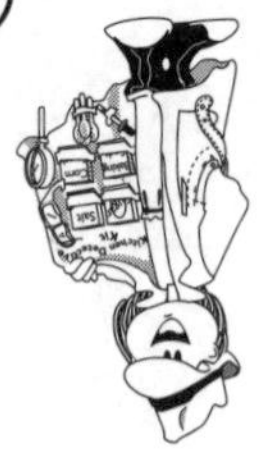

Station 1: Appearance

Roles

#1-Reader

#2-Taskmaster

#3-Quiet Captain

#4-Cleanup Captain

Materials

4 kitchen powders
4 spoons
4 sheets black paper
4 magnifying glasses or hand-held lenses
1 discard cup

Station 1: Appearance

Directions:

1. Taskmaster, give each person 1 sheet of black paper and a magnifying lens or microscope.
2. ***Sugar Expert,*** sprinkle a few grains of sugar on each person's paper.
3. Everyone, observe the grains of sugar closely and discuss the way they look.
4. Everyone, draw a picture of several grains of sugar on your chart.
5. Everyone, brush the sugar into the discard cup.
6. ***Salt Expert,*** give everyone a few grains of salt and lead the team through steps 2-5 above.
7. ***Baking Soda Expert,*** follow the same steps with baking soda.
8. ***Cornstarch Expert,*** follow the same steps with cornstarch.
9. Clean up this station before leaving.

Instruction Tent

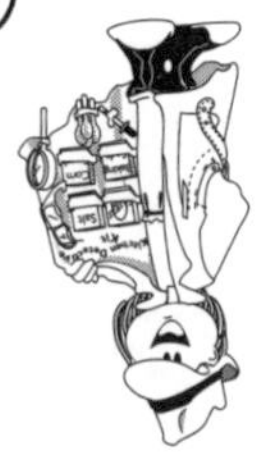

Station 2: Taste

Roles

#1-Taskmaster

#2-Quiet Captain

#3-Cleanup Captain

#4-Reader

Materials

4 kitchen powders

4 spoons

Station 2: Taste

Directions:

1. Everyone, be sure to keep the powders clean by replacing each spoon back into the correct cup. Also, do NOT lick your fingers and stick them into the powders. Follow the directions exactly.

2. ***Salt Expert,*** use the spoon to sprinkle a few grains of salt into each person's hand. Be sure to put the spoon back into the salt cup.

3. Everyone, taste the salt and discuss its flavor.

4. Everyone, write a description of the flavor of salt on the "taste" row of your worksheet. Be sure to write the results in the column for salt.

5. Everyone, brush any remaining salt off your hand.

6. ***Baking Soda Expert,*** lead the team through steps 1-5 above.

7. ***Cornstarch Expert,*** follow steps 1-5 above.

8. ***Sugar Expert,*** follow steps 1-5 above.

Instruction Tent

(The following section appears upside-down on the page)

Materials

4 kitchen powders
4 spoons
1 discard cup

Roles

#1-Quiet Captain
#2-Cleanup Captain
#3-Reader
#4-Taskmaster

Station 3: Texture

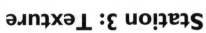

Station 3: Texture

Directions:

1. Everyone, be sure to keep the powders clean by replacing each spoon back into the correct cup.

2. **Baking Soda Expert,** use the spoon to sprinkle a small amount of baking soda into each person's hand.

3. Everyone, rub the powder between your fingertips. How does it feel? Discuss the texture of baking soda.

4. Everyone, write a description of the texture of baking soda on your worksheet in the correct space.

5. Everyone, brush the powder into the discard cup.

6. **Cornstarch Expert,** lead your team through steps 2-5 above.

7. **Sugar Expert,** lead your team through steps 2-5 above.

8. **Salt Expert,** lead your team through steps 2-5 above.

Instruction Tent

Materials

4 kitchen powders
4 spoons
30 waxed paper squares
small cup of water
toothpicks
eyedropper or drinking straw
small trash bag

Roles

#1-Cleanup Captain

#2-Reader

#3-Taskmaster

#4-Quiet Captain

Station 4: Reaction to Water

Station 4: Reaction to Water

Directions:

1. Everyone, be sure to keep the powders clean by replacing each spoon back into the correct cup.

2. **Cornstarch Expert,** take 1 square of waxed paper. Use the eyedropper or straw to drop several drops of water on the waxed paper. Use the spoon to sprinkle a small amount of cornstarch into the water. Stir with the toothpick.

3. Everyone, observe closely and discuss your observations.

4. Everyone, write a description of cornstarch's reaction to water in the correct space on your worksheet.

5. **Sugar, Salt,** and **Baking Soda Experts,** take turns leading the team through steps 2-4 above.

6. Discard all used water and toothpicks by placing them in the small trash bag. Clean up the station.

Lesson **11**
Blackline Master

Instruction Tent

Materials

4 kitchen powders
4 spoons
30 waxed paper squares
small cup of vinegar
toothpicks
eyedropper or drinking straw
small trash bag

Roles

#1-Reader

#2-Taskmaster

#3-Quiet Captain

#4-Clean Up Captain

Station 5: Reaction to Vinegar

Station 5: Reaction to Vinegar

Directions:

1. Everyone, be sure to keep the powders clean by replacing each spoon back into the correct cup.

2. **Sugar Expert,** take 1 square of waxed paper. Use the eyedropper or straw to drop several drops of vinegar onto the waxed paper. Use the spoon to sprinkle a small amount of sugar into the vinegar. Stir with the toothpick.

3. Everyone, observe closely and discuss your observations.

4. Everyone, write a description of sugar's reaction to vinegar in the correct space on your worksheet.

5. **Salt, Baking Soda,** and **Cornstarch Experts,** take turns leading the team through steps 2-4 above.

6. Discard all used waxed paper and toothpicks. Clean up the station.

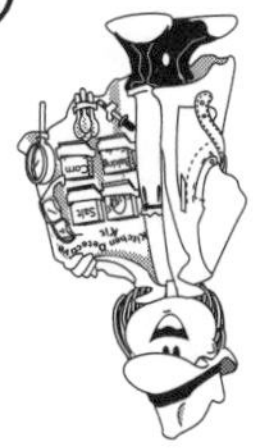

Station 6: Reaction to Iodine

Roles

#1-Taskmaster

#2-Quiet Captain

#3-Cleanup Captain

#4-Reader

Materials

4 kitchen powders
4 spoons
30 waxed paper squares
small cup of diluted iodine
toothpicks
eyedropper or drinking straw
small trash bag

Station 6: Reaction to Iodine

Directions:

1. *Everyone, be sure not to touch or taste anything at this station. Pure iodine is a poison. If you get iodine on your hands, wash them* ***immediately.***

2. ***Salt Expert,*** take 1 square of waxed paper. Use the eyedropper or straw to drop several drops of iodine onto the waxed paper. Use the spoon to sprinkle a small amount of salt into the vinegar. Stir with the toothpick.

3. Everyone, observe closely and discuss your observations.

4. Everyone, write a description of salt's reaction to iodine in the correct space on your worksheet.

5. ***Baking Soda, Cornstarch*** and ***Sugar Experts,*** take turns leading the team through steps 2-4 above.

6. Discard all used waxed paper and toothpicks by placing them in the small trash bag. Clean up the station.

Instruction Tent

Station 7: Reaction to Heat

Materials

matches
metal or glass bowl of water
small trash bag
30 squares of aluminum foil
4 sets of goggles
4 candles in holders
4 spoons
4 kitchen powders

Roles

#4-Taskmaster

#3-Reader

#2-Cleanup Captain

#1-Quiet Captain

Station 7: Reaction to Heat

Directions:

1. **Taskmaster,** give everyone a square of aluminum foil.

2. Everyone, shape your foil into a spoon. Place about 1/2 teaspoon of your powder into the bowl of the aluminum foil spoon.

3. Everyone, put on goggles. Make sure any loose hair or clothing is tied back.

4. **Taskmaster,** when everyone is ready, ask your teacher to light the candles.

5. Hold your foil spoon over your candle for several minutes. If the powder catches on fire, drop the whole spoon into the bowl of water and start over.

6. After 2-3 minutes, carefully blow out the candles.

7. Take turns observing, discussing, and writing about each powder's reaction to heat. Discard spoons by placing them into the small trash bag.

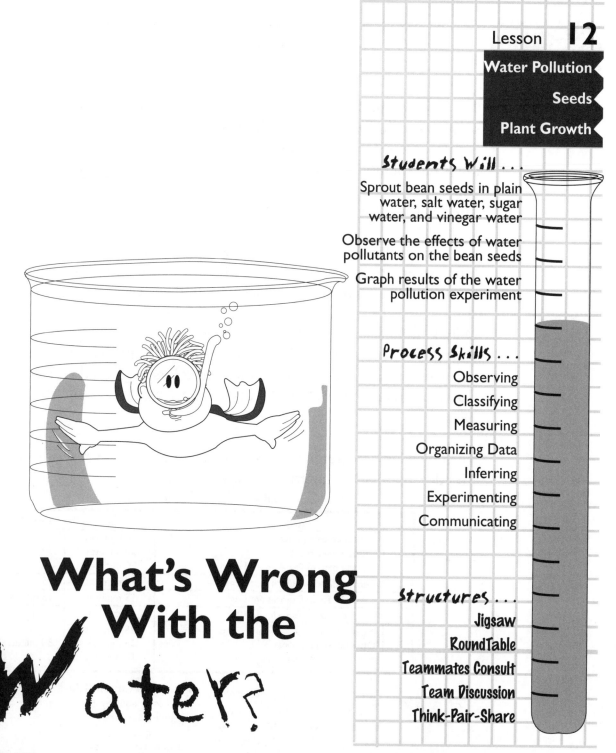

Students Will...

Sprout bean seeds in plain water, salt water, sugar water, and vinegar water

Observe the effects of water pollutants on the bean seeds

Graph results of the water pollution experiment

Process Skills...

Observing

Classifying

Measuring

Organizing Data

Inferring

Experimenting

Communicating

Structures...

Jigsaw

RoundTable

Teammates Consult

Team Discussion

Think-Pair-Share

What's Wrong With the Water?

Many students know in a general sense that the earth's water has become polluted and that we must preserve this natural resource. However, most children have not seen the devastating effect polluted water can have on plant life. In this lesson, students sprout bean seeds in plain water and compare them to beans sprouted in polluted water. Students organize data by keeping daily experiment logs, making a team data table, and graphing the results of the experiment.

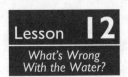

Because seeds take several days to sprout, this lesson will take at least five days to complete. The experiment "Effects of Water Pollutants on Seeds" provides the framework for the whole lesson.

The students sprout bean seeds in four different solutions: plain water, salt water, soapy water, and vinegar water. Seeds sprouted in plain water serve as the "control group" for comparison with the seeds sprouted in the other liquids. The salt water solution represents the salty drainage that flows off roads in the wintertime. The soapy water represents waste water which contains detergents. The vinegar water represents acid rain's effects on our water supply.

Each team will prepare one set of seeds to observe. The students will divide into four "expert groups" who will meet to prepare each part of the experiment. They will then return to their original teams with their seeds.

Only 15 minutes of each of the next three class periods are needed for observing and recording data. On the last day of the lesson, students compile their data using a team data table. They use different colors to graph their results onto one team line graph. Finally, they discuss the experiment and write about their results.

The following time frame is suggested for completing the experiment. Start on a Monday to provide uninterrupted observation.

Daily Procedures and Times

Day	Activity	Time	Total Time
1	Introduce experiment Set up experiment Record data in Experiment Log	10 minutes 20 minutes 20 minutes	50 minutes
2	Record data in Experiment Log	15 minutes	15 minutes
3	Record data in Experiment Log	15 minutes	15 minutes
4	Record data in Experiment Log	15 minutes	15 minutes
5	Make Team Data Table and Graph Discussion questions Writing About Science	25 minutes 15 minutes 10 minutes	50 minutes

Step One: Preparing the seeds
On Sunday night before you begin the lesson on Monday, soak two cups of dried baby lima bean seeds in several quarts of plain water. Drain the beans in the morning and divide them into four watertight baggies.

Materials for the Class:
2 cups dried baby lima beans
plain tap water
2 or 3 quart bowl
4 watertight baggies
4 large beakers (500 ml) or 2-cup containers
4 small beakers or cups marked at 50 ml (1/4 cup)
5 ml (1 tsp.) dish detergent
5 ml (1 tsp.) table salt
75 ml (1/3 cup) white vinegar

Step Two: Preparing the solutions
Prepare one 500 ml container of each test liquid. Be sure to measure the ingredients carefully, because making the solutions too strong will completely kill the seeds. When preparing each container, use the following amounts:
1. Plain Water - 500 ml (2 cups) tap water
2. Soapy Water - 500 ml tap water and 5 ml (1 teaspoon) dish detergent
3. Salt Water - 500 ml tap water and 5 ml (1 teaspoon) table salt
4. Vinegar Water - 500 ml tap water and 75 ml (1/3 cup) vinegar

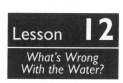
Step Three: Preparing the four Experiment Stations

Before the lesson begins, set up your Expert Group Experiment Stations. Find four locations in the room where your students will be able to prepare their part of the experiment. Duplicate at least four copies of the Expert Group Experiment Instructions. Label them: "Plain Water," "Salt Water," "Soapy Water," and "Vinegar Water."

Materials for the Class:

32 clear plastic cups (8-10 oz. size)
32 paper towels
4 ball-point pens
4 copies of the Expert Group Instructions
4 rolls of masking tape
4 containers test liquid
4 bags of soaked beans
4 small beakers or cups

At each station, place at least one set of materials. The following amounts are the minimum needed for eight teams of four, or 32 students. Adjust the number of items according to the number of students in your class. You may want to duplicate extra sets of instructions so that each station has several instruction sheets. If possible, place extra materials at each station to save experiment preparation time.

Expert Group Station Set Up

1 copy of the Expert Group Experiment Instructions for that station
1 container of the test liquid (plain, salt, soapy, or vinegar water)
1 small beaker (or plastic cups marked at 50 ml- 1/4 cup)
1 bag of soaked beans
1 roll of masking tape
8 paper towels
8 clear plastic cups
1 ball-point pen

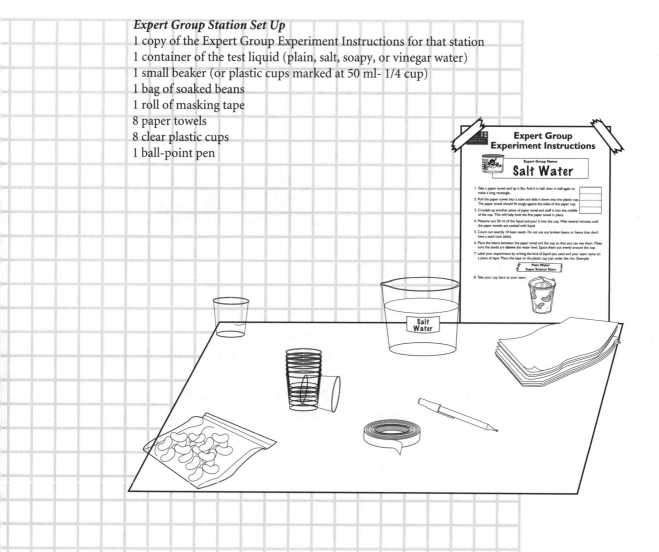

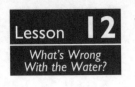

1

Explaining the activity using **TEACHER TALK** | **DAY I** |

Materials for the Class (optional):
I newspaper or magazine article about ocean dumping, oil spills, or other types of water pollution

Tell students that they will spend the week learning how water is important to all living things. They will set up an experiment which they will observe all week.

Ask students to think of a recent situation in the news in which water has become polluted. If possible, read them highlights from a magazine or newspaper article about water pollution. You might discuss an oil spill or trash being dumped into the ocean from ships. Tell students that some water pollution can't be seen, but can still cause harm to living things.

2

Predicting effects of water pollution on seeds using **THINK-PAIR-SHARE** | **DAY I** |

Write the experiment question on the board: *"How will pollutants in water affect the way seeds sprout and grow?"* Explain that a pollutant is anything that isn't normally found in water. Tell students that they will be trying to sprout bean seeds in plain water, soapy water, salt water, and vinegar water. Ask them to think about what effects these pollutants will have on the bean seeds. Students pair with a partner to discuss their ideas. Finally, a few students share their predictions with the class.

3

Setting up the experiment using JIGSAW

| DAY 1 |

Materials for the Class:
4 Expert Group Experiment Stations (see Advanced Preparation)

Divide your class into teams of four students. If a team of five is needed, let two of the students on the team work together as "twins."

To form your expert groups, assign each member of every team to one of the four expert groups: Plain Water, Soapy Water, Salt Water, and Vinegar Water. One of the easiest ways to do this is to have students in teams number off, 1 - 4. Assign all the #1's to the Plain Water expert group, all the #2's to the Salt Water group, the #3's to the Soapy Water group, and the #4's to the Vinegar Water group.

Let the students go to their Expert Group Experiment Stations to prepare their seeds for the experiment. The members of each expert group **RoundRobin** read the instructions as each person prepares one cup of seeds. After the cups are labeled, have students return *with their seeds* to their original teams.

Expert Groups

#1 - Plain Water

#2- Salt Water

#3- Soapy Water

#4- Vinegar Water

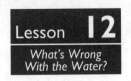

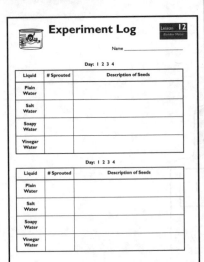

Experiment Log

Lesson 12

Name _____

Day: 1 2 3 4

Liquid	# Sprouted	Description of Seeds
Plain Water		
Salt Water		
Soapy Water		
Vinegar Water		

Day: 1 2 3 4

Liquid	# Sprouted	Description of Seeds
Plain Water		
Salt Water		
Soapy Water		
Vinegar Water		

1 800 WEE CO-OP *Kagan Cooperative Learning*   Laura Candler: *Hands-On Science*   **227**

Observing and recording experiment data using TEAMMATES CONSULT

DAY 1

Materials for each Student:
2 copies of the Experiment Log
1 hand lens (optional)

Materials for each Team:
1 sturdy cup or can

Give each person two copies of the Experiment Log (which provides space to record data on four different days.) Place a sturdy cup or can in the center of the table. Tell everyone to place his or her pencil in the cup. Explain that they will be working in teams to observe their seeds and complete their Experiment Logs. They may discuss what they want to write when everyone's pencil is in the cup, and when they agree on what to write they may remove their pencils. However, while everyone is writing, the team must be silent. Tell them to pay careful attention during the team discussion so they will know what to write.

Lead them through the procedure on the first day. First, everyone circles the number "1" above the first data chart since this is considered "Day 1." The person who has the "Plain Water" seeds places the cup in the center of the table. Since the number of seeds sprouted will be "0," everyone writes "0" on chart next to "Plain Water." Students place their pencils back in the cup and discuss what they want to write for the description. If possible, allow them to use hand lenses to make more detailed observations. The descriptions will be brief on the first day, but some description is necessary to use as a baseline for comparison later. After everyone has agreed on what to write as a description for plain water, students remove their pencils from the cup and individually write their descriptions. No one may talk as the descriptions are written. Monitor carefully to make sure everyone is involved in the discussion, but working independently to write descriptions.

Lead students step-by-step through the same procedure for each of the other three cups. Ask them to notice any differences between the cups and write those differences as a part of the description.

Place the cups with seeds on a countertop, a table, or the floor. The seeds do not need to be in sunlight, but they will grow best in a warm spot.

Each day, check the paper towels to be sure they haven't dried out completely. If the paper towels are almost dry, add a small amount of plain water to each cup. Do not water the seeds too much, however, since they will mildew and begin to rot. Just keep the paper towels damp.

5

*Observing and recording experiment data
using* **TEAMMATES CONSULT**

DAY 2

Materials for each Team:
4 cups of seeds, prepared previously
hand lenses

Students get their cups at the beginning of the class period and bring them back to their teams for observation. Review the steps of **Teammates Consult.** The teams follow the same procedure as the day before to complete their Experiment Logs. Since some seeds should have sprouted, encourage them to invent a method of counting the seeds that will keep them from getting mixed up as they turn the cup.

Notice the quantity and quality of your students' descriptions. If some teams are not writing enough, select several good examples from other teams to read aloud to the class. Or have several students write one of their team's descriptions on the board as an example. Encourage them to observe colors, smells, positions of seeds, presence of tiny roots hairs, direction of plant growth, etc. Remind them to use their hand lenses to make very detailed observations.

Note: If none of the seeds have sprouted, try to find a warmer location for the cups. Don't have your students record any data; wait until some seeds sprout and count that day as Day 2.

6

*Observing and recording experiment data
using* **TEAMMATES CONSULT**

DAY 3

Review the steps of **Teammates Consult** and have the students follow the steps to observe and record their experiment data. Be sure to tell students to write the total number of seeds sprouted in the "# Sprouted" column. The numbers recorded should stay the same or increase each day. For example, if four beans sprout on Day 2 and two more sprout the next day, the student would write "6" in the column for Day 3.

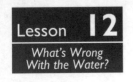

7

Observing and recording experiment data using TEAMMATES CONSULT

DAY 4

Tell students that this will be their final day for recording data. Have them follow the same steps as on previous days. Even though they won't record data the next day, have them return the cups to their storage location. They may want to make additional observations while they are charting their results.

8

Organizing experiment data using ROUNDTABLE

DAY 5

Materials for each Team:
1 Team Data Table
1 Team Line Graph
box of crayons or colored pencils
ruler

Step One: Charting Team Results
The first step in graphing results is to compile the results on one chart. Give each team a Team Data Table. Starting with the person whose beans were sprouted in plain water, each person will complete his or her column of the data table. For each day, have them write the *total* number of beans sprouted. They do not need to write the descriptions of the seeds on the Team Data Tables.

Step Two: Graphing Results
When the Team Data Tables are complete, give each team one Team Line Graph. Each team will also need a pack of crayons or colored pencils. Have everyone choose one color.

(continued on page 223)

Lesson 12
Black Line Master

Team Data Table

Effects of Water Pollution on Seeds

Day	Water	Salt	Soap	Vinegar
1				
2				
3				
4				

Team Name _____

228   Laura Candler: Hands-On Science   Kagan Cooperative Learning | 800 WEE CO-OP

8 cont.

Organizing experiment data
(continued from page 222)

DAY 5

Tell your students that when they finish, each team graph will have four lines to show the growth of the beans in the four different cups. Let them know that some points and lines may end up right on top of each other. Guide students through these steps:

1. Beginning with the person who used Plain Water, each person colors the box in the key with the color they have chosen.

2. Then each person uses that color to plot on the graph the *total* number of seeds sprouted each day of the experiment. For example, the student who grew seeds in Plain Water colors a dot on the "0" line above Day 1. He or she then colors dots on the lines above Days 2, 3, and 4 to show the total seeds sprouted for each day. Then the student with Salt Water plots his or her points in the color that matches the key. In turn, the students with Soapy Water and Vinegar Water do the same.

3. Finally each person, in turn, uses a ruler and their color to connect their points. The result will be four different lines showing the number of seeds that sprouted in each type of water pollution.

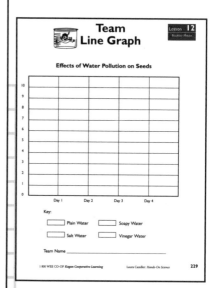

Reflecting on restults using TEAM DISCUSSION

Make sure students have the opportunity to reflect on the results of the experiment. While they are discussing the following questions, let them refer to their Experiment Logs, Data Tables, and Team Graphs. To equalize participation, use Talking Chips (see page 47).

Discuss as many questions as time allows. After each question, randomly call on students from different teams to share ideas with the class.

- *Which of the four liquids provided the best conditions for the seeds?*
- *Which kinds of "pollution" seem to be the worst for bean seeds?*
- *In what ways can water be polluted even when it looks clean?*
- *What kind of pollution does the vinegar represent?*
- *In what way can a large amount of salt get into the environment?*
- *In what ways can detergents (soap) get into the environment?*
- *Can you think of any other pollutants that might be in the earth's water supply that might affect seeds in the same way?*
- *What can you do to keep the earth's water supply from becoming polluted?*

Writing About Science

Have students reflect on what they've learned by writing about the experiment in their Science Journals. Ask them to respond to the following questions:
- *What did you learn about water pollution from this experiment?*
- *What can be done to keep the earth's water supply from becoming polluted?*

For Younger Students

Younger students may have difficulty reading and following the directions at each experiment station. Fortunately, the instructions for each station are exactly the same except for the type of test liquid used. So you can simply read the instructions aloud and demonstrate the method for preparing each cup of seeds.

Younger students may also need more guidance with the Team Data Table and Line Graph. Make an overhead transparency of these pages and use colored transparency pens to demonstrate how to complete them. Lead your students through them in a step-by-step manner.

Materials Check List

For the Class:

- ❏ 1 newspaper or magazine article about ocean dumping, oil spills, or other types of water pollution (optional)
- ❏ 4 Expert Group Experiment Stations (see Advanced Preparation):

  - ❏ 2 cups dried baby lima beans
  - ❏ plain tap water
  - ❏ 2 or 3 quart bowl
  - ❏ 4 watertight baggies
  - ❏ 4 large beakers (500 ml) or 2-cup containers
  - ❏ 4 small beakers or cups marked at 50 ml (1/4 cup)
  - ❏ 5 ml (1 tsp.) dish detergent
  - ❏ 5 ml (1 tsp.) table salt
  - ❏ 75 ml (1/3 cup) white vinegar

  - ❏ 32 clear plastic cups (8-10 oz. size)
  - ❏ 32 paper towels
  - ❏ 4 ball-point pens
  - ❏ 4 copies of the Expert Group Instructions
  - ❏ 4 rolls of masking tape
  - ❏ 4 containers test liquid
  - ❏ 4 bags of soaked beans
  - ❏ 4 small beakers or cups

For each Team:

- ❏ 1 sturdy cup or can
- ❏ 4 cups of seeds, prepared on Day 1
- ❏ 1 Team Data Table
- ❏ 1 Team Line Graph
- ❏ box of crayons or colored pencils
- ❏ ruler

For each Student:

- ❏ 2 copies of the Experiment Log
- ❏ 1 hand lens (optional)

Curriculum Links

1. Literature - Listening to nonfiction
Read *A River Ran Wild* by Lynne Cherry aloud to your students. This story traces the history of the Nashua River. The river once ran wild through New England but became polluted after the settlers arrived and during the industrial revolution. Inspired by a dream, two citizens campaign to clean up the river.

2. Literature - Listening to fiction
Read aloud *The Magic School Bus at the Waterworks* by Joanna Cole. This is a hilarious story of one class's adventures when a magic school bus takes them on a field trip to the city waterworks. Your students will love the story and they'll learn about water treatment plants.

3. Science - Labelling the parts of a bean seed
Show your students how to examine a soaked bean seed and draw the parts. Then show them how to label the seed coat, cotyledons, and embryo. Explain that the cotyledons store food for the baby plant (embryo). The seed coat protects the seed until it begins to sprout.

4. Language Arts - Writing about seeds
Students write stories pretending they are a seed trying to grow in an area polluted by water.

5. Health - Researching water pollution
Every summer beaches all over the country are temporarily or permanently closed because of contaminated water. Lead poisoning has also become a major concern in many communities. Your students might be interested in researching the effects of water pollution on human and animal health.

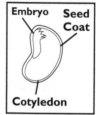

Expert Group Experiment Instructions

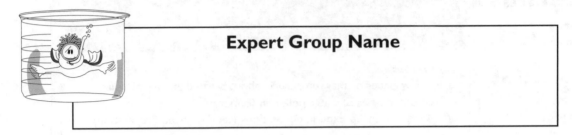

Expert Group Name

1. Take a paper towel and lay it flat. Fold it in half, then in half again to make a long rectangle.

2. Roll the paper towel into a tube and slide it down into the plastic cup. The paper towel should fit snugly against the sides of the paper cup.

3. Crumple up another piece of paper towel and stuff it into the middle of the cup. This will help hold the first paper towel in place.

4. Measure out 50 ml of the liquid and pour it into the cup. Wait several minutes until the paper towels are soaked with liquid.

5. Count out exactly 10 bean seeds. Do not use any broken beans or beans that don't have a seed coat (skin).

6. Place the beans between the paper towel and the cup so that you can see them. Make sure the seeds are **above** the water level. Space them out evenly around the cup.

7. Label your experiment by writing the kind of liquid you used and your team name on a piece of tape. Place the tape on the plastic cup just under the rim. Example:

**Plain Water
Super Science Stars**

8. Take your cup back to your team.

Water Level

Experiment Log

Name _____

Day: 1 2 3 4

Liquid	# Sprouted	Description of Seeds
Plain Water		
Salt Water		
Soapy Water		
Vinegar Water		

Day: 1 2 3 4

Liquid	# Sprouted	Description of Seeds
Plain Water		
Salt Water		
Soapy Water		
Vinegar Water		

Team Data Table

Effects of Water Pollution on Seeds

Day	Water	Salt	Soap	Vinegar
1				
2				
3				
4				

Team Name _____

Team
Line Graph

Effects of Water Pollution on Seeds

	Day 1	Day 2	Day 3	Day 4
10				
9				
8				
7				
6				
5				
4				
3				
2				
1				
0				

Key:

☐ Plain Water   ☐ Soapy Water

☐ Salt Water   ☐ Vinegar Water

Team Name _____

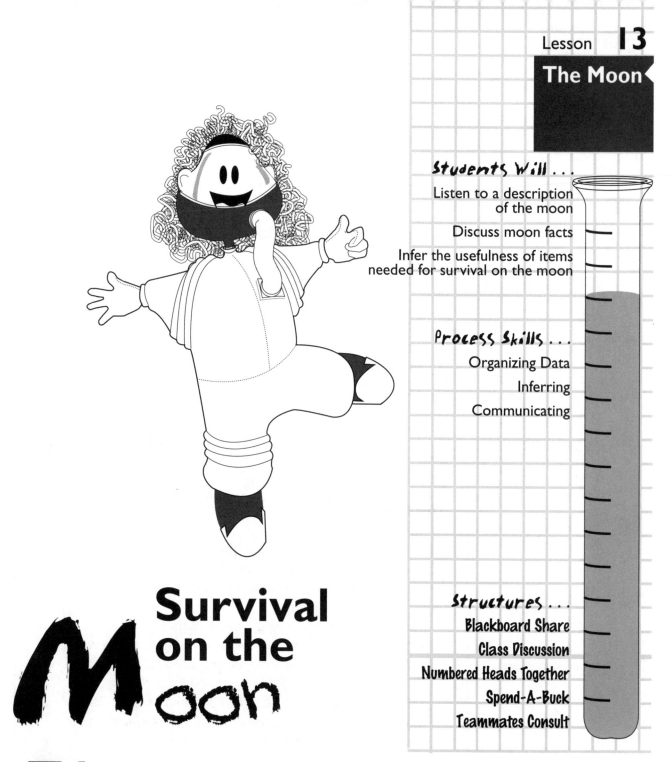

Students Will...

Listen to a description of the moon

Discuss moon facts

Infer the usefulness of items needed for survival on the moon

Process Skills...

Organizing Data

Inferring

Communicating

Structures...

Blackboard Share

Class Discussion

Numbered Heads Together

Spend-A-Buck

Teammates Consult

Survival on the Moon

he moon fascinates children. In this lesson, your students will learn about conditions on the moon as they discuss items needed for survival. You'll read them a description of the moon and then check for understanding with **Numbered Heads Together.** Your students will pretend that they are astronauts stranded on the moon 100 miles from their spaceship. They'll evaluate a selection of items available to bring with them on their return journey. To do this, they must infer the usefulness of those items based on their knowledge of conditions on the moon.

1

Moon Facts

The moon is the brightest object in the night sky, but it does not give off its own light. The moon only reflects light from the sun. The moon is much smaller than the Earth; it's diameter is only about 1/4 the Earth's diameter. For thousands of years man could only dream of visiting the moon, but on July 20, 1969 this dream became a reality for Neil Armstrong. On that day, he became the first man to set foot on the moon's surface. Partly as a result of such ventures, scientists know a great deal about the moon.

Astronauts must wear protective clothing to keep them from feeling the extreme heat and cold. Their special clothing also provides them with oxygen to breathe, necessary because the moon has no atmosphere. Since there is no air or water, the moon does not have clouds, wind, or rain. Without an atmosphere the sky is black, even during the day. The moon's constellations, or star patterns, are always visible from the moon's surface.

Astronauts can move easily on the moon because of the weak force of gravity. Because the moon is much smaller than the Earth, its gravity is only 1/6 the Earth's gravity. This means that a 60 pound boy or girl would weigh only 10 pounds on the moon! Even with their heavy protective clothing and equipment, astronauts almost seem to float as they walk.

The surface of the moon is covered with a thin, rocky soil. There are millions of bowl-shaped craters all over the moon's surface. Some craters are less than a foot in diameter, while others are hundreds of miles across. The large craters have steep, rocky walls. The craters look just as they did when they were formed millions of years ago. This is because the moon doesn't have air or water, so the moon's soil does not erode away as it does on Earth. The moon is also different from the Earth because the moon does not have magnetic poles.

The moon travels around the Earth about once every 29 days. It rotates on it own axis about once every 27 days, making moon days and nights about 14 Earth days long! During a moon day, the rocky surface becomes too hot to touch, about 260 degrees Fahrenheit. During a moon night, temperatures drop to 280 degrees below zero!

Considering the extremely harsh conditions on the moon, it's not surprising that no life exists on its surface.

238   Laura Candler: *Hands-On Science*   *Kagan Cooperative Learning* | 800 WEE CO-OP

Reading the "Moon Facts" description using **TEACHER READS**

Materials for each Team:
1 copy of the Moon Facts description

Ask your students to listen carefully as you read them a description of conditions on the moon. Tell them to think of the many ways that the moon is different from the Earth.

2

Checking for understanding using **NUMBERED HEADS TOGETHER**

Students number off from 1 - 4 within their teams. After you read each question below, allow students to discuss the answer within their teams. Then call out one number and have only the students with that number respond.

• *How does the moon compare to the Earth in size?*
• *Why must astronauts wear special clothing on the moon?*
• *How are astronauts able to view the moon's constellations, even during the day?*
• *How is the moon's surface different from that of the Earth's?*
• *Why are astronauts able to move easily on the moon, even when wearing heavy clothing or equipment?*
• *How long is a moon day?*
• *What conditions make it nearly impossible for living things to survive on the moon?*

3

Introducing the Moon Ventures survival scenario *using* TEACHER READS

Tell your students that they are going to take part in an imaginary survival adventure called "Moon Ventures." They will have to use what they know about conditions on the moon in order to be successful. Read them the following scenario:

"You are a member of a team of astronauts exploring the lighted side of the moon. While traveling in your moon transporter vehicle, you became trapped within a deep crater about 100 miles from your spaceship. Your moon transporter broke down, and now you will have to journey back to the spaceship on foot. There are 12 items in your moon transporter, but you can't take them all with you. You must decide whether each item is 'very useful,' 'somewhat useful,' or 'not useful.' Then you will choose the six most useful items to bring with you on your journey."

4

Evaluating the items *using* TEAMMATES CONSULT

Materials for each Team:
 I sturdy cup
 I copy of the Moon Facts description

Materials for each Student:
 I copy of the Moon Ventures worksheet

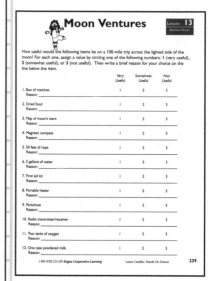

Step One: Discussing the first item (no writing)
This structure always begins with everyone placing their pencils down on their desks or in a cup in the center of the team. Give each student a copy of "Moon Ventures." Tell them that for each item they will assign one of the following values: 1 (very useful), 2 (somewhat useful), or 3 (not useful).

A different student leads the team in answering each item. Ask Person #1 to become the first leader and read the first item aloud, for example, "box of matches." He or she gives everyone time to think of the value they want to assign to that item. When everyone is ready the leader says "Show me!" Simultaneously, everyone holds up the number of fingers that corresponds to their choice. A person who believes a box of matches would be very useful holds up one finger, someone who thinks it is somewhat useful holds up two, and a person who thinks matches are useless would hold up three fingers. The team members then discuss the reasons for their choices. Allow students to refer to the "Moon Facts" description if needed.

(continued on page 234)

4 cont.

Evaluating the items (continued from page 233)

Step Two: Writing responses (no talking)
After several minutes of discussion, the leader asks everyone to pick up their pencils and circle their choice. Everyone does not have to circle the same number. Then, *without talking,* each person writes their reason for that choice. Students may not receive help or copy answers during this part of **Teammates Consult.**

Step Three: Continue evaluating items
Person #2 becomes the leader for the next item. He or she follows the steps listed above. Pencils are down during the discussion; talking is not allowed when students are writing answers. Continue allowing students to take turns being the leader until all items have been evaluated.

Duplicate enough copies of the sheet of paper "Bucks" found on page 44 so that each person will have six bucks. Cut the bucks apart and count out enough for each team of four or five students. Paper clip the sets of bucks together for easy distribution.

5

Lesson **13**	Survival Item Cards	
Box of Matches	Dried Food	Map of Moon's Stars
Magnetic Compass	50 Feet of Rope	Five Gallons of Water
First Aid Kit	Portable Heater	Parachute
Radio Transmitter/ Receiver	Two Tanks of Oxygen	One Case of Powdered Milk

240   Laura Candler: *Hands-On Science*   *Kagan Cooperative Learning* | 800 WEE CO-OP

Choosing the six most useful items using SPEND-A-BUCK

Materials for each Team:
paper "Bucks" (6 per person)
1 copy of the Survival Item Cards
scissors

When all items have been evaluated, ask team members to select the six most useful items needed for the journey back to the spaceship. Give each team one copy of the "Survival Items" page. Ask them to work together to cut the cards apart.

Now each team spreads all twelve cards out in the middle of the group so that everyone can see them. Give each person six paper "bucks" to spend. They place one buck on each item they want to select as the most useful on their imaginary journey.

When all the bucks have been spent, have them work together to count up the number of bucks on each item. Have them write the number of votes for each item on the back of the item card.

Draw a blank Class Graph on the chalkboard or a large sheet of butcher paper. The chart should be a 12 x 8 grid, containing blocks approximately 3" square (see illustration). List the names of the twelve survival items in the bottom row. Students will use this chart to display the results of their **Spend-A-Buck** vote.

6

Displaying the results using BLACKBOARD SHARE

Materials for each Team:
Class Graph on board
Survival Item Cards from each team
masking tape

Give each team a long strip of masking tape. Students work together to make six small loops of tape and place them on the backs of the six items voted on by their team. One team at a time, students come forward and tape their team's item cards in the proper place on the Class Graph.

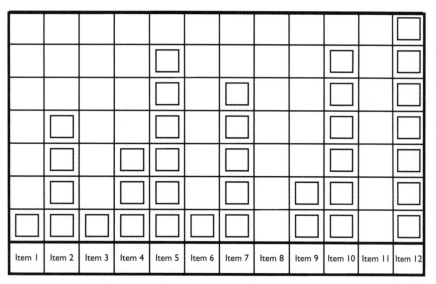

Class Graph

Discussing responses using CLASS DISCUSSION

After all teams have posted their votes, discuss the usefulness of each item. Your students will be amazed at the reasons some materials are very useful and others are almost useless. The explanations offered below are based on the answers to a simulation activity developed by NASA.

Item	Value	Reason
1. Box of matches	3	No air on moon
2. Dried food	1	Supplies daily food requirements
3. Map of moon's stars	1	One of the main ways of finding direction
4. Magnetic compass	3	No magnetic poles
5. 50 feet of rope	1	Climbing out of crater
6. 5 gallons of water	1	Replenishes water lost through sweating
7. First aid kit	2	Needed in the event of injuries
8. Portable heater	3	Not needed on lighted side of moon
9. Parachute	2	Offers protection from the sun
10. Radio	1	Needed for communication
11. Two tanks of oxygen	1	No air on moon
12. Powdered milk	2	Can provide food but heavy to carry

Writing About Science

Have students respond to one or more of the following questions in their Science Journals or on their own paper:
- *How is the moon different from the earth?*
- *What are 3 items that would be important for survival on the moon?*
- *What are 2 items that would be useless on the moon?*
- *Suppose the United States decided to send a small group of people to build a space colony and live on the moon for a year. Would you like to be a member of this group? How might your life be different on the moon than it is now?*
- *If you could choose again, which 6 items do you now think are most useful? Did any of your ideas change? If so, why?*

For Younger Students
Before beginning this lesson with younger students, make sure they are familiar with the following terms and concepts: *magnetism, magnetic poles, Fahrenheit, diameter, atmosphere, constellation, gravity, crater,* and *erosion.*

Materials Check List

For each Team:
- ❏ 1 copy of the Moon Facts description
- ❏ 1 sturdy cup
- ❏ paper "Bucks" (6 per person)
- ❏ 1 copy of the Survival Item Cards
- ❏ scissors
- ❏ Class Graph on board
- ❏ masking tape

For each Student:
- ❏ 1 copy of the Moon Ventures worksheet

Curriculum Links

1. Language Arts - Writing an adventure story
Suggest that students write their own adventure story about being lost on the moon. Have them use their knowledge of moon conditions to make their stories as scientifically accurate as possible.

2. Math - Determining moon weight
Allow students to weigh themselves on a scale. Show them how to figure their moon weight by dividing their Earth weight by 6.

3. Science - Observing the moon's phases
Give each student a blank calendar for the month. Have them go outside at the same time each evening and sketch the moon. At the end of the month, discuss their observations. Try to find an amateur astronomer who can demonstrate the use of a telescope at a final class "moon watch" meeting.

4. Art - Constructing a model of the moon
Allow students to research the moon and construct a paper mache model showing its features.

Moon Facts

The moon is the brightest object in the night sky, but it does not give off its own light. The moon only reflects light from the sun. The moon is much smaller than the Earth; its diameter is only about 1/4 the Earth's diameter. For thousands of years man could only dream of visiting the moon, but on July 20, 1969 this dream became a reality for Neil Armstrong. On that day, he became the first man to set foot on the moon's surface. Partly as a result of such ventures, scientists know a great deal about the moon.

Astronauts must wear protective clothing to keep them from feeling the extreme heat and cold. Their special clothing also provides them with oxygen to breathe, necessary because the moon has no atmosphere. Since there is no air or water, the moon does not have clouds, wind, or rain. Without an atmosphere the sky is black, even during the day. The moon's constellations, or star patterns, are always visible from the moon's surface.

Astronauts can move easily on the moon because of the weak force of gravity. Because the moon is much smaller than the Earth, its gravity is only 1/6 the Earth's gravity. This means that a 60 pound boy or girl would weigh only 10 pounds on the moon! Even with their heavy protective clothing and equipment, astronauts almost seem to float as they walk.

The surface of the moon is covered with a thin, rocky soil. There are millions of bowl-shaped crates all over the moon's surface. Some craters are less than a foot is diameter, while others are hundreds of miles across. The large craters have steep, rocky walls. The craters look just as they did when they were formed millions of years ago. This is because the moon doesn't have air or water, so the moon's soil does not erode away as it does on Earth. The moon is also different from the Earth because the moon does not have magnetic poles.

The moon travels around the Earth about once every 29 days. It rotates on it own axis about once every 27 days, making moon days and nights about 14 Earth days long! During a moon day, the rocky surface becomes too hot to touch, about 260 degrees Fahrenheit. During a moon night, temperatures drop to 280 degrees below zero!

Considering the extremely harsh conditions on the moon, it's not surprising that no life exists on its surface.

Moon Ventures

How useful would the following items be on a 100-mile trip across the lighted side of the moon? For each one, assign a value by circling one of the following numbers: **1** (very useful), **2** (somewhat useful), or **3** (not useful). Then write a brief reason for your choice on the line below the item.

	Very Useful	Somewhat Useful	Not Useful
1. Box of matches	1	2	3
Reason: _____			
2. Dried food	1	2	3
Reason: _____			
3. Map of the moon's stars	1	2	3
Reason: _____			
4. Magnetic compass	1	2	3
Reason: _____			
5. 50 feet of rope	1	2	3
Reason: _____			
6. 5 gallons of water	1	2	3
Reason: _____			
7. First aid kit	1	2	3
Reason: _____			
8. Portable heater	1	2	3
Reason: _____			
9. Parachute	1	2	3
Reason: _____			
10. Radio transmitter/receiver	1	2	3
Reason: _____			
11. Two tanks of oxygen	1	2	3
Reason: _____			
12. One case powdered milk	1	2	3
Reason: _____			

Survival Item Cards

Box of Matches	**Dried Food**	**Map of Moon's Stars**
Magnetic Compass	**50 Feet of Rope**	**Five Gallons of Water**
First Aid Kit	**Portable Heater**	**Parachute**
Radio Transmitter/ Receiver	**Two Tanks of Oxygen**	**One Case of Powdered Milk**

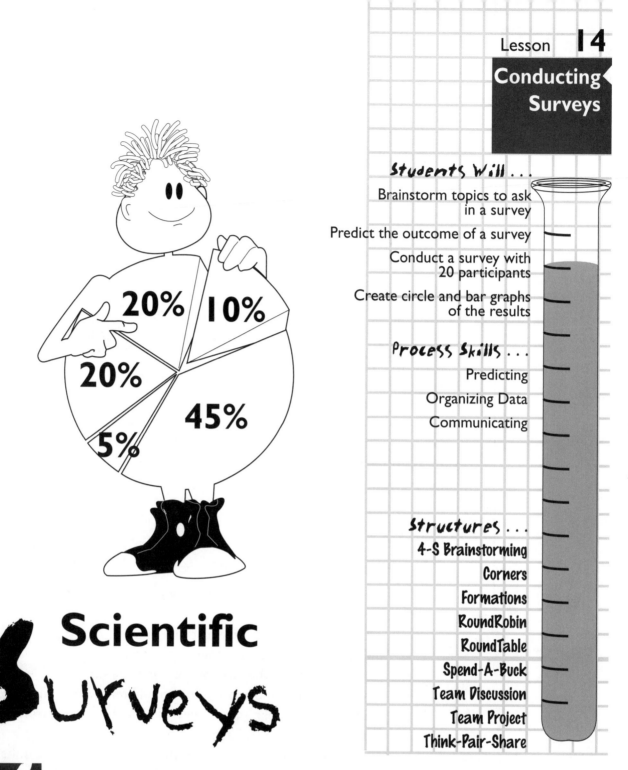

Students Will . . .

Brainstorm topics to ask
in a survey

Predict the outcome of a survey

Conduct a survey with
20 participants

Create circle and bar graphs
of the results

Process Skills . . .

Predicting

Organizing Data

Communicating

Structures . . .

4-S Brainstorming

Corners

Formations

RoundRobin

RoundTable

Spend-A-Buck

Team Discussion

Team Project

Think-Pair-Share

Scientific
Surveys

urveys help scientists gain insight into the thoughts and feelings of
human subjects. However, the data that is collected must be organized
in some way if it is to be useful. In this lesson, your students will conduct a
survey and learn how to display their data in two different forms.

1
Choosing a personal preference using CORNERS

Ask your students to think of their favorite season. Designate four corners of the room to represent: Spring, Summer, Fall, and Winter. Students write their favorite of the four on a slip of paper and then move to the corner that represents their choice.

2
Making a human bar graph using FORMATIONS

The students from each corner line up in four columns to form a human bar graph. Point out the number of students who like each season. Tell the class that bar graphs are useful for comparing information.

3
Introducing scientific surveys using TEACHER TALK

Tell your students that scientists use graphs to compare information, or *data*, that they collect from surveys. Explain to your students that they will be conducting a survey and learning how to show the information in two different ways: with a circle graph and with a bar graph. They will begin by brainstorming topics for their survey. Each team will conduct a survey on a different topic such as favorite animals, favorite foods, number of children in family, etc. Tell them to choose a topic with four or five possible choices.

4

Listing ideas for a survey using **4-S BRAINSTORMING**

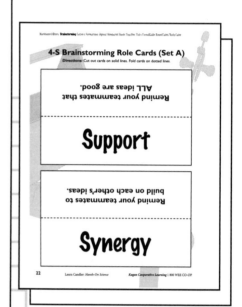

Materials for each Team:
pencils
10-15 slips of paper
1 set of 4-S Brainstorming Role Cards (pages 22 and 23)
scissors

Step 1: Assigning roles

Number students on each team from 1 to 4(or 5). Assign and discuss the roles listed below. Give a set of **4-S Brainstorming** Roles Cards to each team. Each person cuts out his or her role card on the solid line and folds it on the dotted line. Ask students to place their cards in front of them as a reminder of their roles during the brainstorming session.

Role Assignments

#1- Silly (encourages silly and unusual ideas)

#2- Speed (encourages everyone to work fast)

#3 - Support (reminds everyone that all ideas are good)

#4/5 - Synergy (encourages everyone to build on each other's ideas)

Step 2: Recording ideas

Give each team 10 - 15 slips of paper. Ask all students to suggest topics for their team survey. Personal favorites make good topics (TV show, type of music, etc.) As each person calls out a suggestion, have them write it on an individual slip of paper. Remind students that their final topic must have at least four or five options for people to select. Allow the brainstorming session to continue until all teams have at least five possible topics.

 Duplicate and cut apart enough paper "Bucks" so that each student will have five. Paper clip together a stack for each team.

5

Choosing a topic using SPEND-A-BUCK

Materials for each Student:
5 paper "BUCKS" for each student (page 44)

The teams are ready to select their topic from the ideas they brainstormed. Students spread all the ideas out in the center of the team. Everyone has five paper "bucks" to spend on the idea or ideas they like the best. They may place one buck on five ideas, all five bucks on one idea, or any combination in between. Finally, have one person count the bucks on each topic. If there is a tie for the top choices, the counter returns everyone's bucks and they spend their bucks on the top choices only.

6

Writing the survey question using TEAM DISCUSSION

Materials for each Team:
1 pencil
1 slip of paper

Tell your students that the survey topic is usually stated as a question. Students discuss the wording of their question. For example, if their topic is "Favorite Pets," their question would be "What is your favorite pet?" Ask Student #4 to be the Recorder and write the team's survey question on a slip of paper to turn in for your approval. Some teams may need help with wording their question clearly.

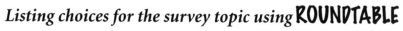

7

Listing choices for the survey topic using ROUNDTABLE

Materials for each Student:
pencils
10-15 slips of paper

Give three slips of paper to each person. Beginning with Student #1, have the teams **RoundTable** as many choices as they can for their topic. Tell them to think of all the possible answers students might give to the survey question. Many students will give only the answer that they like, forgetting that they are going to be surveying *other* people.

As choices are suggested, students write them on individual slips of paper. As each person writes a choice, ask them to say it aloud so that everyone on the team knows what they are writing. They place the slips of paper in the center of the team.

For example, if the topic was "Favorite Foods," Student #1 might write "pizza" and announce the choice as it is placed in the center of the team. Student #2 might write and say "fish," placing that choice in the center also. Students continue until you call time. Give teams enough time to write about ten possible choices, but tell them to stop when they run out of paper. Too many choices make the next step difficult to complete.

8

Choosing 5 options for the topic using SPEND-A-BUCK

Materials for each Team:
5 paper bucks

Students use **Spend-A-Buck** in the same manner as before to select their five favorite choices. Each person places their five bucks on the choice they want included on the survey. If some survey topics have a lot of choices, students choose *only* four topics so they can include "other" as the fifth choice. If they don't do this, they will have nowhere to record some responses. One student counts the bucks to find out which four choices had the most votes. If a tie gives the team more than five choices, have them retrieve their bucks and spend them again to break the tie. Each team may only have five choices, including "other."

9

Preparing survey forms using INDIVIDUALS WRITE

Materials for each Team:
- 1 pencil
- 1 copy of the Individual Survey Results form (half sheet)

Give each person one half-sheet copy of the Individual Survey Results form. Students write their names and the date at the top. Then they write the survey question on the appropriate line. Finally, they write the names of the choices in the five boxes across the top of the chart.

10

Making predictions using ROUNDROBIN

Ask everyone to think of the choice that they believe most people will select. Then ask them to **RoundRobin** their choices to their team.

Decide the names of all possible participants in your students' surveys. You may want to limit the survey to your classroom or your grade level. Complete the "Possible Survey Participants" worksheet by writing one person's name in each block (use more than one sheet if necessary). Duplicate one copy per team. Your students will cut apart the boxes and randomly choose their participants from those names.

11

Conducting the survey using TEAM PROJECT

Materials for each Team:
- 1 copy Possible Survey Participants
- several pairs scissors
- 1 paper lunch bag
- 1 copy Team Survey Results

Step One: Choosing the participants
Tell your students that one way scientists try to make their surveys fair is to randomly choose the people who will take part. Explain that the word *random* means "without a certain pattern or order." Give each

(continued on page 247)

11 cont.

Conducting the survey (continued from page 246)

team one copy of the "Possible Survey Participants" worksheet and tell them that those are all the names of the students who may participate in their survey. Students cut apart the names and place the slips in the paper bag (discarding their own names). Each of the four team members reach in, without looking, and choose five names from the bag. On a five-member team, each person only chooses four names.

Step Two: Recording names
Students list the names they selected on their Individual Survey Results forms.

Step Three: Interviewing participants
Let them take their survey forms with them as they interview each of the people they selected. Tell them to ask each person the survey question and record that person's choice by making a tally mark in the appropriate box next to his or her name. Remind them to record only *one* choice for each person interviewed.

Caution students not to let the participants see the choices of the other people interviewed. The students conducting the surveys should be the only ones to write on their survey forms.

Step Four: Recording results on the team form
Everyone returns to their team when finished. Give each team one copy of the Team Survey Results form. Teams complete the form in **RoundTable** fashion. To begin, ask Student #1 to write the team name at the top, Student #2 to write the date, Student #3 the survey question, and Student #4 the five choices.

Then, they take turns transferring their individual results to the team form. In **RoundTable** fashion, they write the names of their participants and mark their participants' choices in the appropriate columns.

Step Five: Computing totals
Student #1 adds the total number of tally marks for the first choice and records that number at the bottom of the first column. Then Student #2 adds the choices marked in the second column and records the total. Student #3 adds the checks in the third column, Student #4 those in the fourth column, and Student #5 (or #1) the marks in the last column.

12

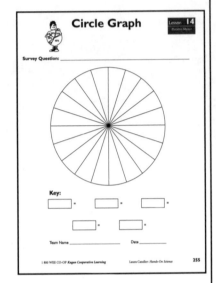

Graphing results using ROUNDTABLE

Materials for each Team:
I copy of the Circle Graph worksheet
I copy of the Bar Graph worksheet
I box colored pencils

Step One: Completing the circle graph

Tell your students that they will display the results of their survey in two different forms. The first way is in a circle graph, sometimes called a pie graph. Give each team one copy of the Circle Graph worksheet.

Assign each person on the team one column of results to graph. For example, on a survey of favorite pets, Student #1 graphs the students who chose "cats," Student #2 graphs those who selected "dogs," etc.

One person begins by writing the team's survey topic at the top of the graph as the title (i.e., Favorite Pets). This person also writes the team name and survey date at the bottom.

Let each person to choose a different color pencil. If a team only has four members, Student #1 will need to choose two different colors. In RoundTable fashion have team members complete the key at the bottom of the page by coloring a box and writing the name of choice they are graphing next to the box. For instance, Student #1 colors the first box green and writes "Cats" next to the box.

(continued on page 249)

12 cont.

Conducting the survey (continued from page 248)

Students then take turns coloring one section of the circle graph for each person who selected that item in the survey. The first person starts at the top and colors the sections of the pie clockwise. The next person begins by coloring the next consecutive section. Make sure your students color the sections consecutively and count carefully. If anyone makes a mistake, the last person will not be able to complete the graph by coloring the correct number of sections. Stress this fact to the students and tell them that they must all watch each other very carefully to be sure the graph is completed properly. When the graph is completed, all 20 sections should be colored.

Step Two: Completing the bar graph

Students will complete the bar graph in much the same manner. Give every team a blank bar graph worksheet and have one person fill in the topic, team name, and date.

Next, tell each person to graph the same item on the bar graph that they completed on the circle graph. Have them use the same color to do this. In **RoundTable** fashion, each person writes the name of that item at the bottom of one column. They take turns coloring one bar for each person who selected that choice.

13

Discussing results using THINK-PAIR-SHARE

When all teams are finished, the teams place both graphs in the center where all members can see them easily. Students discuss some or all of these questions with a partner, then share their ideas with the class:

- *When might a scientist conduct a survey?*
- *Why do scientists usually choose their participants randomly?*
- *Which graph is easier for you to read, a circle graph or a bar graph?*
- *Why might someone show information with a circle graph instead of a bar graph?*
- *When might someone rather use a bar graph than a circle graph?*
- *Were your predictions about the results of your survey correct?*
- *How many more people made the most popular choice than the least popular choice?*
- *Were any items not chosen at all?*
- *Can you think of a question that could be answered by looking at the graphs?*

Writing About Science

In their Science Journals or on a piece of paper, have students respond to some of the questions discussed in the **Think-Pair-Share** activity. You might also want them to sketch a circle or bar graph of their results in their notebooks. They can create two questions that can be answered from the graphs.

Materials Check List

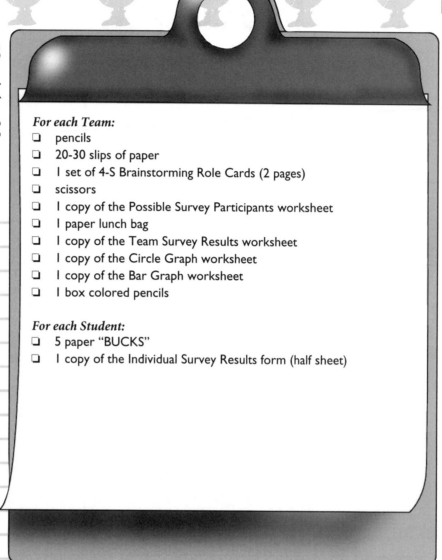

For each Team:
- ❑ pencils
- ❑ 20-30 slips of paper
- ❑ 1 set of 4-S Brainstorming Role Cards (2 pages)
- ❑ scissors
- ❑ 1 copy of the Possible Survey Participants worksheet
- ❑ 1 paper lunch bag
- ❑ 1 copy of the Team Survey Results worksheet
- ❑ 1 copy of the Circle Graph worksheet
- ❑ 1 copy of the Bar Graph worksheet
- ❑ 1 box colored pencils

For each Student:
- ❑ 5 paper "BUCKS"
- ❑ 1 copy of the Individual Survey Results form (half sheet)

Curriculum Links

1. Math - Examining a variety of graphs
Ask students to find an example of any type of graph and bring it to school. One excellent source of up-to-date graphs is *USA Today* newspaper. Each team chooses one graph and use it to create **Send-A-Problem** questions. Follow the directions for **Send-A-Problem** found on pages 40-41.

2. Art - Creating graph posters
Let each team glue their completed circle and bar graphs on a sheet of posterboard. Teams fill the white space around the graphs with appropriate illustrations.

3. Science - Graphing the weather
Students take the outside temperature each day at the same time of day. Show them how to make a line graph of their results.

Possible Survey Participants

Team Survey Results

Team Name _____ Date _____

Survey Question: _____

Names	Choice #1	Choice #2	Choice #3	Choice #4	Choice #5
1.					
2.					
3.					
4.					
5.					
6.					
7.					
8.					
9.					
10.					
11.					
12.					
13.					
14.					
15.					
16.					
17.					
18.					
19.					
20.					
Totals					

Individual Survey Results

Name _____   Date _____

Survey Question: _____

Names	**Choice #1**	**Choice #2**	**Choice #3**	**Choice #4**	**Choice #5**
1.					
2.					
3.					
4.					
5.					
Totals					

Individual Survey Results

Name _____   Date _____

Survey Question: _____

Names	**Choice #1**	**Choice #2**	**Choice #3**	**Choice #4**	**Choice #5**
1.					
2.					
3.					
4.					
5.					
Totals					

Circle Graph

Title: _____

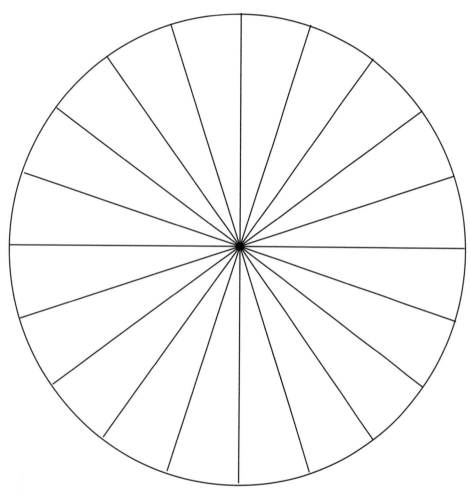

Key:

| | = | | = | | = |

| | = | | = |

Team Name _____   Date _____

Bar Graph

Title: _____

Number of People

15				
14				
13				
12				
11				
10				
9				
8				
7				
6				
5				
4				
3				
2				
1				

Choices

Team Name _____   Date _____

Laura Candler: *Hands-On Science*   1 (800) 933-2667 • *Kagan Publishing*

Students Will...

Observe surface tension

Predict and observe the effects of detergent on surface tension

Predict and observe the number of water drops a penny will hold

Generate a question about surface tension and perform a simple experiment to discover the answer

Process Skills...

Observing

Predicting

Organizing Data

Inferring

Experimenting

Communicating

Structures...

Blackboard Share

4-S Brainstorming

RoundRobin

RoundTable

Spend-A-Buck

Team Discussion

Team Project

Think-Pair-Share

Exploring Surface Tension

his lesson provides an opportunity for students to discover surface tension, a property of water that seldom fails to amaze adults and children alike. Water molecules are strongly attracted to each other and form a thin "skin" on the surface of any body of water. It's this skin that allows water insects to zip across the surface of a pond without sinking below the surface. Surface tension is also the property that causes water drops to form as they drip from a faucet.

During the first investigation, Pepper Predictions, students make and test predictions as you lead them through the steps of the experiment. They sprinkle pepper on the surface of a bowl of water and observe the effects of a soapy toothpick touched to the surface. Students are amazed to see the pepper "jump" away from the toothpick as the surface tension is broken.

In the second investigation, Penny Predictions, each team follows a series of written directions to complete the experiment. In the first part, they predict how many drops of water will fit on the head of a penny. After recording their predictions, they test their guesses. Usually children are astounded to see that the drops of water seem to "pile up" on the penny as if held by an invisible skin. The penny holds many more drops than most predict. In the second part of the activity, team members brainstorm additional questions about surface tension and perform a simple experiment to test one of their ideas.

Finally, students discuss ways that the pepper experiment and the penny experiment are similar. They will infer that the same property of water that allowed the pepper to float caused the drops of water to "pile up" on the penny.

Students need to be in teams of four during both of the experiments. Since both activities involve the use of water, they need to work on a flat surface. If flat-topped tables or desks are not available, have them sit on the floor.

1

Pepper Predictions using ROUNDROBIN/ROUNDTABLE

Materials for each Team:
1 small bowl half-filled with water
1 packet or shaker of black pepper
1 toothpick
2" square of waxed paper with 1 drop of detergent in the middle

Step One: Introducing the experiment
Let one student from each team get the materials for the team. Explain that they will be working together to make some interesting discoveries about a special property of water. Tell them that scientists often make predictions about what they think will happen in an experiment. Say that a prediction made by a scientist before an experiment is called a *hypothesis*. Today they will become scientists and will make hypotheses about each part of their experiment.

(continued on page 259)

Pepper Predictions (continued from page 258)

Step Two: Stating the first hypothesis
Ask the members of each team to **RoundRobin** their responds to the question, *"What do you think will happen when the pepper is sprinkled on top of the water?"* After everyone has responded, point out that they have each stated a hypothesis and they will now test those predictions.

Step Three: Sprinkling pepper on water
Ask Person #1 to pick up the pepper packet and gently sprinkle a small amount of pepper on the surface of the water. Tell everyone else to observe carefully to find out if their hypothesis was correct.

Step Four: Stating the second hypothesis
Next ask students to **RoundRobin** the question, *"What will happen if we touch a clean toothpick to the surface of the water?"* Allow time for everyone to respond.

Step Five: Dipping a clean toothpick in the water
Ask Person #2 to take the toothpick and gently touch it to the surface of the water. Students will probably expect something unusual to happen, but nothing out of the ordinary happens at this step.

Step Six: Stating the third hypothesis
Ask the members of each team to **RoundRobin** a hypothesis for the question, *"What will happen when a soapy toothpick is dipped into the water?"*

Step Seven: Dipping a soapy toothpick into the water
Direct Person #3 to take the toothpick and dip the tip into the drop of detergent. Then tell them to gently touch the soapy tip to the surface of the water. Students who observe carefully will be surprised to see the pepper jump away from the toothpick to the sides of the bowl.

Step Eight: Stating the final hypothesis
The final question to **RoundRobin** is *"What will happen if we sprinkle more pepper on the surface of the water?"* Let everyone state their hypothesis.

Step Nine: Sprinkling pepper
Tell Person #4 to sprinkle a few more pinches of pepper on the surface of the water. Students may expect the pepper to float as it did before, but this time most of it will sink to the bottom of the bowl.

Lesson 15
Exploring Surface Tension

2

Reflecting on results using THINK-PAIR-SHARE

Ask the students to **Think-Pair-Share** their answers to the following questions. Be sure to clear up any misunderstandings which might exist about the scientific reasons for the results.

- *Were you surprised about the results at any point during the activity?*
- *What caused the pepper to float?* (Surface tension of the water.)
- *What caused the pepper to jump away from the toothpick?* (Soap on the toothpick breaks the thin "skin" of the surface tension.)
- *Why didn't the pepper float during the last part of the activity?* (Surface tension was destroyed by the soap.)
- *Would all liquids behave the same way as water?* (No. Different liquids have different surface tensions.)
- *Could you sprinkle anything else besides pepper on the water and get the same results?* (Yes. Many spices will behave in a similar manner)

Duplicate enough paper "Bucks" (see page 44) for each student to have five. Paperclip 20 bucks together for each team. Also duplicate and cut apart a set of Role Cards (see page 266) for each team.

3

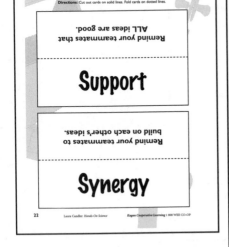

Penny Predictions using TEAM PROJECT

Materials for each Team:
1 penny
1 cup water
1 eyedropper
1 red and 1 blue crayon
scrap paper
paper towels
1 tray or plate
Penny Predictions Instructions
Penny Predictions Record Sheet
1 magic marker
12" x 18" sheet of construction paper
set of 4 Role Cards

Materials for each Student:
5 paper "Bucks" (see pattern on page 44)
1 pin (for role card)

In this activity, your students will lead themselves through another surface tension experiment. You will serve as a monitor rather than as an instructor. Plan to spend one class period on Part One and the next on Part Two.

(continued on page 261)

3 cont.

Penny Predictions (continued from page 260)

Before beginning the activity, assign roles to each team member. The easiest way to do this is to have the students number off from 1 to 4 and assign them the following roles:

        1) Lead Scientist
        2) Materials Monitor
        3) Recorder
        4) Reporter

If you don't have even teams of four, teams of three are preferable to teams of five. In a three-person team, the third person can function as both the Recorder and the Reporter.

Give each team a set of role cards. Have team members pin or tape the cards to their shirts as a reminder of their roles.

Distribute one copy of the Penny Predictions Instruction sheet to each team. Tell them that the Lead Scientist will serve as the reader and the quiet captain for the experiment. *The activity will begin with everyone reading a description of their role, but the rest of the instructions will be read by the Lead Scientist.*

Tell them that after each person completes a step of the activity, that person should put a checkmark in the box next to the step that has been completed. Doing this will help them keep their place. Emphasize that *everyone* will participate in checking off the steps, not just the Lead Scientist.

(continued on page 262)

3 cont.

Penny Predictions (continued from page 261)

Part One: Dropping water on a penny
Put the materials in an easily accessible place and let the students begin working. Monitor closely to be sure they are following directions and checking off each step of the activity.

While they are working, draw a class data table on the chalkboard or overhead projector. Draw a chart similar to the one below, including the example and leaving enough room for each team's results.

Team Name	Guess Range	Results
Example: Whiz Kids	5-10	12

(continued on page 263)

3 cont.

Penny Predictions (continued from page 262)

Part Two: Experimenting with surface tension
If you want to rotate roles for the second day of the activity, make the following changes:

1) Recorder
2) Reporter
3) Materials Monitor
4) Lead Scientist.

During this phase of the experiment, students will be generating their own experiment ideas. They will use **Spend-A-Buck** to choose which of their ideas they want to use for their experiment. You may want them to obtain your approval of their idea before they begin their experiment. Consider the available materials when giving your approval. For example, if they want to test how many drops of vinegar a quarter will hold, they have to be able to obtain some vinegar and a quarter. You may want to provide a variety of liquids and types of coins and ask the students to limit their experiment to the available materials.

For safety's sake, make sure students are not using toxic liquids in their experiments. Many household cleaning materials such as bleach and ammonia are much to strong for classroom use.

You will not draw a class data table for recording the results of the team experiments since all of them will be different. Instead, teams will create posters to report their results. Students may do this on a sheet of construction paper or a section of the chalkboard.

4

Reflecting on results using TEAM DISCUSSION

Be sure to provide closure to this lesson by having students reflect upon what they learned about surface tension. Give them a few minutes for an informal **Team Discussion** on one or more of the following questions. Randomly call on students from different teams to share their team's ideas with the class.

- *How was the pepper experiment similar to the penny experiment?* (Both involved surface tension.)
- *Why did the penny hold more drops of water than you expected?* (Surface tension allowed drops to "pile up.")
- *Would other liquids behave the same way as water?* (No.)
- *Why didn't every team get exactly the same results on the penny experiment?* (Different people using eyedroppers.)
- *How could you make the penny experiment more scientific?* (Repeat experiment and average results, have same person use eyedropper.)
- *How many drops of soapy water do you think a penny would hold? Why?* (Not many because there would not be dry surface tension.)

Writing About Science

Have students describe their team's experiment in their Science Journals. Then they respond to one or more of the **Team Discussion** questions above.

For Younger Students

Younger children will have difficulty completing Penny Predictions on their own. However, they can do the experiment if it is directed by the teacher. Assign roles as usual, but read the directions to the students and monitor their progress very closely. Modify the vocabulary where needed to adapt to your particular students' abilities.

Materials Check List

For each Team:
❏   1 small bowl half-filled with water
❏   1 packet or shaker of black pepper
❏   1 toothpick
❏   2" square of waxed paper with 1 drop of detergent in the middle
❏   Penny Predictions Instructions
❏   Penny Predictions Record Sheet
❏   12" x 18" sheet of construction paper
❏   1 penny
❏   1 cup water
❏   1 eyedropper
❏   1 red and 1 blue crayon
❏   scrap paper
❏   paper towels
❏   1 tray or plate
❏   1 magic marker
❏   set of 4 Role Cards

For each Student:
❏   5 paper "Bucks" (see pattern on page 44)
❏   1 pin (for role card)

Curriculum Links

1. Art - Making Soap-Powered Boats
Students can make models of boats that are powered by changes in surface tension. They should use the wax-covered cardboard from a milk carton to cut a boat similar to the one in the illustration. Place the boat at the end of a pan of water and drop one drop of detergent in the "V" opening. When the surface tension behind the boat is broken by the detergent, the boat is pulled forward by the surface tension in front of it. Children may want to experiment with different shapes and sizes of boats.

2. Science - Dropping paper clips in a glass of water
Fill a glass of water to the very top. Ask students to predict how many paper clips you will be able to drop into the glass before the water overflows. Count together as you gently drop the paper clips in, one at a time. Be sure to have more than one full box of paper clips available or you will be sending a student to borrow some!

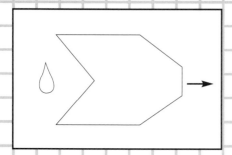

Role Cards

Lead Scientist

Materials Monitor

Recorder

Reporter

Laura Candler: *Hands-On Science*

1 (800) 933-2667 • *Kagan Publishing*

Penny Predictions
Record Sheet

Part One

Question: How many drops of water will the head of a penny hold?

Prediction and Results:

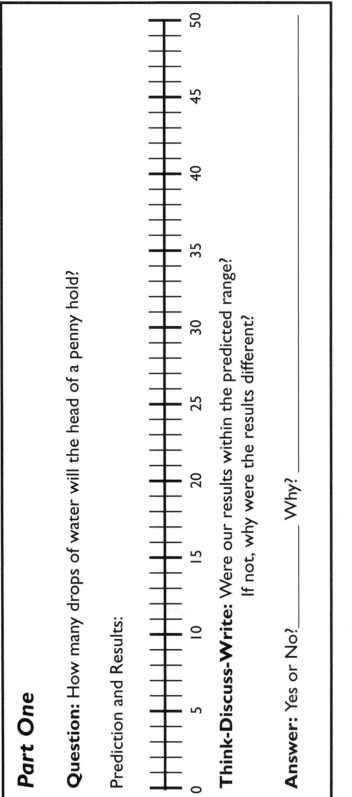

0   5   10   15   20   25   30   35   40   45   50

Think-Discuss-Write: Were our results within the predicted range? If not, why were the results different?

Answer: Yes or No? _____ Why? _____

Part Two

Question: _____

Prediction and Results:

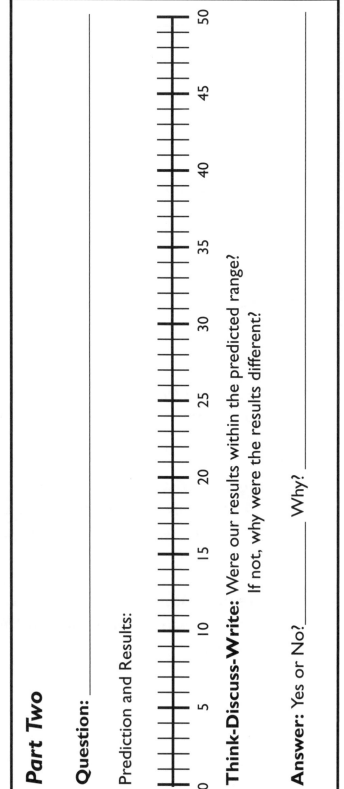

0   5   10   15   20   25   30   35   40   45   50

Think-Discuss-Write: Were our results within the predicted range? If not, why were the results different?

Answer: Yes or No? _____ Why? _____

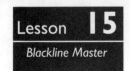

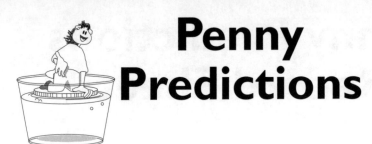

Penny Predictions

RoundRobin: Stating Roles

☐ 1. **Lead Scientist:** *To begin the activity, we will all read our role titles and job descriptions. I am the Lead Scientist and my job will be to read the instructions to the team. I will also make sure that we follow directions and complete the activity one step at a time. It's my job to make sure we all work quietly, too.*

☐ 2. **Materials Monitor:** *I am the Materials Monitor. When it is time, I will get the materials for the team. I will also be the only one handling the materials during this experiment.*

☐ 3. **Recorder:** *I am the Recorder. I will write the team's answers on the Penny Prediction Record Sheet.*

☐ 4. **Reporter:** *I am the Reporter. I will write our team's answers on the chalkboard or overhead projector. I will tell the class about the results of our experiment.*

☐ 5. **Lead Scientist:** *This is a team science investigation about surface tension. We will guess how many drops of water a coin will hold. Then we will perform the experiment to see how our results compare to our guesses.*

☐ 6. **Materials Monitor:** *Put the materials on a tray or plate and bring them back to your team.*

Materials	
1 penny	1 red crayon
1 cup water	1 blue crayon
1 eye dropper	scrap paper
paper towels	20 paper "Bucks"

Penny Predictions

Part One

Think-Write-RoundRobin-Record: Making predictions

☐ 7. **Lead Scientist:** *Take a look at the cup of water. Then look at the face of the penny.* **Do not touch the materials yet; just look and think.** *If we use an eyedropper to drop water onto the coin from 2 centimeters high, how many drops of water will the coin hold before the water spills over the edge? Let's take 10 seconds to think. No talking.* (Wait 10 seconds before continuing.)

☐ 8. **Materials Monitor:** Give everyone one sheet of scrap paper.

☐ 9. **Lead Scientist:** *Now everyone write the number you guessed on your piece of paper. A guess is also called a hypothesis. A hypothesis is what you believe will happen. So let's write down our hypotheses. No discussing.* (Wait 10 seconds before continuing.)

☐ 10. **Lead Scientist:** *One at a time, we will* **RoundRobin** *our ideas. This means we will take turns reading to the team what our guess was. As we talk, the Recorder will use a blue crayon to record our answers on Part One of the Penny Predictions Record Sheet. The Recorder will make a dot on the number line to record each guess.*

☐ 11. **Recorder:** Find Part One on the Penny Predictions Record Sheet. With a blue crayon, make a dot on the number line to record each person's guess. (See example below.)

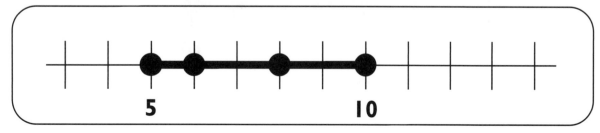

☐ 12. **Recorder:** Now use the same blue crayon to make a solid line from the lowest guess recorded to the highest guess recorded. (See example below.)

Penny Predictions

☐ 13. **Lead Scientist:** *The distance from our lowest guess to our highest guess is called our guess range. Our guess range is shown by the length of the blue line. The guess range can also be reported by stating the lowest and highest numbers. For example, if our guesses were 5, 6, 8 and 10, our guess range would be "5 - 10."*

Blackboard Share: *Sharing Class Guess Ranges*

☐ 14. **Reporter:** Go to the chalkboard (or overhead projector) and write your team's name and guess range in the appropriate place on the chart.

Drop-Count-Record: *Testing predictions*

☐ 15. **Lead Scientist:** *Now we'll test our hypotheses. When I say "Begin," the Materials Monitor will fill up the eyedropper with water from the cup. For dropping water, you need a steady hand. Balance your wrist, and don't drop the water from higher than 2 centimeters. As the drops fall, we will all count aloud together, "One, two, three," and so on. We will count together until the water spills over the side of the coin. Everyone ready? Begin!*

☐ 16. **Materials Monitor:** Drop drops of water onto the head of the penny.

☐ 17. **Lead Scientist:** *The Recorder will record our results on the same line where we recorded our hypotheses. Using a red crayon, the Recorder will make a dark vertical mark 1 centimeter tall on the number of drops that the penny actually held. If the water spilled over on the 13th drop, we would count 12 drops as the actual number of drops the could hold.*

☐ 18. **Recorder:** Using a red crayon, make a dark vertical mark on the line to show the actual number of drops the penny could hold. (See example below.)

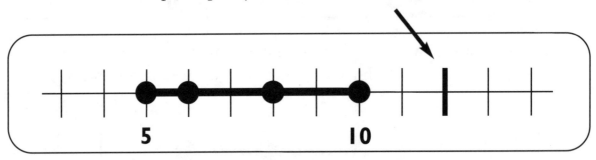

Penny
Predictions

Blackboard Share: Sharing results

☐ 19. **Reporter:** Go to the blackboard (or overhead projector) and write your team's results next to your team name and guess range.

Think-Discuss-Write: Analyzing results

☐ 20. **Lead Scientist:** *Let's all look at the line showing our guess range and results. Now take time to think. Were our results within the predicted range? If not, why were the results different?* (Allow about 10 seconds of think time.)

☐ 21. **Lead Scientist:** *Now let's discuss our ideas. After we reach an answer, the Recorder will write the team answer on the Penny Predictions Record Sheet.*

☐ 22. **Recorder:** Write the team's answer on the line next to the Think-Discuss-Write question for Part One.

Part Two
Brainstorming: Listing experiment ideas

☐ 23. **Lead Scientist:** *Now we're going to think of other experiments like this one that we could do with surface tension. We can think about changing one part of this experiment to make a new one. For example, we could ask "How many drops of water could a nickel hold?" Or we could change other things like the kind of liquid or the way we drop the water. As we think of questions, the Recorder will write each one one a separate piece of scrap paper. Let's see how many questions we can think of.*

☐ 24. **Recorder:** As each idea is called out, write it on a separate piece of paper. **Be sure to write each idea as a question.**

Penny Predictions

Spend-A-Buck: Choosing an experiment

☐ **25. Lead Scientist:** *Now we're going to choose one of these ideas to try as an experiment. We'll use "Spend-A-Buck" to decide which question to use.*

☐ **26. Materials Monitor:** Give each person 5 paper "bucks."

☐ **27. Lead Scientist:** *We are going to use these "bucks" like money to spend on the question we like the best. Each person can spend his or her "bucks" on between one and five different questions. You can place them all on one question. You can put three on the question you like the best and two on your second favorite question. Or you can put one buck on five different questions. Now let's take a minute to look at the questions carefully and spend our bucks.*

☐ **28. Materials Monitor:** Count the number of "bucks" on each question. If there is a tie, do "Spend-A-Buck" again using only the top choices.

Think-Write-RoundRobin-Record: Making predictions

☐ **29. Materials Monitor:** Gather the materials needed to carry out your team's experiment.

☐ **30: Lead Scientist:** *Before we perform our experiment, we need to make our hypotheses, or predictions, about what will happen. Everyone should think and write their ideas on paper. Remember, each of us will write the one number that is our own prediction. (Allow about 10 seconds for everyone to think and write.)*

☐ **31. Lead Scientist:** *Now we will **RoundRobin** our ideas by reading them in turn. As we make our predictions, the Recorder will use the blue crayon to record our guesses on the number line. Then the Recorder will draw a dark line from the lowest to the highest number to show our guess range. Person #1, start by giving your hypotheses.*

☐ **32. Recorder:** Find Part Two of the Penny Prediction Record Sheet. First write your team's experiment question in the space provided. Then record the predictions and the guess range in blue exactly as you did in Part One.

Penny Predictions

Drop-Count-Record: Testing predictions

☐ 33. **Lead Scientist:** *Now the Materials Monitor will drop the drops as before. Let's all count the results out loud.*

☐ 34. **Materials Monitor:** Drop the drops of liquid as everyone counts.

☐ 35. **Recorder:** Record the results using a red crayon. Make a dark mark on the line to show the actual number of drops.

Think-Discuss-Write: Analyzing results

☐ 36. **Lead Scientist:** *Let's look at the line which shows our guess range and our results. Were our results within the predicted range? Why or why not? Let's think before we share our ideas.* (Allow about 15 seconds of think time.)

☐ 37. **Lead Scientist:** *Now let's square our ideas.*

☐ 38. **Recorder:** Write the team's answer to the question in the space provided.

Blackboard Share: Sharing experiment results

☐ 39. **Reporter:** On a section of the chalkboard (or a large sheet of paper), write the following:

      1) your team's name
      2) your team's question
      3) a line showing your guess range in blue and your actual results in red

☐ 40. **Materials Monitor:** While the Reporter is writing the results, supervise clean-up. Make sure everyone on the team is helping to return materials and wipe up spills.

☐ 41. **Reporter:** Stand by your team's results and prepare to report those results to the class.

Professional Organizations

National Science Teachers Association (NSTA)

National Science Teachers
Association
1840 Wilson Blvd.
Arlington, VA 22201
(703) 243-7100

NSTA provides many resources to science teachers at all grade levels. Membership in the organization entitles you to a subscription of *Science and Children, Science Scope, The Science Teacher,* or the *Journal of College Science Teaching.* NSTA also publishes a wealth of materials designed to help the science teacher. The organization sponsors regional and national conventions which provide teachers with up-to-date information and new teaching ideas.

American Association for the Advancement of Science (AAAS)

American Association for the
Advancement of Science
1333 H Street, N.W.
Washington, DC 20005
(202) 326-6400

The AAAS is sponsoring Project 2061, a plan for science education reform. The first two phases are currently complete and are described in two publications: *Science for All Americans* and *Benchmarks for Science Literacy.* Write to Project 2061 at the above address.

Science Material Suppliers

The following companies supply books and/or materials to science educators. Write on school letterhead or call to obtain a catalog.

Carolina Biological Supply Co.
2700 York Road
Burlington, NC 26215
(800) 334-5551

Delta Education, Inc.
P.0. Box 915
Hudson, NH 03051
(800) 258-1302

Idea Factory, Inc.
10710 Dixon Drive
Riverview, FL 33569
(800) 331-6204

NASCO
P. O. Box 901
Fort Atkinson, WI 53538
(800) 558-9595

Sargent-Welch Scientific Co.
911 Commerce Court
Buffalo Grove, IL 60089
(800) SARGENT

Schoolmasters Science
745 State Circle
Box 1941
Ann Arbor, MI 48106
(800) 521-2832

Carle, Eric. *A Tiny Seed*. Natick, MA: Picture Book Studio, 1987.

Cherry, Lynne. *A River Ran Wild*. San Diego, CA: Harcourt Brace Jovanovich, 1992.

Cole, Joanna. *Magic School Bus at the Waterworks*. New York, NY: Scholastic, Inc., 1986.

Cole, Joanna. *Magic School Bus Inside the Earth*. New York, NY: Scholastic, Inc., 1987.

Gibbons, Gail. *From Seed to Plant*. New York, NY: Holiday House, 1991.

Heller, Ruth. *The Reason For a Flower*. New York, NY: Grosset & Dunlap, 1983.

Heller, Ruth. *Animals Born Alive and Well*. New York, NY: Grosset & Dunlap, 1982.

Heller, Ruth. *Chickens Aren't the Only Ones*. New York, NY: Grosset & Dunlap, 1981.

Ziefert, Harriet. *Mystery Day*. Little, Brown, and Company. Boston, MA: 1988.